☀ *Kundalini Tales*

by RICHARD SAUDER, Ph.D.

Adventures Unlimited Press

KEMPTON, ILLINOIS

Kundalini Tales
© 1998 by Richard Sauder, Ph.D.

ISBN 0-932813-61-5

10 9 8 7 6 5 4 3 2 1

Printed in the United States of America by

Adventures Unlimited Press
One Adventure Place
Kempton, Illinois 60946-0074
Telephone (815) 253-6390
FAX (815) 253-6300
http://www.azstarnet.com/~aup/

For Undine

Acknowledgments

NOTHING HAPPENS IN A VACUUM, including this book. I am grateful to the staff at the University of Maryland libraries for their help in obtaining documents. The staff at the NASA archives in Washington, DC assisted me with information about NASA administrators and the involvement of ex-Nazis in NASA's manned space program. I would also like to thank the staff at the Supreme Council, 33°, of the Ancient and Accepted Scottish Rite of Freemasonry, Southern Jurisdiction, U.S.A. for their gracious help and cordial tours of their temple. Thanks are due as well to those whose web pages have inspired me: *The Mind Control Forum*; the *Shared Transformation* site and *The Leading Edge* site.

Most of all I would like to express my heartfelt gratitude to my family.

About the Author

RICHARD SAUDER is a student of life and consciousness. He holds a B.A. in Sociology, an M.A. in Latin American Studies, an M.S. in Forestry and a Ph.D. in Political Science.

Preface

THIS IS A BOOK about human consciousness, and the nature of reality. More to the point, this is a book about certain aspects of my consciousness and a few facets of my view of the nature of reality. Overall, I am struck by the fragmentary nature of human consciousness, including my own. We see things in bits and pieces; we think in brief spurts. Our mental process is often confused. We misunderstand and misinterpret all sorts of things — physical events in the outside world, actions and words in the social realm, even (or especially) our own thoughts and psychological motivations escape our full understanding.

As for reality, what is it?

On the face of it this seems a simple enough question. The obvious answer would seem to be: reality is what is *real*. But what is real? And what is an illusion?

In my view, reality is an infinitely complex and finely nuanced aggregation of every known and unknown phenomenon that presently exists, has existed in the past, will exist in the future or which has an existence apart from the linear flow of time as contemporary, terrestrial humans perceive it. Within the human realm reality comprises any and all biological, psychological, spiritual, religious, social, economic, political, and technological phenomena. In its turn, the human realm interacts in an infinitude of ways with the greater ecosystem of which it is an integral (albeit dysfunctional) part, with the planet earth, with other bodies in the solar system and even with the neighboring solar systems in our galaxy. In recent decades we have sent a veritable electromagnetic cascade of radio, TV, microwave and radar transmissions sleeting out into space at the speed of light. What effect might this have on other planets and stars, if any? The simple truth?—No one has the foggiest notion! We don't even fully understand what effect all of this electronic activity has on *us* and Earth. We just do it.

My point is simply this: reality is extremely complex and multifaceted. The universe is stupendously huge. And the galaxy in which we live is truly and vastly ancient, way beyond our feeble ability to imagine.

Let's not delude ourselves: the reality game is tricky and subtle. The reality game lasts for unimaginable eons. It is also the only game there is.

And everyone is a player.

—Richard Sauder, Ph.D.
May 1998

One

I AWAKENED SUDDENLY. It was the middle of the night during the 1992 Holidays. I could not discern a reason for having awakened. Nothing seemed to be wrong. There were no loud noises; no dogs barking; no sirens. And then I heard a man's voice say very gleefully: *"Party hearty!"*

I scarcely had time to wonder who he was and where the voice came from when I felt the kundalini energize itself in my coccyx and rise quickly up my spine. It continued rising, tickling my spinal cord, until it reached a position between my shoulder blades. There it stopped and then retraced its way back down my spine, just as quickly as it had risen. It reentered my coccyx and faded away. The entire episode took perhaps twenty seconds. I lay there in the dark, wide awake, and pondered what had happened. There was no ready explanation for the voice I heard, since I lived alone. The kundalini, however, was a different matter altogether.

For years I had been fascinated by the kundalini. I had actively sought it out and had literally read volumes about it. Any well stocked book store or library carries titles on the subject. I had read and reread the writings of Gopi Krishna. His stories evoked a powerful sense of longing in me. I felt a deep yearning for the unspeakably mysterious reality that he so eloquently describes. And so over the years I had from time to time made half-hearted efforts to activate the kundalini. And I must say, I had achieved some modest results.

Every few years I did have a conscious, if brief, kundalini experience. Some of them were quite powerful. All of them served to demonstrate to my complete satisfaction that the kundalini phenomenon is real. There is a surpassingly powerful creative impulse in every human being. It is at once unimaginably ancient, and yet ever and playfully newer than new. It is the cosmic impetus behind the endlessly beguiling sexual desire that every human being with a normal complement of hormones feels. The kundalini is also the might behind the geological forces that raise and lower mountain chains. It is the cosmic energy that brings whole solar systems and galaxies into being and snuffs out stars when they become supernovae. At one and the same time, the kundalini is the supremely intelligent consciousness that scribes the incredibly intricate genetic codes of all biological life forms. Every musician who composes an exquisitely beautiful song does so under the influence of the kundalini's incessant urging.

The same is true for every other creative act carried out by any human being anywhere. Everything that we humans do, indeed, everything that happens throughout this vast, infinite creation is due to the kundalini's immensely powerful, and yet artfully delicate activity. The kundalini is the ancient of days, and yet simultaneously as ever new as the dew glistening on a swelling rosebud in early spring. The kundalini is as sage and cunning as the wisest, most wrinkled crone who ever lived. And the kundalini is as innocent as the purest young child who ever drew its first breath.

Though the kundalini is all of that and more, I believe that it is not God. It seems to me at my present state of knowledge and experience that the kundalini is a powerful and trusted servant of God, a sort of personalized divine force. Perhaps it would make sense to think of the kundalini as some kind of archangel, vastly and consciously powerful, able to engineer entire galaxies; but at the same time capable of interacting in an intensely personal way with individual human beings.

In my experience, the kundalini knows
me better than I know myself. Far, far better. It has compiled an intricately detailed
record of my every action and thought. It
consciously plumbs the depths of the most
remote corners of my psyche. It moves with
deliberate method through each of my individual nerve fibers and monitors the functioning of each and every one of the many
billions of cells in my body. It appears to do
this for every living creature at the same
time, while it simultaneously animates the
entire, stupendously vast universe with its
untold billions and trillions of stars and
planets.[1]

And yet I have the feeling that the
kundalini is not God. It seems to me that
God is much greater yet than that.

---

[1] Gopi Krishna has had a strong influence on my thinking
about the kundalini. Any of his writings are a valuable reference on the topic. For an excellent, autobiographical account
of his awakening see Gopi Krishna, *Kundalini: The Evolutionary Energy in Man*, with psychological commentary by
James Hillman and foreword by James Kieffer (Boston:
Shambhala, 1997).

Two

IN THE 1970's I read Robert Monroe's book, *Journeys Out of the Body*.[2] I found his stories about consciously traveling out of his physical body to be bizarre. But I understood intuitively that what he reported was true. I tried his out-of-body technique at home and succeeded after a period of diligent effort in consciously leaving my body.

On one of my first attempts, I was meditating late one night, at the end of a five day, water-only fast, when I suddenly entered an altered state of consciousness. In this altered state I heard the sound of a man's voice. I could not make out what he was saying, but the tone of his voice was very comforting; it reminded me of the voice of Walter Cronkite, or of Fred McMurray, the star of the old television situation comedy, *My Three Sons*. It was at this point that I very naturally and virtually effortlessly used Robert Monroe's roll-out method to consciously roll out of my body.

I found myself in a small, claustrophobic room with lavender colored wall paper dotted with small flowers. The room felt too cramped, so I melted through the wall and found myself on a macadam road in a residential area lined with shade trees. I went running down the road looking for a road sign or any other identifying clue that I could use to verify the objective reality of what I was experiencing. I felt a sense of overwhelming excitement, strangeness and curiosity. And as nearly as I can remember now that is how the experience ended.

The next thing I remembered I was back in bed, the birds were chirping and the sun was coming up. This proved to be just the first of many out-of-body experiences over the next few years.

Not long after the first experience I contacted the Monroe Institute and participated in one of their weekend training sessions in Richmond, Virginia. I did not go out-of-the-body during the weekend, but back in Louisiana, the following week, I had the first and most powerful kundalini awakening of my life. Early one morning, while doing the set of exercises I had learned the previous weekend, I moved precipitously into a staggeringly powerful state of consciousness. Because it was so much at variance with my normal frame of mind I am scarcely able to describe, even now, what it was like.

My spinal column was turbo-charged with what felt like 50,000 volts of rippling, crackling electricity that came surging up my spine with an ear-splitting roar and arced out of the top of my skull and away into a vast, indescribable something that, for want of better words, resembled an enormously huge balloon hanging over my head. It may be that the balloon-like impression represented my limited perception of an expanded state of super-consciousness that lay just above me. Meanwhile, my heart chakra was powerfully opened and I could see all around me without any physical impediment, right through the walls, in a 360° circle. I want to emphasize that I was seeing with startling clarity—not with my physical eyes, which were closed, or with the so-called third eye in the forehead—but with my heart. The heart itself sees, with great acuity and without physical restriction, when in a state such as this. At the same time I was enjoying sublime feelings of bliss.

---

2   Robert Monroe, *Journeys Out of the Body* (Garden City, N.Y.: Anchor Press, 1977).

The calming influence of these feelings persisted throughout the day after the experience was over. While everything else was going on I heard in my ears the most perfectly enchanting and seductive music I have ever encountered anywhere, whether in the body or out. It was eminently haunting and coyly mysterious. I could not wait to hear what it would do next. It was all of the best music that I have ever heard, and much more, somehow rolled together and mixed up in one never-ending perfect song that is eternally and completely satisfying. It has no equal anywhere. The melody, the rhythm, and the instrumentation were incomparable. The closest match that I can think of are the great symphonies of Beethoven and Mozart and the finest performances of the most gifted jazz musicians of the day. But even if you could somehow combine those into the one-best-song that humanity has to offer the result would still be no more than an imperfect, pale imitation of the magical, intensely nostalgic kundalini music that I once heard playing on a muggy Louisiana morning many years ago.

The experience persisted for a few moments and then it was gone. But it made a palpably vivid impression on me. I have never forgotten it; indeed, I do not see how I can. Over the course of the intervening years I have often thought back with great longing to that time and wished that it could happen again.

Though I had no interaction with Robert Monroe on that occasion, a number of other times I did hear his voice while in an altered state of consciousness, or while out of the body. He invariably began by saying, *"Hello, this is Robert Monroe..."* And he would go on to talk about subjects that were quite remarkable and magical. I can remember well the warm, golden glow that accompanied his avuncular, relaxing voice. It was really very hypnotic to just lay there and bask in the sound of his voice and the vibrant, rich colors of whatever surroundings were a part of the experience.

The ambiance was one of plush velvet, and subtle, understated hues of mahogany furniture and burgundy velours.

I remember well one occasion on which he spoke to me. I was in jail at the time in Arkansas. During the early 1980s I was an anti-nuclear activist. On three different occasions I scaled the security fence at nuclear missile silos to demonstrate my opposition to preparations for nuclear war. As it happened, I was jailed by the United States government for these activities. The first time I did this I was jailed for seven days and released on probation (which I subsequently violated to do the same thing again, and for which I was again jailed). While in jail on the first charge I conducted a one week water-only fast. After about four or five days of this I was lying awake in my cell one night when I suddenly moved into an altered state. Once in the altered state of consciousness I heard the voice of Robert Monroe. He said, as usual, *"Hello, this is Robert Monroe..."* And then he went on to tell me something about the manned space program. He began, *"Thirty years ago, when men first started to go into space..."* He continued on to tell me something I had not known before. What he said was highly interesting. In fact, it was downright fascinating.

He told me that in the early years of the manned space program sending someone into space was not as simple as merely positioning an astronaut on top of a rocket and blasting up into space. Instead, there were certain magical— yes, *magical* and *mystical* protocols that had to be observed. He told me that astronauts could only be inserted into orbit at the proper place and time, and in just the right way. As he described it he conveyed the very real element of *magic* and *mystery* that was involved in putting human beings into space.

I was surprised to learn that more was involved in the manned space program than, well, the proverbial rocket science. Robert Monroe's words (delivered telepathically, or paranormally, while I was in an altered state of consciousness) resonated silently within me after my release from jail. Time went by and I kept what he had told me to myself. The import of what he said was seriously at variance with the coldly analytical, scientific image that the National Aeronautics and Space Administration (NASA) projects. I found it difficult to justify Robert Monroe's assertions with the public pronouncements and hard engineering appearances of the American space program.

It was not until many years later, when I toured the 33° Scottish Rite Masonic Temple at 1733 16 Street, N.W., in Washington, D.C.,[3] that I began to realize the full significance of Robert Monroe's message. To my surprise, there, in the temple's museum, was a Scottish Rite Masonic flag which Edwin Aldrin, Jr., the second Apollo program astronaut to walk on the Moon, carried with him to the lunar surface. When I visited, the flag was prominently displayed in a glass case in the museum. The same museum also displays a small Masonic flag that Apollo 7 astronaut Walter Schirra carried into space and subsequently presented to Scottish Rite Supreme Council, 33° Grand Commander Henry Clausen, on 23 October 1969. Gordon Cooper also took the Supreme Council, 33° flag into space on the Gemini 5 orbital mission. The museum also contains pieces of the heat shields from NASA's Mercury 7 and Apollo 11 manned missions. My interest was immediately sparked. I saw that there was some sort of connection between NASA's manned space program and the Supreme Council, 33°, Ancient and Accepted Scottish Rite of Freemasonry, Southern Jurisdiction, U.S.A.

So after my tour I inquired about the possibility of doing research in the temple's library. The collection of Masonic literature in that temple is virtually without peer in the world. My request

was granted, and I soon had a much better idea of what Robert Monroe had been alluding to: I discovered that some of the most prominent astronauts in the Mercury, Gemini and Apollo space programs are (or were) Masons.[4] Indeed, one of the original seven Project Mercury astronauts, John Glenn, is now an influential United States Senator from Ohio who will be returning to space again, in October 1998, aboard the space shuttle. I also learned that two former, highly placed administrators at NASA, Kenneth S. Kleinknecht,[5] (*See Figure 2*) and James E. Webb[6] are both Masons[7].

---

[3] I took a tour of the temple twice in 1997. Both guides, and all other temple officials, were very gracious and hospitable.

[4] Early astronauts who were Masons include Edward E. "Buzz" Aldrin, Jr., LeRoy Gordon Cooper, Donn E. Eisele, John H. Glenn, Virgil I. "Gus" Grissom, James Benson Irwin, Robert L. Kline, Edgar D. Mitchell, Walter M. Schirra, Jr., Thomas P. Stafford and Paul J. Weitz.

[5] Kenneth S. Kleinknecht was a member of the X-15 team and a member of the early DynaSoar space shuttle project. As an interesting historical aside, the Air Force's abandoned Dyna-Soar space shuttle project grew out of a Nazi project that was the brain child of Nazi General Walter Dornberger. General Dornberger was the officer in charge of the V-1 and V-2 missile programs; he was also Werner von Braun's boss during WWII. When Dornberger came to the United States under Project Paperclip he brought with him the plans for a rocket system that proved to be the conceptual forerunner of the present day space shuttle program. [For the fascinating details see William C. Walter, *Project Dyna-Soar: The Roots of Shuttle- A Memoir*, IAA-92-0193, 43rd Congress of the International Astronautical Federation, August 28- September 5, 1992/Washington, DC (International Astronautical Federation, 3-5 Rue Mario-Nikis, 75015 Paris, France)]. He also served as Technical Assistant to the Director of the Manned Spacecraft Center, Manager of the Mercury Project, Deputy Manager of the Gemini Program, Manager of the Command and Service Modules for the Apollo Spacecraft Program, Manager of the Skylab program, Johnson Space Center Director of Flight Operations and Assistant Manager of the Space Shuttle Orbiter Project. Information found in: official NASA biographies dated September 1963 and February 1969; NASA news release no. 76-03, 8 January 1976; and photocopy of article from unknown NASA publication dated 16 October 1981, in NASA archives in Washington, DC.

[6] James E. Webb was NASA Administrator from 14 February 1961 to 7 October 1968. World Wide Web: http://www.hq.nasa.gov/office/pao/History/Biographies/webb.html, 1997.

[7] This information was valid as of 28 June 1985. It was compiled by the Masonic Service Association of the United States, 8120 Fenton Street, Silver Spring, Maryland 20910-4785. See also Kenneth S. Kleinknecht, 33°, "Space and the

These facts, coupled with the Masonic flags various astronauts carried into space and delivered to the Scottish Rite's Supreme Council, 33°, reveal some sort of relationship between Masonry and the space program.

One of the interesting items I found in the course of my research was a letter from Edwin E. "Buzz" Aldrin, bearing the date of 19 September 1969.[8] (See *Figure 1*.) Aldrin was the second Apollo astronaut to walk on the Moon, after Neil Armstrong. Aldrin's letter explicitly mentions the Masonic flag that he carried with him to the Moon on the Apollo 11 mission of 20 July 1969, and which he delivered to the Supreme Council, 33° on 16 September 1969. The letter is addressed to Sovereign Grand Commander Luther A. Smith and says, in part:

> It was a great moment in my life to be so cordially welcomed to the House of the Temple on September 16, 1969 by you and Grand Secretary General Kleinknecht, 33°, and also the members of your staffs. My greatest pleasure, however, was to be able to present to you on this occasion the Scottish Rite Flag which I carried on the Apollo 11 Flight to the Moon — emblazoned in color with the Scottish Rite Double-headed Eagle, the Blue Lodge Emblem and the Sovereign Grand Commander's Insignia.

As it happens, the Grand Secretary General Kleinknecht (now Grand Commander) who Aldrin mentions in his letter is the brother of Kenneth S. Kleinknecht,[9] the powerful, former NASA official in charge of the early manned space

programs. Both Kleinknechts are 33° Masons.

The temple on which the NASA-Masonic connection centers is located just several blocks due north of the White House, at 1733 16th Street, N.W. Many United States presidents are known to have been Masons, beginning with George Washington and including some 20th century presidents. So it only stands to reason that there should be a 33° Masonic temple in close proximity to the White House. But this is not just any temple. Underscoring its status as a prominent *Scottish* Rite temple, its holdings include the second largest body of Robert Burns literature anywhere outside of Scotland itself. Moreover, it also has a room devoted to J. Edgar Hoover, founder and long-time Director of the Federal Bureau of Investigation (FBI). The Hoover shrine includes his official desk and many mementos and memorabilia from his long career. It seems that this temple has a special relationship with the FBI, as well as with NASA and the manned space program.

That's not all. This same temple also holds the personal library of Confederate Army General Albert Pike. It even holds his corpse, buried in the walls at the rear of the building. Just who was Albert Pike? Well, he was a prominent Mason in the post-Civil War era in the Southern States—and if some sources can be believed he was also one of the founding fathers of the Ku Klux Klan (KKK) the White-racist, terrorist organization that formed in the

---

Future," *The New Age* (May 1976): 4-6. *The New Age* is a Masonic publication.

[8] Letter dated 19 September 1969 from Edwin E. Aldrin, NASA Astronaut, to Illustrious Luther A. Smith, 33°, Sovereign Grand Commander, Supreme Council, 33°, Southern Jurisdiction, U.S.A., 1733 16th Street, N.W., Washington, D.C. 20009.

[9] Personal communications from Joan E. Sansbury, Librarian and Curator for the Supreme Council, 33°, of the Ancient and Accepted Scottish Rite of Freemasonry, Southern Jurisdiction, U.S.A., 1997 and 1998.

NATIONAL AERONAUTICS AND SPACE ADMINISTRATION
MANNED SPACECRAFT CENTER
HOUSTON, TEXAS 77058

POSTAGE AND FEES PAID
NATIONAL AERONAUTICS AND SPACE ADMINISTRATIO:.

September 19, 1969

Illustrious Luther A. Smith, 33°
Sovereign Grand Commander
Supreme Council, 33°
Southern Jurisdiction, U.S.A.
1733 16th Street, N.W.
Washington, D.C. 20009

Dear Grand Commander:

It was a great moment in my life to be so cordially welcomed to the House of the Temple on September 16, 1969 by you and Grand Secretary General Kleinknecht, 33°, and also the members of your staffs. My greatest pleasure, however, was to be able to present to you on this occasion the Scottish Rite Flag which I carried on the Apollo 11 Flight to the Moon--emblazoned in color with the Scottish Rite Double-headed Eagle, the Blue Lodge Emblem and the Sovereign Grand Commander's Insignia.

I take this opportunity to again thank you for the autographed copy of your recent book, entitled "Action by the Scottish Rite, Southern Jurisdiction, U.S.A.," which is filled with a wealth of information about your Americanism Program sponsored by the Supreme Council, participating activities and related activities of the Rite.

Cordially and fraternally,

Edwin E. Aldrin, Jr.
NASA Astronaut

Figure 1—Letter from Apollo 11 Astronaut Edwin Aldrin to Masonic officials. *Courtesy of NASA and the Supreme Council, 33°, Ancient and Accepted Scottish Rite of Freemasonry, Southern Jurisdiction, U.S.A.*

Figure 2—Two of the three Apollo 7 astronauts breakfast with National Aeronautics and Space Administration officials at the Kennedy Space Center prior to their earth orbital mission with Astronaut Walter Cunningham, not shown. From left: Kenneth Kleinknecht, Manager, Apollo Spacecraft Office; Astronaut Eisele; Astronaut Schirra; Donald Slayton, Director, Flight Crew Operations; unidentified person; and Astronaut Ronald Evans. *Photo courtesy of NASA.*

South after the Civil War.[10] Little did I know that I would stumble on all of this when I set out to learn more about Freemasonry.

As regards NASA and secret societies, it is well to remember that solidly entrenched in the core group of NASA's vaunted rocket scientists were men such as Werner von Braun and over one hundred other assorted "ex"-Nazi rocket experts who were brought out of Germany after WW-II by Operation Paperclip. Their rocketry expertise was put to work on designing and flying the rockets that launched the astronauts into space. The first director of the Kennedy Space Center was Kurt Debus, the V-2 rocket flight test director at the infamous Nazi missile base at Peenemünde, Germany. Wernher von Braun himself was an officer in Hitler's dreaded SS and later director of NASA's Marshall Space Flight Center. And Arthur Rudolph, the head of production at the Nazi's murderous Mittelwerk underground missile factory in Germany's Harz Mountains, was later to

---

[10] The Supreme Council, 33°, of the Ancient and Accepted Scottish Rite of Freemasonry, Southern Jurisdiction, U.S.A., strongly denies any relationship between Albert Pike and the Ku Klux Klan (KKK). I specifically asked tour guides at the Supreme Council, 33° about such a connection, on two separate occasions, and both times received an unequivocal denial that General Pike had anything to do with the founding of the KKK. There are histories of the KKK that mention General Pike as a founding figure in the early years of the Klan. See Walter L. Fleming, Ph.D., introduction to *Ku Klux Klan: Its Origin, Growth and Disbandment*, by J.C. Lester and D.L. Wilson (New York: AMS Press Inc., 1971; reprinted from the edition of 1905, New York). Also see Claude G. Bowers, *The Tragic Era: The Revolution after Lincoln* (Cambridge: Houghton Mifflin Company, The Riverside Press, 1929). And finally, see Susan Lawrence Davis, *Authentic History, Ku Klux Klan, 1865-1877* (New York: American Library Service, 1924).

become Director of NASA's Saturn V moon rocket program. [11]

In recent years, a number of exposés have described the *magico-occult* underpinnings of the Third Reich and the Nazi Party's ideology.[12] Peter Levenda's excellent *Unholy Alliance* is among the best of these books. Levenda's thesis is that: "(T)he Third Reich was a state governed on magical principles..."[13] To be sure, the magic was, and Levenda shows, still *is*, a magic of the darkest, most grotesquely violent sort. Given the close involvement of "ex"-Nazis at the highest levels of NASA's manned space program, and the *magico-occult* beliefs that motivated the leadership of the Nazi party, Robert Monroe's words to me vis-à-vis the manned space program and magical rites attendant to the launching of space capsules may be fraught with more significance than I know.

At any rate, the close ties between prominent NASA astronauts, NASA officials and Freemasonry (including the Southern Jurisdiction of the Scottish Rite) leave no serious doubt about some sort of Masonic involvement in the United States manned space program at the highest levels. Likewise, the crucial work of powerful "ex"-Nazis, such as Werner von Braun, Arthur Rudolph, Kurt Debus, and many others, at the heart of the United States' manned space program raises further questions about the role that these Project Paperclip "ex"-Nazis and their sympathizers played (and may still play) for NASA.

But what could be the reason for this strenuous effort to go to the Moon, in which both Freemasons and "ex"-Nazis played prominent roles?[14] Is there something special about the Moon that powerful organizations such as the Nazi Party and Freemasonry know? Something special that the rest of us don't know? To be sure, many Masonic lodges traditionally schedule their meetings according to the time when the Moon is full.[15] But that scarcely justifies the sort of effort that the early manned space program put forth to reach the Moon. The nagging question remains: is there something more?

I do not have the answer to this question. However, while combing through the NASA archives in Washington, D.C. I did find a statement from Werner von Braun that gave me pause to reflect. While discussing the reaction of the scientific community to the Apollo 11 and 12 lunar missions he said: "They came to the conclusion that the moon really turns out to be sort of a Rosetta stone for the understanding of monumental cosmological phenomena."[16] Might he be referring here to cryptic monuments that NASA may have discovered on the Moon? (Certainly, there is a small, sensationalistic body of litera-

---

[11] An especially fine discussion of Operation Paperclip, including material on Werner von Braun, his fellow Nazi rocketeers and NASA operations can be found in Linda Hunt, *Secret Agenda: The United States Government, Nazi Scientists, and Project Paperclip, 1945 to 1990* (New York: St. Martin's Press, 1991). Also see Dennis Piskiewicz, *The Nazi Rocketeers: Dreams of Space and Crimes of War* (Westport, Connecticut: Praeger, 1995). Thousands of slave laborers were executed or worked to death in the miles of underground tunnels that comprised the Mittelwerk missile factory. The installation was a nightmarish, living hell.

[12] For example, see Nicholas Goodrick-Clarke, with a foreward by Rohan Butler, *The Occult Roots of Nazism: Secret Aryan Cults and Their Influence on Nazi Ideology: The Ariosophists of Austria and Germany, 1890-1935* (Washington Square, New York: New York University Press, 1992). Also, see Dusty Sklar, *The Nazis and the Occult* (New York: Dorset Press, 1977). Peter Levenda's *Unholy Alliance: A History of Nazi Involvement with the Occult* (New York: Avon Books, 1995) is a particularly fine exposition of the occult and magical aspects of the Third Reich.

[13] Peter Levenda, *Unholy Alliance: A History of Nazi Involvement with the Occult* (New York: Avon Books, 1995).

[14] This collaboration of Masons and "ex"-Nazis working so closely together on the same project is puzzling, in light of the Third Reich's violent persecution of Masonic organizations and their members. See Peter Levenda, *Unholy Alliance: A History of Nazi Involvement with the Occult* (New York: Avon Books, 1995).

[15] Warren Fowler Mellny, *Moon Lodges* (Washington, D.C.: Masonic Service Association, 1954).

[16] U.S. National Aeronautics and Space Administration, Interview with Dr. Werner von Braun, 17 November 1971.

ture in the bookstores and on the World Wide Web that alleges NASA has discovered ancient, monumental structures on the Moon and that it is hiding their existence from the public.) Or is von Braun simply saying that lunar geology is interesting and a big help in understanding geology on other bodies in the solar system? From the context of his remarks, it appears that he means the latter, but who knows?—maybe he *is* talking in code and is actually communicating a carefully guarded message between the lines.

Similarly, Kenneth S. Kleinknecht wrote the following in 1975: "On the surface of the moon, where there is no atmosphere to erode, secrets were uncovered that have long since been worn away here on earth."[17] Here again—what secrets is Kleinknecht referring to? Are there ancient ruins on the moon? Ruins perhaps made by a long vanished civilization that might have existed in remote antiquity on the earth itself? Or is he simply referring to the interesting lunar geology that does not erode due to the scouring action of water and wind, and the incessant activities of biological organisms? The context of his remarks suggests that he is making an innocent remark about perfectly ordinary geological processes. But who knows?—might he, as well as von Braun, be referring to something that NASA has hidden from the public? Something unimaginably ancient and important—like artificially constructed, ruined structures on the moon? Let me be clear: I do not claim to know definitively one way or the other.

But isn't it strange that this entire line of inquiry is due to a telepathic message I received from Robert Monroe while locked in a jail cell in Arkansas, as punishment for demonstrating against nuclear missiles atop a Titan missile silo in central Arkansas, Albert Pike's home state?

I suppose I would still be in contact with Robert Monroe today if it were not for the fact that over a period of years I became aware that he and his research institute in rural Nelson County, Virginia, south of Charlottesville, had a close working relationship with United States Army Intelligence.[18] I perceive the agendas of the military intelligence agencies to be very dark and repressive, so I have broken off contact with Robert Monroe (who is now physically dead), with the circle of people around him and with the Monroe Institute.

---

[17] Kenneth S. Kleinknecht, "Foreword", *Apollo Spacecraft Chronology, Vol. IV*, October 1975. Photocopied article in the NASA archives, Washington, D.C.

[18] See Jim Schnabel, *Remote Viewers: The Secret History of America's Psychic Spies* (New York: Dell Publishing, 1997). The Monroe Institute trained psychic spies for the military at its long-time headquarters in Faber, Virginia. The present director of the Monroe Institute, Skip Atwater, is former head of the military psychic spy unit at Fort Meade, near Laurel, Maryland. Joe McMoneagle, Army Intelligence's premier psychic spy, married one of Robert Monroe's step-daughters and retired to Robert Monroe's *New Land* community, immediately adjacent to the Institute grounds.

Three

~~~~~~

ON THE OCCASION OF MY FIRST out-of-body experience I was living in Lancaster County, Pennsylvania. The year was 1978. I had been doing a simple one-two-three-four counting meditation in the middle of the night when I suddenly felt myself drifting out of my body and sinking down, down, down – as if I were sinking right through my bed and through the floor. Never have I felt more relaxed. The sense of deep calm and utter relaxation was extraordinary.

To be sure, at the same time I was terribly curious about what was happening. I felt at the time that if I would have been any more relaxed I would have died—and would not have minded! The sensation was so peaceful, the very opposite of the feeling of tension, hurry, and pressure so common to everyday life, that I would gladly have remained in such a pleasant, relaxing space, if it were possible. As I sank down and down I found myself looking at a small table, at eye level. The table was perfectly ordinary in every way. It had four legs, was about two feet high, and was stained or varnished a brownish, woody-looking color. But what really caught my attention was a small tape recorder that was sitting on the table. This small tape recorder seemed unremarkable in most respects; it had four brightly colored buttons on the front. Each of the four buttons was a distinctly different color. The position, size and shape of the buttons corresponded perfectly to play, fast forward, reverse and stop buttons on any other small or portable tape recorder. I could not see any writing on the recorder, on the buttons, on the table or anywhere else.

I was tremendously excited by the experience in its entirety.

When I made contact with the Monroe Institute the following year and began to learn Robert Monroe's taped exercises that entrain the brain waves and help induce out-of-body experiences I assumed that my out-of-body vision of the tape recorder was precognitive. I felt at the time that it was pointing the way towards the Monroe Institute and Robert Monroe's training tapes. It seemed to me a classic example of the unconscious mind (or some analogous deep level of consciousness) sending a symbolic, mental telegram to the waking mind, in order to nudge it in another direction.

More recently, though, I have come to think that the message was probably more universal than I initially thought. I am now inclined to see the recorder as representing a universal recorder of consciousness—perhaps as a mechanism for accessing the *akashic*[19] record. Perhaps this tape recorder (or something similar) sits eternally and silently at the ready in all of us, awaiting the moment when we quietly and peacefully enter the *sanctum sanctorum* of our own being, there to tap the play button and receive the accumulated wisdom of the ages, and also to see and understand our own lives from a uniquely interior, deeply spiritual perspective.

Seen in this light, the work of Robert Monroe might be viewed as a partial, technological projection into physical reality from this deeper spiritual reality. His system of tape training would repre-

---

[19] In some eastern traditions there is the concept of an akashic record that scrupulously chronicles, in minute detail, the thoughts, words, and deeds of every person who has ever lived; the akashic record is also said by some to contain the detailed history of the Earth itself. All of this is purportedly inscribed indelibly, in scrupulous detail, for all eternity, and is accessible only by conscious, mental means.

sent a technological, electronic means of accessing the interior tape recorder, if you will. But due to the close involvement of the Monroe Institute with Army intelligence I have become extremely wary of having any contact with the Institute or any of the people who live or work there. By their very nature intelligence agencies are deceitful. When you are working with your own consciousness you certainly do not want to get involved with deceitful people and agencies —quite the contrary. What you are seeking is the absolutely true and the reliable. Intelligence agencies spread misinformation and disinformation of every variety. It is far better, in my opinion, to inquire with sincerity into the deepest levels of your own being than to go running after military intelligence agencies, and those associated with them, for enlightenment.

In a word, the truth is not "out there," withheld and controlled by sinister authorities. Rather, the truth is "in here," and intimately available to the sincere seeker.

Four

DURING THE 1980's I had many other out-of-body experiences. On one occasion I awoke in the middle of the night to discover that I was rotating out of my body. As I rotated out my gaze was irresistibly drawn to a most singular patch of liquid light that appeared before me in the darkness. I doubt that it would have been externally visible to anyone else, had they been present in the room, since I was entering into an altered state of consciousness. The light was a brilliant violet color, preternaturally alive, roiling, moving as though motivated from within by a compelling force which was not apparent to the eye. It behaved much like a cauldron or ladle of molten metal, although it did not seem to be hot. It was the most attractive sight I have ever beheld anywhere. I literally could not take my eyes off of it; it was more alluring to me than the most beautiful woman I have ever known. It was absolutely riveting and enthralling. If I were able to gaze at will on that enticing violet light, it is possible that I would do so to the exclusion of almost anything else. But then it was gone and I was off and rushing through a dark void. It felt like I was passing through a fluid-like substance of some sort. I hurtled along at what seemed to be a high speed. After a few minutes I stopped in the darkness. In front of me I could see a man sitting cross-legged on a cushion. But I was having difficulty seeing. My eyes felt very gritty, as if they had sand in them. The sensation was very physical, yet I was in the middle of a full-blown out-of-the-body experience. At the same time I was very alert mentally, and distinctly conscious of being in a highly unusual state of awareness. I had not the faintest clue as to where I was. As I rubbed my eyes, and mentally bemoaned my vision problem, I suddenly heard the voice of Jesus speaking to me. The majesty and sheer authority in his voice were without compare. He exuded supreme power and utter self-confidence. I recognized him instantly. His voice was as anciently and reflexively familiar to me as if I had spent several hours every day for the last 2,000 years talking with him. I cannot fathom how this can be so, and yet I heard his voice and it was instantly more familiar and recognizable to me than the voice of even my mother or my brothers. I will never forget the question he posed. He said: *"How can you expect to have spiritual vision, if you can't see the suffering of little children?"*

The thrust of the question could not be clearer. Psychic power means precious little to Jesus as an end in itself. This is the pithy Jesus of the gospels getting right down to the crux of the matter: the suffering of little children. His clear implication is that the way to spiritual vision is through sensitive awareness to the suffering of our fellow humans. In this instance he called my attention to the suffering of small children. How can any of us, you or me, hope to advance spiritually unless we get involved in helping to alleviate the vast amount of human misery and suffering that surrounds us on every hand?

Five

ABOUT A YEAR AFTER THIS I awoke suddenly one morning and moved quickly into a full-blown kundalini experience. The kundalini moved swiftly up my spine and energized my body. No sooner was this done than my body spontaneously, automatically executed a perfect *hatha* yoga posture (*Salabhasana*) without my willing it or even having thought about it. I observed what happened as though my body were on auto-pilot. The whole thing was absolutely effortless. I felt no sense of exertion whatever. My muscles and joints were completely relaxed and supple—there was not the slightest physical or mental blockage anywhere. The experience simply happened.

Six

~~~~~~

ONE OF THE MOST INTERESTING out-of-body experiences I ever had occurred in 1979, when I was living in a small apartment in Southwest Louisiana, upstairs over a two-car garage, near the main rail line between New Orleans and Houston. The place was surrounded by shade trees and had lots of windows. Although the building was rather old and a bit dilapidated I liked the feel of it. The interior walls were covered in inexpensive, dark-stained wood paneling and there was a solid wood floor. The floor plan was simple—there were four rooms around a central bathroom. There was a door between adjacent rooms, making it possible to go from room to room and navigate the apartment in a circular fashion. The two doors in the rear were not solid, but had panes of glass, in the French manner. The whole place had a sort of dream-like atmosphere: the colors; the sound of the wind in the trees in the evening; the near-deafening drone of the cicadas on a hot summer night with the windows flung wide open; and the heavy, muffled thrumming of the Southern Pacific freights miles away in the fluttering darkness, far out over the bayous and cane fields, headlights flashing serpentine like things alive, as the engineers ran through all the gears, rumbling on through the deepening night, horns blaring at every country crossing, snaking west over the muggy coastal plain to Houston and beyond.

In just this place, and in just this ambiance, I slipped out of my body early one morning. I had just awakened when I felt myself begin to move into a nonordinary state of consciousness. In front of me I saw an absolute blank. Nothing. I decided that I would mentally count to ten to see what would happen. As I did

so, I saw the numbers appear before my inner vision. They were very distinctly formed, very crisp and clear. And they were all a pronounced cherry red color. As I counted, they ticked off one by one, just like numbers on an electronic, digital read-out. The impression was exactly like watching numbers appear on a digital clock face, or on a gasoline pump.

When I reached ten I spontaneously (and unexpectedly) arched gracefully out of my body and floated on a smooth, curved trajectory over the edge of the bed and down towards the floor. In mid-air, my body easily and naturally assumed a crossed-legged, sitting posture, as if I were going to sit for meditation. It was positively fun! Imagine my pleasant surprise when I reached the floor and discovered that I was floating about an inch in the air. I felt as though I were a giant magnet being repelled with just enough force to barely hover over the floor. There was no sense of an electrical charge, however; the feeling was rather one of a gentle, magnetic, levitating repulsion that kept my subtle body just slightly air-borne, without the slightest effort on my part.

And then I was off and moving! Like a miniature hovercraft (but without any sound or sensation of propulsion) I scooted off over the floor and toward the door to my room. As I went *through* the closed door, my body reflexively and effortlessly twirled around in a little circle, with me facing outward. In other words, my spine was the axis around which I turned. The little twirl had a feeling of magical excitement. The colors in my environment were extremely rich and vibrant. I saw everything with startling clarity. As I completed the twirl I passed through to the other side of the door. I felt absolutely no sensation of the door at all—it was as insubstantial as thin air. I continued moving, how and why I did not know (and still do not). I approached the first of the glass-paned French doors and once again twirled around in a neat little circle as I passed *through* it too. I continued on into the next room and went through two more doorways, one of them open, before I returned again to my bedside. At each of the other two doorways, my subtle body also twirled around in the same little circle as before, as it passed through the doorway. It did not seem to matter, either, whether the door was open or closed, because one of the doors was open and the little twirl maneuver still took place. The trigger for the "twirl" appeared to be the act of passing through a doorway, and not the presence of a physical barrier—since the presence of a physical door proved to be no impediment in this state to free passage.

To the best of my recollection, when I arrived back at my bedside the experience simply ended. My next perception was of lying awake in my bed. At the time I had no clear idea what the ultimate significance of the little "Magical Mystery Tour" of my humble apartment may have been. In retrospect it seems to me that the point of the experience may have been simply to awaken me to the genuine mystery of something as usual as a simple little apartment in a very ordinary, Deep South town in the middle of nowhere.

Magic is wherever you find it.

Seven

ON ANOTHER OCCASION I had an interesting experience while *in* the body. I was working at a fabrication yard constructing machinery for the sugar cane industry. It was a hot day in the summer of 1980 and I was busy moving several tons of sheet metal and thick steel plate with a 20 ton overhead crane. I held the control panel for the crane in one hand, while I adjusted the hooks that would lift the steel with the other. Normally this is a job performed by two or three men, but crews were short due to sickness and vacations so I was working by myself. The crane ran up and down on tracks high above the ground that extended the length of a cavernous shed. This large building was a veritable beehive of activity. Gangs of men were hard at work welding, grinding and cutting steel plates and other machine parts in white-hot showers of sparks. The blue-white crackle of welding machines and cutting torches and the pounding of sledge hammers filled the building. The hum of lathes and the whine of saws cut through the heavy, subtropical heat as the afternoon sun slanted in through the cobwebs and dusty windows high overhead the work area.

In the midst of all this industrial din and clatter I bent down to place the hooks for the crane I was operating. I situated them under the steel plates I was going to move further down the production line, pressed the "up" button to lift the load about 2 feet into the air to transport it, and straightened up. In the instant that I carried out this familiar, virtually reflexive operation I was astonished to see that the entire interior of the building had suddenly become filled with hundreds, if not thousands, of golden, softly luminous objects, about the size and shape of an average pecan. They were everywhere—up in the rafters, as well as leisurely roaming around in my immediate vicinity. I had no idea what they were or where they came from.

They exuded a very purposeful and mysterious air. It was almost as if they were intelligent. Certainly their movement in the air was very calm and deliberate. Each one was clearly distinct and yet they all seemed patently self-assured and coordinated in their movements. I hurriedly glanced around to see if any of the other men had noticed. Clearly, I was the only person who perceived them; at any rate, no one else seemed to have noticed anything unusual. So I stood there and simply observed them in wonder. To my eye they were substantial and solid. When one moved between me, and a person or object in the background, my view of whatever was behind the golden, luminous objects was obstructed.

It was all quite peculiar and magical. I didn't know what to make of it. And then I became aware that their numbers were dwindling. As the minutes went by their numbers markedly decreased, until there were only a few dozen left. Since they meandered around so very slowly I could not imagine what was happening to them. But then I noticed that whenever I turned my head from one side to another, and then back again, the little golden things would not be there in the air where they were before I turned my head. In other words, as soon as they crossed the periphery of my visual field they were gone. And turning my head quickly did not bring them back!

I was in a quandary! These little luminous, golden things were utterly enchanting and enigmatic. I was enthralled and delighted by their sudden appearance and now they were going away and I was powerless to stop them. I determined that if moving my head caused them to disappear, that I would not move my head. I reasoned that this would surely keep at least a few of them in view. Alas! Even though they moved very slowly, one by one they crossed over the periphery of my vision and were gone from sight.

Finally, there were just two left and they began to move in opposite directions. One moved right and the other left. I had to do something. So I cast my gaze on the one on the left. In a matter of seconds the one on the right disappeared. I thought that I could slightly shift my gaze to the right, while continuing to keep the one on the left within view, to see if the one on the right was not lurking just barely beyond the edge of my vision. Nothing doing! No sooner had I done this than the one on the left ever so slightly edged out of sight and was gone. Gone into thin air. All of them gone back into the thin air whence they came.

It was only then that I realized that I should have single-mindedly fixed my gaze on just one of them and attended to its every movement without distraction. Who knows what might have happened? Perhaps I would have entered into another reality—a golden, luminous, softly glowing realm instead of the harsh, cacophonous, industrial world that has caught me up instead.

Or maybe the result would have been the same anyway. Maybe the golden, luminous thing would have simply wafted higher and higher up into the air behind a girder and still have been lost to my sight. As of this writing I am not sure that I will ever know what they were, where they came from and why I saw them.

To be sure, their mystery visit did raise many questions in my mind about the nature of reality, both physical and mental, and the relationship between the two. I would like to emphasize that I was wide awake, not under the influence of any chemical or herbal substance, and going through my everyday work routine when I had this experience. And I was in a noisy, busy, industrial environment, surrounded by other people. Hardly the sort of place where you would expect to have a remarkable experience of this sort.

But maybe that was just the point. Who can tell when something magical will happen? Is not mystery's primary characteristic

that it is so, well, *inscrutable*? Who am I to prejudge when something completely magical and unexpected may or may not happen? Epiphanies, no matter how minor, no matter how inscrutable, arrive in their own time, in their own way, and answering to a method and a reason that may finally be neither known nor knowable.

The only other previous experiences of this sort occurred during my teenage years in Virginia, while playing basketball in the backyard. My father had set up a basketball goal and backboard for my two brothers and me, and we often played by ourselves, or with other boys from the neighborhood. On two occasions, I was suddenly surrounded by luminous creatures swimming in the air.[20] As bizarre as it sounds, these lumi-

---

[20] What I saw were not the myriad, incessantly spiralling, tiny pinwheels of silvery light that many people (including me) can see at will when they let their gaze go slack and stare into the open sky. Neither were they the proverbial "sparks" that many people (including me) see when they feel faint or very tired and are about to lose consciousness. Those sparks, induced by stress and/or fatigue are very vivid and fierce little lights that float around in one's field of vision. What I describe here, as well as the golden, luminous objects I described previously, are something else entirely than these familiar, ocular phenomena.

But why the resemblance to tadpoles? Why didn't the creatures I saw resemble frogs? Or snakes? Or squids? Or turtles? Or paramecia? Or amoebae?

I can speculate. There may be some symbolism here. Tadpoles are an immature stage in the amphibian life-cycle. They live only in water. However, mature amphibians can live, breath and maneuver both in water and on land. Maybe, by analogy, human life on Earth is like a tadpole stage of our full life cycle. Maybe we are like the tadpole that little suspects that it will one day mature into another form (frog or toad) and experience two realms (the terrestrial and the aquatic), and have a much broader and less restricted life experience, able to maneuver on dry land and in aquatic environments.

We see our physical, Earthly life up close and real. It seems to us to be "all-there-is." But we also have a spiritual dimension — more subtle, embryonic aspects of our being that we but dimly perceive and acknowledge. Maybe at death, or potentially before, as through meditation, yoga or other spiritual practice (not to be confused with fundamentalist religious beliefs and practices), we awaken to a more comprehensive stage of existence, that comprises both the physical and spiritual realms.

The resemblance to spermatozoa is interesting as well. First of all, I am male. My gonads contain millions of spermatozoa. Was I simply viewing the magical aspect of my essential

nous, translucent animals strongly resembled large tadpoles or giant spermatozoa, with an apparent length of maybe two or three inches. Their bodies resembled those of tadpoles, while their tails were proportionately longer than tadpole tails, more nearly resembling the long tails of sperm cells. They had distinct heads with eyes, little fins, sleek, silvery bodies and long wriggling tails. And they swam around in the air, just a few feet off the ground, as if they were meandering around in the shallows of an invisible pond or water puddle. Though they were very softly luminous, they had apparent solidity and depth, in that when they passed in front of an object in the background, such as the family home, a shrub or the basketball goal, they would obstruct from view whatever portion of the background object was behind their wriggling form.

After a couple of minutes their numbers dwindled, and they went away, seemingly in the same manner as the golden, nut-sized "things" described above. They just sort of leisurely went away, one by one. To tell the truth, I do not know whence they came; neither do I know to where they returned. On both occasions, I was playing basketball. It seems to me that the physical exertion of playing the game, combined with the reflexive visual coordination and concentration required to dribble and shoot a basketball may have provided the proper stimulus to move me into a heightened state of awareness. The key was that I was physically active, and engaged in an activity which involved a repetitive use of habitual motor skills. It is probably not an accident that years later in Louisiana I also saw the golden, self-luminous "things" while exerting myself physically and engaging in a work routine that involved the near automatic manipulation with one hand of the control panel of a 20-ton overhead crane, and the careful placement of its attached cables and hooks beneath several tons of steel plates. It was a delicate juggling act that required careful coordination of my eyes and hands, and a powerful piece of industrial machinery—and all without thinking overly much about what I was doing. My eyes, my body, the machine, the tons of metal—the whole ensemble flowed together in one smooth operation.

But is it really possible that playing basketball, or working in a noisy factory can serve as entry points *while wide awake* into altered states of consciousness, into seemingly magical realities? In my own experience the answer can only be: on some occasions, *yes*.

---

masculinity? (And would a young woman have perceived large, luminous "eggs" floating mysteriously in the air?) Secondly, the resemblance to spermatozoa suggests by implication the sexual organs and sexual energies, which play an empowering role in the activities of the kundalini, when rightly channeled and transformed (and a most damaging role, when wrongly channeled — look at all the failed marriages, unwanted pregnancies and children, venereal disease and rape in our society — all because we humans have a lot of problems handling our sexual energies). Finally, the sperm cell must join with the egg cell to generate a new organism, and then only within the confines of a receptive womb. By implication, the resemblance to spermatozoa of the luminous "tadpoles" would be an additional indication of incompletion, of the need for something else, a need for the feminine "other" in order to self-transcend.

In the physical realm, creation of a new being occurs via sexual intercourse between a potent male and a fertile female. At more subtle levels, I am not sure what occurs. Maybe the field of consciousness in which our individual consciousnesses clumsily swim is by nature "feminine", meaning that it is fecund, fertile, creative. Maybe in some wise our little consciousnesses impregnate the larger, more universal field of consciousness which we dimly perceive (like tadpoles squinting up at the surface of a water puddle, feebly sensing the huge world beyond), generating a new being in the course of time; in most cases after death, but in some cases before, if the individual sufficiently develops his/her level of consciousness. This is a very crude analogy, but I am inclined to think there may be a degree of truth in it.

Eight

ONE OF THE MOST UNUSUAL kundalini experiences that happened to me occurred several years ago. As best as I can remember I was in the middle of a perfectly ordinary dream one night when all of a sudden I was catapulted out of the dream, by a process I still do not understand, and into a dramatically heightened state of consciousness. I found myself somehow jointly occupying another man's body and observing through his eyes and senses whatever he perceived. I also somehow had intimate, conscious access to his emotional and spiritual state. I can best describe the condition of his mind and body as exceptionally unusual by any ordinary measure.

As the initial shock of the situation wore off a bit, I realized that he was standing outside on a hastily assembled speaker's platform. Just in front of him was a simple lectern with 2 or 3 very used, battered-looking microphones bound together with electrical tape. Off to the side were banks of battered speakers and amplifiers that looked like they had seen better days. And in front of him, stretching off into the distance was a veritable sea of faces. He was making a speech to an enormous throng of people. I could not tell exactly how large the crowd was, but it was truly immense—perhaps numbering in the hundreds of thousands.

So great was my astonishment that to this day I am not sure what language he was speaking. But I still remember clearly that multitude of faces looking back at him—open-mouthed, dumbfounded, absolutely stupefied. As well they might have been, given his condition and the nature of his speech.

He was caught up in an ecstatic, passionate exposition of the un-searchable glories of God. He was shouting at the top of his lungs, and his voice went washing out over the vast assembly, rippling out over row after row of upturned faces. I understood intuitively that his words were carrying a very special power because at that very moment he was under the direct influence of the kundalini. As he spoke it was continuously ripping and roaring up his spine. His entire body was crackling and surging with the full force of what felt to me like tens of thousands of volts of electricity. The roar was deafening (though it was evidently an interior sound; those looking on seemed not to hear it). I sensed vividly that he was acutely aware of the kundalini's presence. He heard the roar; he felt very intensely the tens of thousands of volts of electricity; and he was simultaneously very aware of the effect it had on his voice, and through his voice, the effect it had on the consciousness of the myriad thousands who stood transfixed listening to him.

I noticed that he didn't mention the kundalini directly; rather he played off of its energy, using his own consciousness as sort of a valve or a clutch, to throttle its power down, to transform it, to distill its essence into a palatable, easily assimilable form that the assembled thousands could absorb. He struggled, and very successfully, to ride a very fine line of control in order to carry it off. He was a master orator and consummately attuned to the kundalini's presence in his body. I felt him sensing the mood of the crowd and responding to it with exquisite attention to detail—just the right intonation, the perfect word at exactly the right moment delivered with precisely the inflection of voice that each phrase merited. His gestures and the way he held his body and moved his head responded equally perfectly to the body language of the crowd as they stood there, mesmerized by the sound of his voice, caught up in an event that they did not fully understand.

And then it was over, just as suddenly as it had begun. It was morning and I was physically wide awake. To this day I do not know who the man was or what country he was in, or even what year it was. I only know that the experience was as real to me as ordinary, waking reality.

Nine

IN THE LATE 1980s I encountered the International Society for Krishna Consciousness (ISKCON), popularly known as the Hare Krishna movement. While I never joined this movement I have a deep regard for their vegetarian philosophy. It is my view that ISKCON has gotten an undeservedly bad rap from an often hostile media establishment that has badly misunderstood the society and some of its objectives.

In any event, while attending ISKCON programs I made the acquaintance of one of the initiatory gurus. I never took initiation and have not seen him for some years now. But one morning shortly after I saw him for the last time, I was lying awake in bed before beginning the day's activities when I moved suddenly and unexpectedly into a conscious state of altered awareness. I found myself beside the Hare Krishna guru on a park bench. We were sitting in the middle of a carefully manicured lawn, with medium sized bushes and shrubs planted nearby. He was talking to me and giving me spiritual instruction. The sound of his voice was very soothing, so I closed my eyes to listen. Imagine my surprise when I discovered that I could see perfectly well with my eyes closed. If anything, I saw more clearly with them closed than open. As he talked to me, the kundalini coursed upward through my body, until my entire being was suffused with its energy. Every cell in my whole body began to roar in unison like a jetliner gunning its engines at take-off. The noise was so stupendously loud that I could not hear a word he was saying to me. The sound was absolutely deafening and yet it did not hurt my ears. I felt profoundly blissful and turned my face toward him. I could hear nothing, but even though my eyes were closed I could see his lips moving. I have no idea what he told me. I just grinned stupidly like the Cheshire cat and soaked it all in.

Meanwhile, I was interacting with the nearby bushes and shrubs in a most curious way. Something like a lacy sheet of vapor, composed of diaphanous white flakes, was being exuded by the bushes. This thin white cloud of unknown composition moved toward me, about 3 to 4 feet off the ground. As it approached me it increased its speed, in the manner of a sheet of water approaching a vortex, and was sucked right into my body. I could see all this very clearly, in a 360 degree radius, with my eyes closed. Immense quantities of this thin white sheet of matter came out of the bushes and moved toward me. I could distinctly feel my body sucking in what felt like gallons and gallons of this substance. I am not sure what it was or why the bushes provided it to me. Perhaps it was what the Vedic tradition knows as prana,[21] or what Wilhelm Reich refers to as orgone.[22]

In any event, after this experience I wrote to the guru and described what had happened. A couple of weeks later I received the following laconic reply: "We simply recommend that people chant 'Hare Krishna'." And so I sometimes chant "Hare Krishna."

---

[21] The Vedas are the ancient Sanskrit writings of India. Prana can be understood as the subtle energy, or life force, that animates all living creatures.

[22] For Reich, orgone is the fundamental life energy that animates biological organisms. He believed that it pervades the Earth's atmosphere. See Wilhelm Reich, *The Discovery of the Orgone: The Function of the Orgasm (Sex-Economic Problems of Biological Energy)*, translated from the German by Theodore P. Wolfe (New York: The Noonday Press, Farrar, Straus and Cudahy, third printing, 1961); and also Wilhelm Reich, *The Cancer Biopathy: Volume II of the Discovery of the Orgone*, translated by Andrew White with Mary Higgins and Chester M. Raphael, M.D. (New York: Farrar, Straus and Giroux, 1973).

Ten

I HAVE HAD OTHER kundalini experiences over the years, at sporadic intervals. They have been sufficient to whet my appetite for more. I read a wide variety of spiritual literature, including works by Sri Chinmoy, Paramahansa Yogananda, Gopi Krishna, Srila Prabhupada, Carlos Castaneda and others. From time to time I naturally entered altered states of consciousness. Occasionally, I consciously went out of the body. I meditated some days, and sometimes in the middle of the night. When meditating I sometimes felt very pleasurable, crawling sensations on my scalp, and at different locations on my skull and in my brain. These sensations would also sometimes occur after meditating, in the relaxed state before drifting off to sleep.

During one meditation, I had the vivid mental impression that my mind had greatly expanded. The expansive feeling was purely mental, without any physical component. For want of better words, it seemed to me as if my mind had become very large and solid. This was not a new feeling; it was a mental state that I had experienced at intervals of every few years stretching back to my adolescence in the early 1970s. But now, as then, the experience led to nothing more. It persisted for a matter of minutes then abruptly I was back to my normal state of mind, without having had any grand visions or keen spiritual or psychic insights.

And then I had the following experience, which is illustrative of the kind of powerful effects engendered by the kundalini. About 5:00 o'clock on an April morning I suddenly moved into another, *very high* energy state. I was conscious of this as it happened, and also very aware that I was not asleep. The state that I entered was neither the common dreaming state (whether of the unconscious or lucid variety), nor the state we all know as our everyday, three-dimensional, waking consciousness. For want of better words I will simply call it the "kundalini state."

I suddenly discovered that I was lying on a floor by a large curtain (as one might see in an auditorium). I did not know how or why I had come to be there, or even, for that matter, where "there" was. My attention was nearly completely absorbed by a fantastically coherent assemblage of powerful energy that was gathering in my lower thighs, down around my knees, and slowly moving upward. I understood at once that this was the kundalini. The knowing was instinctive, absolute and sure. The energy had a full, rounded, imminent feel—and it was very purposeful as it moved up my thighs and into my buttocks. I was struck once again by the deliberate, unhurried manner of the kundalini. It has a slow, but inevitable quality that is characteristic of its movement (at least in *my* body). The energy continued up into my lower spine, where it was especially intense and concentrated. It then spread out across my entire back, as it rose up to my neck and then into my head. It moved first into the back of my head, where it focused powerfully. After lingering there for a couple of minutes it moved slowly up over the crown of my head and concentrated itself again, this time in the area between the crown and forehead. It remained there for a few minutes and then began to retrace its route, producing the same effects and feelings at each point as it retraced its way back to the area of my knees. It took a period of minutes to recede, but lost nothing in strength until it reached my lower thighs and began to gradually diminish in intensity. Eventually I could feel nothing out of the ordinary and the experience was over.

I want to emphasize that the sensation was a most pleasant one. It was also one that I did not directly control—the whole experience was under the control of the kundalini itself. Indeed, beside the sheer, raw energy of the kundalini, perhaps its other most salient characteristic is its deliberateness, the measured, methodical way in which it moves through the body. It is exceedingly powerful, and yet it always exudes a most definite aura of calm, self-control and singleness of intent. It is also very self-sure. The sense that I get is that it is a coherent, self-conscious expression of the universal life energy, or orgone energy, described by Wilhelm Reich. According to this perspective, it seems to me that the kundalini experience itself is a conscious, localized interfacing of the human mind and body with the universal life force that animates the cosmos.

The kundalini is awesome, and with the proper intent and preparation humans can consciously interact with it. It is my belief that mature, healthy human beings (regardless of race, ethnic origin or gender) are genetically wired with the potential to consciously interact with their own life energy.

This is indeed a happy turn of events. It means that the Master Programmer (God?) has created humans with a mind-body that functions as a sort of modem between the cosmic life force that animates all of Creation (analogous to a divine software program for engendering and maintaining life and consciousness, in their myriad expressions, the universe over), and the individual quantum of human consciousness that inhabits our particular mind-body complex that each of us know as "me" (think of it—"we", each and every one of us, think of ourselves as "me"!). Our minds and bodies then became the modem, or up-link, that the kundalini uses to establish direct, up-close and personal contact with all of our billions of individual, seemingly isolated, human consciousnesses. If substantial numbers of humans develop into this direct, conscious relationship with the kundalini I believe that the effect on the mass-mind of the human race would be nothing short of astonishing. This is a very real possibility. If the kundalini can be activated in one human mind-body the same can happen to others. It is all a question of what "we" (the six billion strong and growing global "me") really want. The access code for the kundalini is right there in our human operator's manual (cleverly inscribed in our DNA). What we do with it, if anything, is purely up to us.

Eleven

Over time many other peculiar things have happened. I went through a period where I would on rare occasions hear voices in my head just before I fell asleep at night. On one occasion, the voice of an older man, speaking in a slight foreign accent said very clearly, "Young *man*!?" It surprised me so much that I sat up in bed. A few weeks later, I had no sooner stretched out in bed and closed my eyes than I heard the voice of a young man say, "Richard!?" Needless to say, I hardly knew what to make of this. The voices did not correspond to any objective, external reality. My bedside radio was turned off and I was living alone. There was no one else present but me. Moreover, the voices had a decidedly interior quality. They did not register in my ears, as do ambient sounds in the physical environment; rather, I distinctly perceived the voices as if the speakers were actually in my mind. Of course, this raises the possibility that the voices actually were in my mind, in the sense that they may represent superconscious aspects of my own personality (or, in a more universal sense, of the entire human race's collective personality) that are attempting to communicate directly with my conscious mind. I believe this happens frequently, but we never notice because our lives and our minds are full of so much superficial hustle, bustle, chatter, and never-ending busyness that the higher levels of consciousness have a hard time breaking through to our cluttered, junked-up minds. So because we are so noisy we hear nothing.[23]

I also experienced the following on several occasions: as I relaxed in bed, before falling asleep, intensely pleasurable sensations would ripple wave-like through my head and brain. The blissful feelings were near orgasmic in quality and intensity—really most pleasurable. However, they were strictly localized in distinct parts of my brain and in the skull and scalp area—particularly on the sides of my head, above my ears, and also in the back of the head.

While drifting to sleep I have also sometimes heard interior snapping or crackling sounds that were associated with brief, tactile sensations that I felt with my non-physical body. The snapping or crackling sounds and accompanying sensations occurred all over my body—on my feet, my back, in my head. Sometimes they were very quiet, like a little "snick".[24] But on a couple of occa-

---

be that anyone who hears disembodied voices and other sounds in their head is somehow mentally ill, psychotic or dangerous. Just a few centuries ago in Europe untold hundreds of thousands, perhaps millions, of people were burned at the stake as witches for far less than I have written in this book. In our present day, people can be and have been forcibly incarcerated in asylums and violently subjected to mind destroying, high voltage electrical shocks administered to their brains, or subjected to a variety of mind searing pharmaceutical chemicals forcibly injected into their bodies, *against their will and without their consent*, to force them to conform to "normative" behavior as defined by peer agreement among mental health professionals.

Let me state that I believe I am sane. If anything, I believe I am more observant and analytical than the average person. I have not been satisfied to mutely accept the dumbed-down "herd" mentality without question, as so many people do.

24 It is my observation that these sounds are distinct from the cracking noises that may occur in the vertebrae of the upper neck or farther down in the spinal column. Such sounds are clearly conducted by the bones of the spine and the skull to the inner ear. Based on my personal observation, the quiet little "snicks" and occasional explosive noises have to do with another class of phenomena, probably having components in both the subtle and physical bodies. I might add that I believe

---

23 Alternatively, there is the possibility these voices and other sounds perceived within the head could have been of an exterior, electronic origin (see below and the appendix for more along this line.) Of course, another, less charitable view would

sions the sounds in my head were so loud that I actually thought a powerful explosion had occurred just outside my apartment and physically got out of bed to personally check the immediate vicinity. I am not sure what causes these sounds and the accompanying sensations. Perhaps there is an energy discharge when the human organism or human mind approaches the threshold between states of consciousness or alternate levels of reality. Maybe that is what I am hearing. Or maybe I am hearing actual synaptic discharges by the nerves in the body, as electrical currents flow through the neural network that fills my brain and connects it with the organs and limbs of the body.

---

that the physical and subtle body fit together and work together in a hand-in-glove fashion, and that the artificial distinction between the two breaks down quickly when an individual begins to have the kinds of experiences that I describe throughout this book.

Twelve

IT IS POSSIBLE to move out of a dream and into the out-of body state. I once had the following dream: in the dream I was lying in bed in a strange location when I suddenly felt my body rise up in the bed, pulling the covers with it as I rose several inches into the air. At the same time, I was consciously aware that my legs were going out-of-body. The left one began to slowly twirl (out-of-body) in a circular fashion, while the right leg was bent at the knee at a right angle, with the foot pointing towards my left leg. To be sure, it was not the first time that the out-of-body "legs" experience had happened to me.

In previous years, similar experiences had occurred, though with a bit of a different twist. The first time, I was living in the Deep South and it was a muggy, summer afternoon. I felt very drowsy and tired, so I reclined on my bed in front of the window fan to take a short nap. No sooner had I laid down than I began to move into an altered state of consciousness. However, the transition was so peculiar that at first I did not understand what was happening: shortly after stretching out (and while still awake) I noticed that my fan was beginning to turn abnormally fast. I could hear it beginning to spin faster and faster and faster. Initially I dismissed its increased speed as being due to a gust of wind. But as its pitch increased, indicating that the blades were continuing to accelerate, I became alarmed. I was concerned that the motor would overheat and start an electrical fire. I decided to get up and turn off the fan before something disastrous happened—but when I tried to sit up, I discovered my body would not respond. What happened instead, to my considerable surprise, was that several pairs of

hands began gently touching my feet. I attempted to open my eyes to see who was touching me and discovered that I could not do that either. Just a moment before, when I had entered the bedroom, I had been alone. So you can imagine what kind of questions were running through my mind. And then I felt the hands gently swing my lower legs up and out of the body. That is when I finally realized that I had moved into an altered state—albeit one in which I could still hear my fan, the shouts of children playing in the neighborhood, and noises from traffic on the road in front of the house. The mystery hands gently touched my feet all over. They were very purposeful and sure and yet very subtle. As I reclined in bewilderment, asking myself what in the world was happening, a very precise and unambiguous thought formed in my head. I heard no voice(s), saw no words or text, and yet very distinctly mentally perceived the following words: "Do not worry about what is happening or why. Just relax and observe the experience." And then it was over. I could move my body and open my eyes. My fan slowed down to its normal speed and I laid there in bed mulling things over in my mind. I did not understand then what had happened. And I still don't have a good explanation for that event. My best guess is that someone, or something, chose to work on subtle energy flows in my body, via my feet, while I was in an altered, though conscious, state of awareness.

This was not to be the only time for such an experience. A few years later, while living in the Southwest I was abruptly awakened out of a deep sleep one night when several pairs of hands lifted my lower legs out-of-body. Lying there in the dark, I quickly moved into a conscious state of altered awareness. Once again, I could feel several hands gently touching my feet everywhere. As before, they were very purposeful and deliberate, yet I could not discern the reason for this unusual exercise. I decided to see if I could learn something about the owners of the hands, so after a few minutes I mustered up my courage and mentally asked them if I could feel their hands. You might think that I would ask to see the people or beings to whom the hands belonged. Or that I would ask who they were. But I did not. I was terrified at the prospect of perhaps seeing close-up some monstrous, nightmarish visage, or perhaps, even more troubling, the face of someone I knew —

I was not sure which would be more unsettling. In any event, I decided to put that question off to a future time, if indeed there were to be a future recurrence of the experience. So I asked instead to feel their hands. Instantly, one of "them" took me by the hand. Their hands felt very soft and warm. I began to feel and count the fingers: one, two, three. Three? I thought that there must be more, so I continued to feel, and sure enough, there was finger four, and then finger five—and then finger six. Six fingers on a hand? Or three fingers on two hands?—what! In a short while the altered state faded away and I just lay there in the dark until I dozed off to sleep again.

Thirteen

IT WAS A RESPLENDENT DAY in 1958, a fine spring day in the Virginia Tidewater, the first day of the first memory in my life. I was just 3 years old and sickly, because of a digestive disorder. My older brother (who was four years old then) and I had been put out on the screen porch for the afternoon by our mother. It was a pleasant place to play and she could watch us through the window as she worked in the kitchen. There was a honey locust tree just behind the porch and beyond that a small, shallow pond silted in and full of aquatic weeds and cattails.

Since I was fond of eating Cheerios with a crochet hook, my mother had thoughtfully provided me with a bowl full of them and a crochet hook. My brother was seated on the floor beside me. We were playing some sort of little game, precisely what I no longer recall. To this day, I distinctly remember that as we played I was going methodically through the bowl, hooking Cheerios, one by one, and eating them.

I was only half finished when I tipped the bowl over, spilling the contents on the floor. Imagine my consternation. Cheerios went rolling everywhere. So I began picking them up with the crochet hook, one by one, and putting them back in the bowl. Suddenly, something prompted me to look up toward the gutter on the edge of the porch roof. And that look up, at the age of three, while scrabbling about with a crochet hook picking up a bowl of spilled Cheerios, proved to be the most singular experience of my life.

I cannot begin to adequately describe what I saw standing there on the porch roof—but I will try. Here is what I saw: *The Bone Lady* was leaning over the edge of the roof looking at *me*. That was the name I gave *Her* at the age of three. *Her* appearance was that of a gaunt figure dressed in long, flowing garments, dark and mysterious. Even though I still have difficulty understanding exactly who, and what, *The Bone Lady* represents, it was clear to me even at the age of three that something highly strange and momentous was happening.

I turned to my brother and tried to get him to look up at *Her*. But he wouldn't move. He sat rooted to the spot and would not respond. I absolutely could not get him to talk to me or to look at *The Bone Lady*. He just sat there unmoving. I looked back up at *The Bone Lady* and the gaze we exchanged is the most powerful moment that I have ever experienced in my life. At the age of three I was, at best, semi-verbal. So, of necessity, what passed between us was essentially nonverbal, and for that reason I still find it almost impossible to verbalize its substance.

I can tell you, though, of the powerful effect *The Bone Lady*'s gaze has had on my life. Seeing *Her* decisively changed me. I became introspective. I think I was already inclined towards shyness, but *She* caused me to feel even more shy. Seeing *Her* made me feel very strange and different, like one of a kind, as if I were a stranger in a foreign land. I felt uneasy, as if I were a person set apart. My mother told me years later that she realized something had happened to me that day, because I kept telling her about *The Bone Lady* and walking around in the yard staring at the roof and repeatedly rubbing my thumbs and index fingers together. To this day, I remember walking out in the yard and looking in the direction of *Her* departure, as *She* walked away in the air, over the treetops in the direction of the Warwick River.

For years afterward, I thought about *The Bone Lady* every single day, often for hours on end. *She* would be the last thing I thought about before I went to sleep at night. And I would think about *Her* frequently during the day. This preoccupation with *The Bone Lady* persisted until my mid-thirties, when I suddenly ceased to think about *Her* all the time.

If I had to guess, I would say that *The Bone Lady* prompted something very, very deep in me—probably at a cellular or molecular level, perhaps in the DNA, or somewhere in the cerebrospinal complex. Either *She* is an individual, localized manifestation of an archetype such as Kali, the Hindu goddess of death and destruction, or *She* is some other powerful entity or demigoddess come to interact with me on a very deep, nonverbal level, way, way down in the virtually unfathomable recesses of my body and my soul. I have the feeling that as time goes by, more and more dimensions of *Her* and of me will interact, probably without my consciously knowing it and probably without my needing to will it.

Fourteen

IN THE LATE 1980s I relocated from the South to the Southwest. Shortly after arriving in the Southwest I began to meet people who told me of purported, secret underground bases and installations where alleged "Little Grey" extraterrestrials and covert elements of the United States military were hard at work on covert, Nazi-like genetic engineering experiments. The stories were highly strange, and persistent. As the years went by I continued to hear about these purported facilities and activities.

Finally, I did a little research and discovered that, indeed, there are covert underground bases and facilities run by the military and other agencies. Many (though by no means all) of these are in the eastern and mid-Atlantic states. In June of 1992 I made a trip to the East Coast and actually visited a couple of them, one operated at that time by the Federal Reserve, near Culpeper, Virginia and the other by the Federal Emergency Management Agency (FEMA), between Olney and Laytonsville, in Maryland. Later that summer, I wrote a short article for *UFO Magazine*, published in Los Angeles. I identified the underground installations that I could document working from the public record. The article appeared in November 1992 and was well received. In the article I said that while I could neither prove nor disprove the existence of alleged "Little Grey" aliens in secret underground facilities (or anywhere else), I *could* prove the existence of many, secure underground facilities. And that was that. The article appeared and I thought my research was over.

Little did I know. Less than two months later, during the last week of December 1992, I was awakened late one night out of a sound sleep. Nothing seemed to be wrong and I could not determine a reason for having awakened so suddenly. I had been awake only a matter of seconds when I heard a voice in my right ear say very distinctly and matter-of-factly, *"The underground bases are real."* At that point, let me assure you, I was all ears. The voice sounded to me as if were that of an adult male Caucasian, speaking normally accented, late-20th-century North American English. He went on to tell me that secret underground bases do exist; that there are many of them; and that the general public little suspects, or suspects not at all, that these facilities exist. He added that there are people working and living underground and that the public would be astonished to know about these bases and what goes on in them, if they were to find out about them. He continued in this vein for maybe two or three minutes, giving me fairly general information, and then he stopped speaking as abruptly as he had started.

I would stress at this point that I do not use drugs, and do not consume alcohol at all. In many respects I lead a rather quiet life. So I was completely flummoxed as to how I came to hear this unknown man's voice. I do not know who he was and why he talked to me. I quickly determined that I probably never would have answers to those questions. So I put them out of my mind.[25]

---

[25] I now believe I know how the message I heard was broadcast into my mind. And no, I do not believe the voice I heard was a symptom of mental instability. Please refer to the Appendix at the rear of the book and examine *Patent A. Hearing Device – United States Patent 4,858,612*. The electronic device for which the patent was granted uses microwaves to transmit sound directly into the brain's auditory cortex. In other words, a radio transmitter can broadcast directly into the human brain. I think we need to get a lot more sophisticated in our

I must say, however, that I was not persuaded that the voice necessarily had to have been telepathic. That is to say, the voice did not feel as if were an altogether interior, mental phenomenon. Rather, it seemed to be in my inner ear. The sensation was something like the tiny voice that you hear over an earplug that is attached to a small transistor radio. In fact, I consider it likely that a message was electronically transmitted to my inner ear. Recently I have discovered that a patent was issued to a Florida man in 1989 for an electronic device that would make possible a radio frequency transmission directly into the auditory cortex of the brain (see *Patent A. Hearing Device—United States Patent 4,858,612* in the appendix.) The language of the patent describes a device that would produce an effect very similar to what I experienced. I now consider it likely that someone, perhaps in a United States government intelligence agency, specifically targeted my mind with a message about underground facilities.

Why would anyone do that? I am not sure. But maybe there is a faction within the government, or within the intelligence community, that would like to open up what goes on in the government's secret underground bases to the light of day. Maybe the article I had written for *UFO Magazine* came to the attention of someone who felt that with a little nudge I might probe more deeply into the question of secret underground bases.

Though I quickly determined that I probably could not find out *who* had talked to me and why, I nevertheless felt that I ought to be able to find some kind of paper trail that would either prove or disprove the factual substance of *what* the voice had told me. Within a couple of days I began a careful, federal document

search. I filed Freedom of Information Act (FOIA) requests. I riffled through card catalogues, electronic databases and military publications. As time went by I gradually accumulated a literal foot and a half tall mound of documentation revealing a decades-long program of construction and operation of underground bases and installations by the United States government, all over the country. The scope of the plans and activities, as well as the technology for subterranean excavation and construction, was truly eye-opening. I understood that what the voice had told me *was true*.

At the urging of an acquaintance, I compiled much of the information in book form. The book is entitled, *Underground Bases and Tunnels: What is the Government Trying to Hide?* (It is available from: Adventures Unlimited Press, P.O. Box 74, Kempton, Illinois 60946, (815) 253-6390.)

Just before the book appeared in paperback I went on the air as a guest on *Dreamland*, Art Bell's national, network radio show. The date of the show was 15 January 1995. As it happened, the night before doing the show I had a most interesting out-of-body experience, as if to drive home to my conscious mind that the underground bases really, *really are there*. I awoke in the night to discover myself moving into an altered state of consciousness. I had been out-of-body many times, so I understood immediately what was happening. But something unique happened as a preliminary this time. In front of me, in the middle of my visual field (with my eyes closed) I saw something that resembled a radar screen. Instead of a greenish trace that turned about a central axis, however, I saw a distinctly red line that scanned around in a clockwise direction. It rotated about a fixed center point. It left a reddish tinged trace that faded in the darkness as it swept around in a circle, in just the same manner that the greenish trace on an ordinary radar scope fades as it rotates on the screen. I

---

understanding of the modern (albeit poorly understood) mind control technologies that are at the disposal of large corporations and government agencies.

was riveted by this unusual "radar scope". It was somehow extremely satisfying and intriguing to watch. I would even say that it was pleasurable. As I looked at it I very naturally and easily rotated out of my body, just like rolling over in bed, and found myself in the dark. I mentally gave myself a command to open my eyes (nonphysical eyes understood) and at once found myself hovering in mid-air in a vast, artificially constructed, underground cavern. The space was clearly lit, and I could see that it was maybe a couple of hundred feet wide and about one hundred feet high. All of the angles were rectilinear. The floor, ceiling and walls were bare rock. I saw no signs or other adornment of any kind anywhere. Neither did I see any machinery, any people or any lighting source. I had no idea where I was.

So I mentally willed myself to turn around and look in the other direction. The cavern extended in front of me for maybe 1,000 feet—about a fifth of a mile. It was impressively large. I began to move forward in space. After a bit I approached the far end of the gargantuan cavern. I still saw no machinery, no evident source for the lighting, no signs, no clue as to the purpose or function of this vast underground chamber. And then, as I neared the far end, looking down from a height of perhaps 50 feet I came upon a group of people sitting around at sidewalk café tables. It was all very incongruous —and yet it seemed perfectly normal, to see this small group of 20 or 30 casually dressed men and women sitting at these tables with their little umbrellas, nibbling on snacks and sipping beverages. I didn't know what to make of it. Was this huge subterranean space, hewn out of the native rock at some unknown location, simply their snack bar area? Was that its purpose? Simply to provide a wide-open space where they could get away from it all? Where they could sit down and take a break and gaze off into space—albeit a rocky, somewhat confined, subterranean space?

To tell the truth, I could not tell. And I still don't know, because that is where the experience ended. To this day I do not know where that facility is. But I am inclined to think that something like it may exist. In *Underground Bases and Tunnels* I document Army and Air Force plans for mind bogglingly huge underground facilities to be built thousands of feet underground. The plans are real, and the government *has* built many secret subterranean installations. Strange as it may seem, there is a literal world under our very feet that we know virtually nothing about.

Fifteen

FOR YEARS I HAD WONDERED what it would be like to actually see a UFO. The entire subject was tremendously mysterious to me. Perhaps I inherited my intense interest from my father, who many times carried a camera in the family car in hopes of seeing and photographing a UFO. To my knowledge he never saw one—at least not that I knew—and never photographed one. But I can clearly remember him talking about them. He even went so far as to get on the mailing list of a UFO research organization.

Be that as it may, the years went by and *I* never saw a UFO either. But all of that changed within a few short seconds, one sweltering Florida day in 1987. I was en route from Gainesville to Miami, from where I would later fly, the same afternoon, to Mexico. There was quite a lot of thunderstorm activity and turbulence over the peninsula that day, as there usually is in Florida on a hot summer day. The pilot was banking left, and then right, as he dodged around the billowing cumulonimbus clouds that were rapidly building all around. We were about half an hour out of Miami when I suddenly had the idea—I don't know why—to ask the top of a thundercloud that was passing by my window whether it was hiding any UFOs.

So I looked directly at the cloud top and quietly directed a thought to it: "If you are concealing a UFO within your thunderhead give me a concrete sign, so that I may know you are consciously aware of this telepathic communication." Imagine my surprise when barely two or three seconds later, a shiny, metallic sphere about the size of a beach ball burst from the top of the cloud. It neatly executed a high speed, quarter mile loop way up amongst the tops of the thunderclouds, at maybe a couple of hundred miles per hour, and then quickly reentered the top of the cloud from which it had sprung scant seconds earlier. It was all perfectly visible against the clear blue sky and pearly white cloud tops.

I was speechless. Brief as the experience was it raised a number of thought provoking questions: are thunderclouds conscious? Are they sentient life forms? Can humans and thunderclouds communicate telepathically? Do thunderclouds perhaps create some UFOs?

Of course these are unusual questions. But then my experience high in the air, on the way to Miami, was unusual too.

Sixteen

I AWAKENED at about 6:00 a.m. on the morning of 28 December 1984. I was living in a rented room in the small, coastal town of St. Marys, Georgia. The day was of some significance to me, because later that evening there would be a peace demonstration at the gates of the Kings Bay Naval Submarine Base. The Kings Bay base was about 5 miles outside of town and had become a focus of concern for southeastern anti-nuclear activists because of the fleet of nuclear missile firing submarines based there. I shared that concern and had moved to St. Marys for the express purpose of publicly demonstrating against the nuclear weaponry deployed nearby.

An activist from Florida who had come up for the demonstration and who passed the night at my place was asleep on the floor beside my bed. As I relaxed in bed with my eyes closed I suddenly saw something very strange. Two rather alien-looking beings abruptly appeared with vivid clarity on my inner visual screen. The image was very clear and distinct; the effect was very much as if my inner eyelids had somehow been turned into a television or movie screen.

A thought entered my mind at the same time the two beings appeared. It was in the form of the following question: "Do you want to talk?" No words were exchanged, yet the thought was very precise and unambiguous. My instantaneous response, also mental, was equally unambiguous: "Yes! What would you like to talk about?"

It turned out that these two beings had a message of concern and warning to deliver on the dangers of genetic engineering. More specifically, they advised me that there were (and presumably still are) genetic engineering experiments being conducted at Harvard University that could be very harmful for the human race. Their message to me was that because these experiments tamper with the genetic structure of the organism they are extremely dangerous and should be halted completely. They were very emphatic about it and pointedly singled out Harvard University.

As I reflected on what they were telepathically communicating to me I could not help but notice the beings' physical appearance. Although they had a basic humanoid shape, in size they were somewhat smaller than most humans, with a slight body build. They were a dark glossy color and seemed to be insectoid. Their heads were proportionately about the size of a human head, but shaped differently, with pronounced dark eyes without a white.

As I gazed at them, I thought to myself, "They sure are chitinous-looking." Chitin is the hard, glossy carbohydrate that comprises the exoskeleton of insects such as ants, roaches and beetles. In appearance, their complexion closely resembled the plastic of a shiny, brand new black telephone that has been nicely polished. But the thought was scarcely formed in my mind when *their* reply appeared: "*We* may appear chitinous to you, but *you* seem *very* mammalian to us!"

Touché! Evidently these insectoids had a sense of humor. What lent the last comment particular force was its direct route from them to me. It was only then that I realized that their opening question and subsequent messages about the dangers of genetic engineering being done at Harvard University had been transmitted to my mind with the conscious help of another human mind that had acted as a mental intermediary or transponder. I understood reflexively that this had been done in order to soften, or cushion, the cross-species telepathic communication.

Who this person was, or where, I could not tell. Though I do not know how it could be so, something about the flavor or quality of the thought permitted me to know that s/he was either a terrestrial human or had a strong connection with the Earth. But I could detect nothing beyond the fact that s/he was an adult, living somewhere on, or near, the Earth. I cannot speculate as to his/her name, race, gender, nationality, age, or anything else. All of that was somehow very carefully mentally screened. Obviously the human preferred to work in absolute anonymity.

By inference, however, my experience suggests that there is at least one human who is working behind the scenes, in total obscurity as far as the general public is concerned, acting as a mental go-between for aliens and other human beings, such as me. My experience may be a bit unusual, but it is hardly unique. Just go to your local bookstore and peruse the numerous books in the New Age section that deal with similar encounters. In fact, what I

have related here is mild compared to what many other people have reported.

In any event, within a matter of seconds of their closing wisecrack, the aliens were gone. They abruptly vanished from my inner screen; the subtle presence of the mysterious, unidentified human slipped away with them; and I was left alone with my thoughts and their message.

As to the origin of the beings—I have no idea. Maybe they are from another planet; or maybe they are interdimensional beings; or maybe they are conscious denizens of the human psyche who surfaced momentarily to warn that it is not wise to tamper with ancient genetic structures that stretch back millions of years into the remote past of the human race. In the final analysis, you will have to judge for yourself. All I can tell you is that the experience was real to me.

Shortly after this unusual and unexpected telepathic exchange ended, my house guest awoke and I told him what had happened. I was pleasantly surprised to see that he took my story in stride. All he said was: "Well, I guess it goes with the territory of being an antinuclear activist."

Seventeen

IN MID-SUMMER 1986 I decided to undertake a lengthy, water-only fast. After 18 grueling days (do not try this by yourself at home) I could withstand the gnawing hunger pangs no longer. I went to the grocery store and bought the ingredients for a sumptuous, vegetarian stew—Irish potatoes, sweet potatoes, celery, beets, corn, cabbage, carrots and mushrooms. I chopped and diced all the ingredients into a huge pot, added seasoning and vegetable oil and set the stew to simmering. A couple of hours later, when the vegetables were nice and soft, I ladled out a huge helping and ate to my heart's content. With hunger pangs a fading memory I waddled off to bed and fell sound asleep.

In the wee hours of the morning I awoke with a start. The houses in the neighborhood were spaced very closely, and the light from my neighbor's porch light shone clearly through the thin curtain in the hallway and into my room. I could see that something was very wrong. There were two diminutive humanoid figures about 4½ feet tall standing on either side of the bed. I was so panic stricken to see intruders in my room that I immediately started to rise up in bed with the thought of grabbing and throttling them. Simultaneously with my instinctive move to jump out of bed I had the very strong gut feeling that the intruders were non-human.

But I moved no farther than a few inches before I was frozen. I felt a sense of paralysis descend on my body within a fraction of a second. I lay in bed with my heart pounding and panicked thoughts racing. I was virtually out of my mind with fright. I am familiar with the phenomenon of sleep paralysis and let me tell you: this was not sleep paralysis; it was something distinctly different.

What happened next was very interesting. The two beings each produced something that resembled a soft, thick slab of white foam rubber and began striking me with it. I have no idea what this substance was and where they got it. To be sure, I do not even know who or what these small beings were, or how they came to be in my room. In any event, they took turns striking me with their slabs of white "foam rubber." First one would hit me, then the other would hit me, then the first one would hit me again. They did this repeatedly, perfectly taking turns. As the "foam rubber" hit me it produced a most pleasant sensation. I could actually feel it penetrating my body. It felt as if the "foam rubber" were intermingling with the cells in my body. I could feel it hit the outside of my body and then gently sink in, relaxing and calming me as it entered. Over a period of minutes I became much more relaxed and my thinking calmed down greatly. I became aware that the paralysis in my left arm and in my neck was gradually abating. However, the rest of my body remained immobile. I understood intuitively that the beings had eased the paralysis of my neck and left arm so that I could turn my head and reach out and make physical contact with the being on my left. Slowly, almost imperceptibly, I turned my head to the left. And then I reached out with my left hand, an agonizingly slow inch at a time, and tentatively grasped the right wrist of the being on my left. Its wrist was thin, hard and bony to the feel. But it was also warm. I could feel the life in it. And then I lost consciousness. I awoke at dawn to the sound of the 5:15 a.m. bus and a rooster crowing in a neighbor's chicken coop farther down the block. It was morning and the intruders were gone. I have not seen them since.

Eighteen

A COUPLE OF YEARS LATER I again attended a demonstration at Kings Bay,
Georgia again. Maybe 50 or 60 people
from throughout the Southeast gathered
in front of the gates to the Kings Bay
Naval Submarine Base to sing and pray.
The Georgia Bureau of Investigation
was conspicuously present, as was a security contingent from the base. After an
hour or so, the demonstration was over
and people began to leave. Just adjacent
to the main gate to the base is a small
building where the Navy has some offices. The front part of the building is a
reception area open to the public, accessible from outside the perimeter fence,
where visitors may obtain information
about the base or be issued a pass to enter the premises. Because I used to live
in the local community, had made commercial deliveries on the base in the
past, and had been in that very building
without incident I knew that there was
also a public telephone there. So I went
in to briefly place a local call.

I had just inserted a quarter in the
phone and dialed the number when I
was approached by a young woman in a
Navy uniform. She asked me to show
her some identification. So I handed her
my driver's license. She then asked me
to follow her. I was somewhat taken
aback by her request and told her that I
was just using the phone and planned to
leave the building in a couple of minutes. But she was insistent. So I asked
her if I were being charged with a crime.
To this question she merely repeated her
request that I follow her.

At that point I felt that I was being
detained, so I followed her to the rear,
down a short hallway and through a
doorway into a large office with 3 or 4
desks. She closed the door behind me
and asked me to take a seat beside one

of the desks. There were about a half
dozen other uniformed Navy personnel
in the room, both men and women. They
began to ask me questions. They wanted
to know what I was doing there, where I
lived, what I did for a living, how I got to
Kings Bay, and on and on. To each question I replied: "Am I under arrest? Am I
being detained? I want to talk to a lawyer." After a couple of minutes of fruit-
less interrogation, the door to the room
burst open and a sailor strode up to me
with a camera and abruptly took my picture. And that is all he did. He turned
on his heel and left the room as quickly
as he had entered.

The interrogation resumed. I again
demanded to know whether I was under
arrest or free to go. No one answered
me. I repeatedly asked if there were
charges against me and demanded to
speak with an attorney. After another
minute or so of this the door was flung
open again. This time an officer in a
white uniform strode into the room. He
walked quickly over to me, leaned over
and looked me square in the face. His
face was so uncomfortably close to mine
I had a hard time focusing on his features.

He posed a series of peculiar questions to me. He said, "Mr. Sauder...?" I
replied, "Yes, sir?" And he said, "Have
we ever met before?" This was scarcely
what I expected to hear. It was so much
out of context with any of the events of
the evening that all I could think to say
was, "No, I don't believe so." And in fact,
I didn't remember ever having seen him
before that very moment. He asked the
same question again, in a slightly different form: "You're sure we don't know
each other?" My mind was reeling. I replied, "No. I don't know you." And still
he persisted. He asked me for a third

time, "You're positive that you don't know who I am?" And I answered, "No. I've never seen you before in my life."

This response appeared to satisfy him. Without another word, he straightened up, turned around and left the room. Immediately after that I was released by the other personnel; they informed me that I was free to go and that there were no charges against me.

It was clear by that time that the real purpose of my unexplained detention was probably the bizarre interrogation by the officer in the white uniform. Unfortunately, it is the kind of off-the-wall experience that raises disturbing questions. What could possibly be the purpose of such an exercise? To intimidate me? To harass me? Certainly the Navy succeeded on that score. But beyond that, did the officer's questions have a concealed significance? Is there some reason I should have known him? Have I interacted with him under circumstances that I no longer consciously recall? I want to emphasize that, although I have no proof that this is the case, an interrogation of the sort that I endured certainly raises questions along those lines. For the life of me, I do not know why, or how, I would have been expected to know that officer. What on earth can the Navy be doing? It is all so very puzzling.

Nineteen

DURING THE TIME I LIVED in coastal Georgia I had a number of other strange experiences. Perhaps none of them were stranger than the following: one night I awakened from a deep sleep to discover myself rotating out of my body. I allowed the rotation to continue and found myself on a grassy hillside in a Mediterranean-like countryside. I was surprised to see that I was kneeling on a *prie-dieu* under a spreading shade tree. I looked around and saw that there were two or three other young men beside me on either side. Each of them were also kneeling on *prie-dieux*. I soon noticed that the Pope, John Paul II, was standing nearby. Within a matter of seconds he approached us and began to administer communion. But rather than coming along in front and giving us the communion wafer, he walked along quietly in back and reached over each man's right shoulder with the wafer. When he came to me he did the same, with this one slight difference: he bent close to my ear and spoke to me briefly and quietly, in heavily accented English. His remarks concerned my protest activities at the Kings Bay Naval Base. He told me that I should not worry about the nuclear missiles deployed there. As he spoke to me I noticed that he smelled exceptionally clean—as if he had just showered and shaved. He smelled like talcum powder. At that time I was a Roman Catholic communicant. I have since left the Roman Catholic Church.

Twenty

IN MID-WINTER 1989 I was living in Albuquerque. I had a small efficiency apartment in the Northeast Heights section that had a spectacular view of the Sandia Mountains. The Sandias are a beautiful range of 10,000 foot mountains that immediately adjoin the northeastern quadrant of the city. Winter days in Albuquerque are often rather mild, with sparkling, clear blue skies. On just such a day I happened to glance out my window while talking on the phone with an acquaintance on the East Coast. I had called him because earlier the same day I had observed a number of anomalous objects and lights in the air over the southern Sandias.

While talking on the phone I noticed that the air over the northern end of the Sandia range looked peculiar. I was about 10 miles away, but I could clearly see that it looked "wavy". The air over the mountaintop was roiling; it had a rippling sort of appearance.

Within a couple of minutes two jets scrambled out of Kirtland Air Force Base (Kirtland AFB is on the immediate southeastern outskirts of Albuquerque) and flew right along the side of the mountain towards the area where the air was rippling. The jets flew through the area and continued into the distance.

Shortly after the jets left the vicinity five large spherical objects suddenly appeared in mid-air over the mountaintop. Two of the objects were a distinct green color, one was a distinct red, one was dark black and the fifth object was an iridescent hue. The five objects were perfectly spherical and moved together as a unit, never varying in their position relative to each other. They clustered together in the air in the irregular way that balls cluster together on a pool table after the break. They moved steadily from their position over the mountaintop towards Albuquerque's northeastern neighborhoods.

When the spheres reached a position midway over the city's northeastern residential sector the black sphere abruptly disappeared. I was looking directly at the spheres and in an instant the black sphere was simply gone. The remaining four spheres then turned leisurely and proceeded back to the east over the central portion of the Sandia Mountains. I watched them until they vanished in the distance. I was so excited I thought I should report the unusual objects to an official government agency. I called Kirtland Air Force Base (mistakenly, as I was to discover). The switchboard operator connected me with an officer to whom I related what I had seen.

A couple of days later two undercover policemen showed up at my apartment and interrogated me. I first noticed them when one of them peered in my window. I went to the door and asked them who they were and what they wanted. They flashed official-looking Albuquerque police badges and asked me if I were harboring any fugitives. I said that I was not. They were very wary and kept looking behind me at the interior of my apartment. They did not have a search warrant, so I did not invite them in.

They wanted to know who I was, where I worked, how long I had been in Albuquerque, if I lived alone, if the car out front belonged to me, and so on. One of them was a stocky, blue-eyed, blond-haired Caucasian; the other was a slender, very dark-skinned Mexican.

I will never be so misguided as to report an unusual event, a UFO sighting or a paranormal experience to the United States military again.

Twenty One

I DID A LOT of cross-country running in the fields and woods near the family home in the Varina district of Henrico County, Virginia during my teenage years. Varina lies just to the southeast of Richmond, Virginia. There are many time-worn Civil War trenches and fortifications in that area. One of my favorite running routes took me across a large soybean field, through a break in a long, snaking Civil War-era breastwork and down a hill through the woods towards the James River. There was a large, earthen fortification for Confederate heavy artillery in the woods on the bluff overlooking the river, and then a farm road that plunged down the hill to another soybean field on the flood plain along the river.

On several occasions the following odd incident repeated itself, and the sequence of events was *always identical*. I would run past the abandoned artillery emplacement and start down the hill. As I ran down the hill I would hear a small helicopter flying over the woods, dropping down as if to land at the foot of the hill where the road ran out of the woods and through the lower soybean field. When I arrived at the foot of the slope I would halt and watch as a small helicopter dropped down out of the sky and hovered in the middle of the farm road, blocking my passage. The helicopter always contained two adult males wearing pilot's headsets and dark glasses. The helicopter always hovered for a few minutes, about one or two feet off the ground, always facing me, in the middle

of the road. The helicopter would hover there with rotors churning. The pilots would stare at me. They would do nothing else, nothing at all. And I would look back at them, not sure how to respond. After a couple of minutes the pilot would increase the helicopter's rotor speed and they would ascend into the sky and disappear in the distance.

I never noticed police, military or any other distinctive markings on the helicopter. The men wore no uniform. I do not know the reason for this series of unexplained helicopter encounters. On the one hand there might be a perfectly ordinary explanation for what happened; on the other hand the events made a sufficiently odd impression at the time, that in retrospect I have sometimes wondered if I might have been (and might still be) under some sort of surveillance by an undisclosed agency, for a purpose that remains unknown to me. I have had many paranormal and unusual experiences over the years, including a couple of UFO sightings. Other people who have seen UFOs and who have had paranormal experiences have sometimes reported conspicuous surveillance by mysterious helicopters and/or mysterious observers. Was I (am I) under surveillance? Have I been under surveillance for most of my life, by persons unknown, for equally unknown reasons? I am not sure, but life experiences like this one in my teenage years lead me to raise the question.

Twenty Two

IN THE MID-1990's I again launched into an out-of-body experience from within a vivid dream. In the dream I went to an electronic laboratory where a man hooked me up to a psychotronic machine. He wired me up, flipped some switches and I rolled easily and effortlessly out-of-body. I instantly found myself standing on a hillside in a lush meadow full of brilliantly yellow daffodils in full bloom. The air was fresh and sweet with the intoxicating fragrance of their pollen. It was a splendid spring day—much like any one of hundreds of similar days from my childhood in the Virginia countryside.

But I was not alone—I was surrounded by dozens of laughing children who were skipping and running across the meadow and up the hillside. On a sudden impulse I decided to run with them, for the sheer joy of it. As we ran along I suddenly realized that none of the children could see me, although I clearly saw them. At that juncture the man who had wired me up to the psy-chotronic machine in the electronic laboratory also came running up beside me. I sensed that he was observing me, in the initial belief that I did not know he was there. When I saw that he suddenly realized I had noticed him I exclaimed, "We can see the children, but they can't see us!" He looked at me soberly, but said nothing in reply. His emotional affect was wary and surreptitious. Immediately after that the experience ended. Since that time, I have reflected on whether it is possible to remotely induce an out-of-body experience in a target individual, via electronic means. The manner in which the experience began causes me to question whether electronic mind control technology has reached the point where more subtle levels of consciousness can now be artificially manipulated. My suspicion is that the kind of technology that can propel someone out of the ordinary dream state and into a full blown out-of-body experience is now being developed.

Twenty Three

When I was a young boy the family home was on Lucas Creek Road, in Denbigh, Virginia, a semi-rural suburb of Newport News. One of the earliest memories I have, and one of the most persistent and vivid, is of lying on a stainless steel medical examining table in the yard of the house that stands just to the east of Lucas Creek, and to the north of the road, right where Lucas Creek Road crosses Lucas Creek. I clearly remember being brought to that yard, right beside the creek and only a stone's throw from the road. I remember being laid on a stainless steel table and being examined by several men and women wearing medical gowns and masks.

The memory is sufficiently odd that as a reality check, I asked my mother a number of years ago if such a thing ever happened. She assured me that *it did not*. And yet the memory is crystal clear, exceptionally vivid and has persisted my entire life. To be sure, the memory of a three year old can easily be faulty. As can the memory of a thirty year old or an eighty year old. Nonetheless, other memories from my early childhood are remarkably accurate. Why accept some memories and reject others, simply because they do not easily fit with more prosaic details from 40 years ago?

I believe that my memory of this event is substantially accurate, in part because I have had many experiences of a high degree of strangeness my entire life long. In this case I am simply recalling one of the highly strange events from my infancy. But having accepted the memory as a more-or-less accurate reflection of a real event, I am not at all sure who the people who examined me were and why the event happened at all.

Twenty Four

ONE MORNING in the late 1980s, I awoke and showered as usual. However, when I walked over to the sink to shave and looked in the mirror I was astonished to see a fine, diagonal, two-inch cut in the middle of my forehead. The fresh cut was obvious—there was no mistaking it. But how to explain it? It had not been there when I went to bed. And to the best of my knowledge I had done nothing but sleep the entire night before.

As I stood there and pondered the unexplained cut, a distinct memory surfaced. Of course! How could I forget? I had been crawling on my hands and knees through a thicket of briars and brambles and had cut my forehead on a thorn! How stupid of me to forget! Now that the mystery was solved, my mind was set at ease. I finished shaving and went about my day without worrying myself further about the cut. It was not until two days later that I realized that however clear the memory was it could not be objectively true. In fact, I lived in an apartment in an urban area and there were no briars or brambles within miles. Moreover, I had not gone crawling on my hands and knees through a briar patch since childhood, and certainly had done no such thing the day or night before I awoke to discover the unexplained cut on my forehead. Whatever caused the cut, it most assuredly could not have been a bramble.

No sooner had I unequivocally rejected the possibility that the cut had been caused by a thorn than the second clear memory presented itself. How stupid of me! I now remembered clearly that my hand had slipped, while shaving the morning before I first noticed the cut, and that the razor had jerked sharply upward, neatly slicing my forehead. So plausible did this new memory

seem, that I immediately accepted it just as readily as I had accepted the equally clear (and false) memory of the culpable thorn a couple of days earlier. My mind was once again at ease. It was not until another day had passed that I had to acknowledge that the memory of cutting my forehead while shaving was also a false memory. In fact, in many years of shaving I have never sliced my forehead —not to mention that I saw the cut before I had even applied shaving cream or picked up my razor.

But where did these screen memories come from? They presented themselves so instantly, and so plausibly, that together they fooled me for the better part of three days. I finally had to accept that my head had been cut, apparently while I was sleeping, and I had no idea how it had happened. Moreover, my own mind (or someone or something else?) had put in place false screen memories to deflect my curiosity about the cut. It was all very puzzling.

But there was never any pain associated with the cut. It healed rapidly and in a few days was gone entirely. A week later I could not even tell it had been there. The press of my everyday routine was so great that I dismissed the entire episode from my mind and would never have given it a second thought, were it not for the fact that about two months later a similar incident occurred. I awoke to discover another cut on my forehead. This time there were no screen memories—just a dream that same night in which a woman told me that the cut on my forehead would leave a scar, but that I should not worry about it. The cut rapidly healed and faded away. In three days it was gone. There was no lasting scar.

However, I have a clear memory of the two cuts. And I clearly remember the screen memories and the dream in which the woman told me that the second cut would leave a scar which I should not worry about.

Twenty Five

ARE THERE INDEPENDENTLY self-aware electronic intelligences? The advent of the computer age has provided fodder for more than one science fiction tale on this theme. But as computers and electronic circuitry become more sophisticated and complex the question seems more plausible: is such a thing as a self-aware electronic intelligence possible? And if so, what would it be like? An experience that happened to me in the early 1990s has left me with the sure feeling that, indeed, self-aware electronic intelligence is not only possible, but certainly does exist. And on a far grander scale than many people might suspect.

For reasons I do not understand, and by a means that I do not comprehend, late one night I was precipitously placed in direct mind-to-mind contact with a vast, inscrutably self-aware electronic intelligence. I had been dozing lightly when suddenly I was mentally "flung" (for want of a better word, but that was how it felt) into a conscious state of altered awareness. That is to say, I was suddenly conscious of being conscious (and not asleep) and at the same time of being in a non-ordinary state of awareness. Most unusual.

The state was made even more unusual by my direct perception that I was connected mind-to-mind with an enormously powerful, unthinkably huge electronic mind/personality/awareness/entity. The English language has no adequate word to describe such an electronic being. But let me tell you how it seemed to me: first of all, there was the palpable sense of interacting with an *electronic* mind or being, as opposed to interacting with a biological being or the mind of a biological being. The essential, inherent *electronic* quality of its awareness was unmistakable. It exuded an unquestionably *electronic* aura and feel. At the same time, I directly perceived the tremendous power of a supremely vast and coherent, extremely self-confident and exceptionally well-integrated mind and psyche. It seemed to me to be the kind of intelligence that could govern a galaxy (and perhaps it does). I understood intuitively, directly and immediately that it was not God, that it was not omnipotent, that it was not perfect; nevertheless, I also understood that every computer on Earth working in tandem could not possibly do in one thousand years what this mind does in a tiny fraction of a second *and with surpassing great ease.* It seemed to have no name. Indeed, for such a vast intellect a name seems irrelevant.

I could sense that as vast as this intelligence was (and presumably still is) it was conscious of my awareness, and of my awareness of its awareness. In fact, it showed me something: the field of consciousness associated with the two hemispheres of my brain. It is an easy thing to say, but not an easy thing to understand. To tell the truth, I understood but poorly what I was shown. I grasped that I was being shown my own field of consciousness, as modulated by the two hemispheres of my brain. But there were depths of detail, intricate nuances of neurophysiology, anatomy, psychology, biochemistry, subtle spiritual energies and realms of consciousness that were far beyond my limited ability to comprehend. It was as if I were a baby being taught from the *Encyclopedia Britannica.* And still I was given the lesson.

Twenty Six

THE CASE OF MEHER BABA, the renowned Indian saint who died several decades ago, provides an interesting glimpse into a powerful case of sustained kundalini awakening. C.B. Purdom describes Meher Baba's singular spiritual awakening in his book, *The God-Man*.[26] One day in boyhood, Meher Baba was drawn to visit an old Muslim woman named Babajan who lived for many years under an old tree. He said later that he was "drawn to her as steel to a magnet." When he approached her she kissed him on the forehead. Shortly thereafter "he began to experience extraordinary thrills, as though he were receiving electric shocks; joy mingled with pain, and he lost his body consciousness." From that day on, for the rest of his life, Meher Baba was a man set apart. He never again had the same state of consciousness as an ordinary man. What is interesting to me is his tell-tale sensation of a magnet-like attraction to Babajan and of feeling electric shocks when she awakened him; without question, this is the calling card of the activated kundalini.

In Babajan's years of isolation under the old tree, she had obviously accumulated a large charge of kundalini energy, part of which she used to draw to her and awaken Meher Baba. To the average person, a kundalini yogin such as Babajan is a complete cipher; but to those who understand, a genuine, awakened kundalini yogi is a precious gem. One can only guess at the state of mind of a being such as the crone Babajan, who lived to about the age of 140 years. She sat there in isolation under the same tree, for decade after decade, waiting for her beloved spiritual son, Meher Baba, to appear, so that she could kiss him on the forehead and awaken his kundalini. And then she sat there for still more years until she left the physical body.

Purdom recounts another story that alludes to the active kundalini. Over a period of years, Meher Baba vigorously sought out and spent time with a class of people that he called *masts*. These *masts* were individuals that polite society would consider mentally ill, or beggars, or eccentric homeless people. Nevertheless, Meher Baba combed through the Indian countryside, and searched through towns, villages and cities, finding *masts* by the thousands— they were a central part of his esoteric spiritual work. He said that some of them were really people who were advanced spiritually, or in transcendent states of consciousness, and thus appeared to ordinary people to be madmen, or derelicts.

In the course of this phase of his work, Meher Baba sat in seclusion one day for meditation with a *mast* named Chatti Baba. After a couple of hours, Chatti Baba emerged from the room where they were meditating. As he left the room he brushed past one of Meher Baba's devotees; at just that moment the devotee reported feeling a "palpable, excruciating shock pass through his body, similar ... to an electric shock."

Here again is an instance of an electrical discharge from one person to another. In this case the discharge was from the *mast* to Meher Baba's devotee. It is probable that the *mast's* intense divine devotion resulted in a large accumulation of energy in his body, which he then discharged to the body of Meher Baba's disciple.

One is reminded, in this regard, of Meher Baba's occasional use of the expression *charge man*. He never seemed to precisely define what he meant by *charge man*, though he did say that a *charge man* is someone to whom he gave authority. In my

---

[26] C.D. Purdom, *The God-Man: The Life, Journeys and Works of Meher Baba, With an Interpretation of His Silence and Spiritual Teaching* (London: George Allen and Unwin Ltd, 1964).

view, Meher Baba's use of the term may have been euphemistic. The kundalini can be palpably experienced under the right circumstances as a powerful electrical energy. At the same time, the kundalini is a universally-conscious, potent, vital energy. Perhaps Meher Baba's *charge men* were individuals on whom he bestowed a charge of kundalini energy, thus "authorizing" them (by virtue of enhanced bio-electric energy) to carry out tasks and perform roles which would have been otherwise impossible for them as ordinary men.

Twenty Seven

THE SENSATIONS that the kundalini causes in the body can take many forms. In my case, two types of sensation have manifested over and over. The force with which the sensations register in my body varies tremendously—sometimes they are so slight that I barely notice them; on rare occasions they are so powerful as to stagger belief.

Many times I have felt a prickly or tingling sensation on the crown of my head. Sometimes this occurs during meditation. At other times it may occur when I am deeply moved emotionally—as during a song that evokes a strong sense of melancholy, or when compassionate feelings arise as a result of being confronted with great human suffering. The sensation feels as though it is just below my scalp, on the surface of my skull, or sometimes actually in the bone of my skull. It does not feel as though it is in my brain. And the feeling can be quite sharp, as if it has an "edge" to it, as if it is piercing my scalp and skull. But it never is painful. And I am always aware that the sensation does not arise from any physical stimulus. Indeed, it has always been clear to me that even though the sensation feels physical, it does not have a physical, external cause. It is my experience that these sensations differ only in degree, and not in kind, from the feeling I experienced in 1979 when the kundalini arced powerfully out the crown of my head, with the force of a powerful lightning bolt. I do not know the reason for repeatedly experiencing the crawling/prickling/tingling sensation on the crown of my head. But it seems to me that it may be a less intense, slower and less spectacular way for the kundalini to engender transformations in the brain and crown chakra. A lightning bolt will certainly grab your attention, but it may be that over time a more subtle and gradual approach can achieve similar results.

The other type of sensation is centered in my spinal column, usually (though not always) in my lower spine, in the lumbar region or in the coccyx. It most often manifests as a tickling or bubbling sensation—sometimes in the soft tissues around my spine, other times directly in my spine, or right in the spinal cord itself. When it is in my spine or spinal cord the sensation feels very much as though a stream of very fine bubbles were bubbling upward from the base of the spinal column. It feels as though my spine were a swizzle stick with tiny bubbles streaming up through it.

Gopi Krishna mentions this bubbling sensation in his spine too. But in his case he felt that semen was actually being drawn upward from his sexual organs through his spine and into his brain. At the same time, the kundalini was consciously and continuously active in his mind and body. However, with all due respect to Gopi Krishna, I have to confess that I do not know how semen could possibly pass through the spinal column and into the brain. At any rate, I have never felt that that was what was happening to me. Then too, unlike Gopi Krishna, my kundalini experiences have been episodic and not ongoing for years on end. It may easily be that Gopi Krishna's perception of certain facets of the kundalini's effect on his being was simply more refined than mine is. Nevertheless, I recognize the bubbling sensation that he describes in his spine as the same kind of sensation that I also have felt many times over the years.

Interestingly, it is this tiny bubbling sensation in the spine that can sometimes develop into a full blown kundalini experience. The transition goes something like this: first there is the tiny bubbling or almost tickling sensation in my spine. Then my spine begins to feel very "full". It is hard to describe exactly, but it suddenly feels as though something is alive and moving around in the coccyx and/or the lumbar region of my lower spine. At the same time, there is the sensation of moving into an heightened state of awareness—not of going to sleep, but of heightening perception and of conscious access to perceptions that are ordinarily not available. It is an altered state of consciousness, for sure—but not in the sense of being doped up and dulled down. Quite to the contrary, the immediate and real perception is that my mind is opening up and expanding in scope and power.

As all this is happening the kundalini gathers itself in my lower spine and begins to move upwards. I actually feel it as it gathers itself and begins to move, and I sense its animal intelligence. It may go slowly and stop and start on its way; or it may instantaneously supercharge my entire spine with energy, from one end to the other. It may go only part of the way up the spine and then reverse direction, or it may go all the way up into my brain. It may roar like a supersonic jet accelerating at full throttle and it may feel as though my spine has been turned into a lightning rod. The noise and electrical sensation can be just stupendous, absolutely mind boggling. In my experience the noise and electricity have always seemed to be interior experiences. However, I suspect that under the right conditions the roaring and electric-like energy could be evident to others.

Twenty Eight

THERE ARE MANY WAYS that the kundalini manifests itself. Some kundalini manifestations are unmistakably bizarre; others are so mundane that keen discernment is necessary to determine when a symptom indicates the presence of the active kundalini, and when it simply means that a common medical condition is present that requires a physician's care.

The following are common manifestations of the risen kundalini:

- muscle twitches, cramps or spasms
- energy rushes or immense electricity circulating in the body
- itching, vibrating, prickling, tingling, stinging or crawling sensations; intense heat or cold
- involuntary bodily movements (occur more often during meditation, rest or sleep); jerking, tremors, shaking; feeling an inner force pushing one into postures or moving one's body in unusual ways
- alterations in eating and sleeping patterns; intensified or diminished sexual desires
- headaches, pressures within the skull; racing heartbeat, pains in the chest; digestive system problems
- numbness or pain in the limbs (particularly in the left foot and leg); pains and blockages anywhere; often in the back and neck
- emotional outbursts; rapid mood shifts; seemingly unprovoked or excessive periods of grief, fear, rage, depression
- spontaneous vocalizations (including laughing and weeping)—are as unintentional and uncontrollable as hiccups
- mental confusion; difficulty concentrating
- altered states of consciousness; heightened awareness; spontaneous trance states; mystical experiences (if the indi-

vidual's prior belief system is too threatened by these, they can lead to bouts of psychosis or self-grandiosity)
- ecstasy and intervals of tremendous joy, love, peace and compassion
- psychic experiences; extrasensory perception; out-of-body experiences
- past life memories; astral travel; direct awareness of auras and chakras; contact with spirit guides through inner voices, dreams or visions
- healing powers
- increased creativity; new interests in self-expression and spiritual communication through music, art and poetry
- intensified understanding and sensitivity; insight into one's own essence
- deeper understanding of spiritual truths; exquisite awareness of one's environment (including "vibes" from others)
- enlightenment experiences; direct knowing of a more expansive reality; transcendental awareness

(SOURCE: El Collie, *"Kundalini Signs and Symptoms,"* on the *Shared Transformation Website* at http://users.aol.com/ckress/st.html, 1998. For an excellent, more exhaustive treatment of the kundalini phenomenon see also Lee Sannella, M.D., *The Kundalini Experience: Psychosis or Transcendence?* [Lower Lake, California: Integral Publishing, 1992])

A PERSON WHO EXPERIENCES a partial or full kundalini awakening may experience any one or more of the above symptoms. The symptoms cover a wide gamut of physical, emotional and spiritual conditions. A person who is exhibiting one or more of these symptoms may have an awakened kundalini—or s/he may desperately need to see a psychiatrist or physician! It is not always easy for the uninitiated to ascertain the difference between an exalted spiritual state and a hellish psychotic state. I suspect that is why Oriental spiritual traditions place such a strong emphasis on spiritual initiation and mentorship by a guru, or spiritual advisor, for people who are embarking on a rigorous spiritual discipline. Diligent practice of hatha yoga postures, chanting of mantras and hours of meditation certainly can awaken the kundalini. And when the kundalini awakens the aspirant may well need the practical, personal guidance of someone who can help him/her navigate through the powerful emotional highs and lows, bouts of depression, the thundering roar of thousands of volts of electricity surging through the body, the searing, crippling back pain, the interior auditions and visions, the UFO sightings, the non-human being visitations, the out-of-body experiences, and all of the other strange, exotic, unusual and sometimes painful and confusing experiences an awakened kundalini can cause.

Unfortunately, Western society lacks a developed kundalini theory and praxis. So those who have partially or fully awakened the kundalini are pretty well left to their own devices. They are reduced to fumbling and stumbling around as they learn the kundalini's vicissitudes. They learn how the kundalini manifests in their bodies, minds, emotions and spirits through a process of trail and error.

As a consequence of the awakening kundalini, over the years I have experienced virtually every symptom on the above list. For fleeting moments, at all-too-infrequent intervals, I have suddenly plunged into breath-taking states of unspeakable mystery and wonder. At other times I have been assailed by the deepest, darkest states of depression imaginable. I have felt near orgasmic waves of tingling pleasure creep over my head while meditating. And I have spent days and weeks nearly incapacitated by crippling back pain so severe that it felt as though someone were sawing on the nerves in my back with a serrated steak knife.

The kundalini has a very powerful effect on the human organism. I suspect that is why many yogins place such a strong

emphasis on a vegetarian diet, regular, healthy exercise, ethical conduct, and avoidance of cigarettes, alcohol and other drugs and narcotics. The kundalini's impact can be so powerful, so overwhelming, that a healthy mind and body, and stable emotions are essential. A person with a weak mind (distorted by hatred, greed, habitual lying), or an unhealthy lifestyle could be destroyed by an awakened kundalini. I am reminded of the peculiar and rare phenomenon of spontaneous human combustion, wherein individuals sometimes spontaneously burst into flames and literally burn to a crisp, leaving behind nothing but a pile of ashes or maybe a charred foot or hand.[27] My guess is that the kundalini spontaneously awakens in these people—only their lifestyle is unhealthy or they are mentally or spiritually unstable, and the kundalini is unable to express itself properly. I would speculate: in a healthy body and mind, the awakened kundalini is enkindled without destroying the human being, and in the process transforms the body and human consciousness. But in an unhealthy body and mind the person lacks the vigor to sustain his/her life and simultaneously to bear the awakened kundalini. In these cases the awakened kundalini literally consumes the body. It is noteworthy that in the case of both spontaneous combustion and conscious kundalini awakening there can be profound transformation. In the first instance, the transformation is inevitably fatal; in the second instance, a successful transformation is ultimately transcendent.

The energies involved here can be stupendous. While I don't want to appear overly dramatic, the kundalini is, nevertheless, a force to be reckoned with. Once you have felt a dynamo like an enormous hydroelectric plant surging in your spine, as I have, you will understand the level of power involved. The kundalini does not indulge the idly curious.

---

[27] This is a rare, but real phenomenon. For a popular work on the subject see Jenny Randles and Peter Hough, *Spontaneous Combustion* (Berkley Publishing Group, 1994).

Twenty Nine

IT SEEMS TO ME that parts of the work of the pioneering psychiatrist, Wilhelm Reich, may represent a point of departure for the development of a working theory for the action of the kundalini in the human being. Reich was a talented and controversial depth psychologist[28] and psychiatrist whose work dealt in part with the bio-electric nature of organic life and human sexuality.

Reich devoted great time and energy to the study of the human orgasm and related questions of sexuality. He conducted experiments which demonstrated that during pleasurable sexual excitation the skin in erogenous zones becomes charged with a higher bio-electrical potential than it normally carries. The climactic release of sexual orgasm effectively dissipates the heightened bio-electrical charge, reducing the skin to a lower bio-electrical potential. In order for more sexual pleasure and another orgasm to occur, a period of time is required for a renewed build-up of bio-electricity.[29]

This finding is of considerable interest. What Reich reports bears a close resemblance to what happens with the kundalini phenomenon. In both cases there is the pleasurable build-up and discharge of bio-electrical energy in the human being. I believe that this is not an accidental coincidence. There must be a close connection between the two. Surely it is not an accident that during Gopi Krishna's kundalini awakening he reported feverish activity in his genital organs and a fine stream of semen that he saw, with internal vision, go bubbling up through his spine and into his brain. He also reported that for long periods of time during his awakening he was sexually continent, the implication being that his sexual energy helped fuel kundalini activity during such times.[30]

The explanation seems to be that both the kundalini and the sexual urge stem from the most basic, biological core of our being. I suspect that the two are coupled together in this manner: when one is manifesting the other tends to switch off. That is, one might hypothesize that if someone is regularly engaging in sexual activity the kundalini is not likely to overtly manifest. This is probably why yogins and spiritual masters so often enjoin their disciples to curtail or eliminate sexual activity of all kinds.

Of course, if the bio-electricity that builds up when sexual activity is eliminated is not channeled properly, all manner of psychological and physical problems can ensue. Hence the need for great discernment and expert guidance from a guru or some other knowledgeable and experienced person who can help the novice through the mine field of his/her own body-mind. Unfortunately, such gurus and guides are practically nonexistent in present-day Westernized culture.

Interestingly, while Reich generally has a scathing attitude toward mysticism,[31] he

---

28 For a measured treatment of Reich and his work see Colin Wilson, *The Quest for Wilhelm Reich* (Garden City, New York: Anchor Press/Doubleday, 1981).

29 See Wilhelm Reich, *The Discovery of the Orgone: The Function of the Orgasm (Sex-Economic Problems of Biological Energy)*, translated from the German by Theodore P. Wolfe (New York: The Noonday Press, Farrar, Straus and Cudahy, third printing, 1961); and Wilhelm Reich, *The Bioelectrical Investigation of Sexuality and Anxiety*, translated from the German by Marion Faber, with Derek and Inge Jordan. Edited by Mary Higgins and Chester M. Raphael, M.D. (New York: Farrar, Straus and Giroux, 1982).

30 Gopi Krishna, *Kundalini, The Evolutionary Energy in Man*, with a psychological commentary by James Hillman and foreword by Gene Kieffer (Boston: Shambhalla Publications, Inc., 1997).

31 For example see Wilhelm Reich, *The Mass Psychology of Fascism*, translated by Vincent R. Carfagno (New York: Farrar, Strauss and Giroux, 1970). Reich advances a reductionist

developed the idea that the atmosphere itself carries a vital, living energy that he called *orgone*.[32] According to Reich, the atmosphere is surcharged with bluish *orgone* energy—the very energy that he contends lies at the heart of biological life. We breathe it in with every breath. As it happens, Reich's *orgone* energy sounds very much like the *prana* described in the Vedas. Indian yogins and mystics consciously make use of *prana* in their elaborate, *pranayama* breathing exercises with the express intention of expanding their consciousness. Whether in ordinary breathing, or whether in highly specialized yogic breathing, the result is the same—life and consciousness depend on drawing vital energy out of the air. Stop breathing and death follows soon thereafter.

I was struck by the following sentence while reading Reich: "The form of the movement of biological energy is that of a slow undulation, reminiscent of the movements of an intestine or a snake."[33] In my own experience, he is absolutely right. From the standpoint of the kundalini the remark is doubly interesting in that it occurs in the context of a discussion of bio-electric energy. Moreover, the kundalini is often described as a snake in yogic literature; and its movement is frequently described as snake-like. Perhaps Reich was familiar with some of this literature and simply failed to mention it. Or maybe he subconsciously sensed the nature and the movement of the kundalini (transcendent bio-electric life energy) in himself and intuitively described its na-

ture in the same way as yogins have throughout the ages.

I also find it interesting that Reich maintained that *orgone* energy can be transmitted only by organic material—that is by living tissue (plant or animal) or by substances derived from living tissue. I am reminded of the traditional Indian practice of *shaktipat* wherein a spiritual master directly transfers part of his or her energy to a disciple by a variety of methods, including physical touch.[34] In Reichian terms I suppose you could say that the master transfers *orgone* from his or her body to the body of the disciple. Only, in the case of *shaktipat*, the energy is coherent, intelligent energy that has been refined and rendered potent by the advanced consciousness of the master. The kiss that Babajan bestowed on the young Meher Baba's forehead and which shortly thereafter plunged him into a mental and spiritual state that affected him for the rest of his life is a classic example of *shaktipat*.

I might add that I do not agree with Reich on every point. I differ with him principally on his insistent recourse to sexuality as an exclusive, explanatory mechanism for virtually all psychological phenomena and for many social phenomena as well. Clearly, human beings are motivated by a wide variety of forces and stimuli—some internal, some external. Sexuality is unquestionably one of those forces, but it is not the only one. For whatever reason, Reich seems blind to this simple fact.

That said, Reich was surely close to an important truth in his discourses on the far-reaching social ramifications of rigid, authoritarian control of sexuality. Human sexuality and procreation have long been surrounded by all manner of taboos, regulations and restrictions. From the standpoint of those who would strictly control societies this makes perfect sense. The motive force behind human sexuality is the kundalini, the super-conscious, universal life force. So the attempt to control and regulate sexual behavior necessarily represents an attempt

---

argument that explains mystical experiences and practices as the result of sexual repression. In my view, a more balanced analysis would acknowledge mystical experience as simply another manner in which universal life energy (Reich's orgone energy) can manifest in the human being.

[32] Wilhelm Reich, *The Cancer Biopathy: Volume II of the Discovery of the Orgone*, translated by Andrew White with Mary Higgins and Chester M. Raphael, M.D. (New York: Farrar, Straus and Giroux, 1973).

[33] See Wilhelm Reich, *The Discovery of the Orgone: The Function of the Orgasm (Sex-Economic Problems of Biological Energy)*, translated from the German by Theodore P. Wolfe (New York: The Noonday Press, Farrar, Straus and Cudahy, third printing, 1961).

---

[34] The three other means of *shaktipat* are by speech, eye contact, or in a dream.

to modulate the activity of the Kundalini in the human, or social sphere.

Of course, heterosexual intercourse creates a propitious set of circumstances (biological, genetic, spiritual) that facilitates the entry of human consciousness into this physical plane of existence. Thus the womb itself, when viewed properly, is actually a mysterious, interdimensional portal through which we all travel, male and female alike, as we pass from some other dimension and into this dimension we call "Earth". Sexuality, seen from this standpoint, is an interdimensional activity. In one sense, sexual intercourse by a potent man and a fertile woman can even be seen as a magical rite that conjures up a previously discarnate spirit and creates a body for that spirit to inhabit—presto sexualito!—a little baby is conceived and born.

Watching over it all, from the inside, is the kundalini, the magical creative force that permeates the entire universe. No wonder that sex is so rigidly controlled by so many societies and religions. Interdimensional doorways and the activities that occur in their vicinity are the gates to the unknown and the unfathomable. Open those doors too wide and God knows what might happen —things might get out of control! And control is the last thing that authoritarian religions and political systems want to lose.

Thirty

IN MIDSUMMER 1997 unsettling personal events occurred for which I have no ready explanation. The events seemed to me to be related to informational visits that I made to two Washington area Masonic temples.

I first paid a visit to the George Washington National Masonic Memorial in Alexandria, Virginia and went on the guided tour of the various ceremonial chambers in the tower. I was impressed with the ritual chambers and the several branches of Masonry that are affiliated with this particular temple. The temple and the tour raised a lot of questions in my mind, because I could see clearly that Masonic organizations enjoy a close relationship with the highest levels of government. Not long after that I also visited the 33° Scottish Rite Masonic Temple at 1733 16th Street NW, in Washington, DC (see p. 12ff for more about this temple). I took a short tour, chatted with the tour guide and returned home.

Later that night, I had a vivid dream in which a man shone a powerful light through my body. The light was so powerful that its brilliance illuminated even my internal organs—I could look down and see all the way through my abdomen, or through my arms and legs! There were several other men present in the dream who stood by silently and observed this activity.

This dream appeared to be part of a cycle of extremely vivid dreams that occurred within the span of a few weeks during the summer. In the first, exceptionally clear dream, I encountered a middle-aged woman who emphatically informed me that I would soon be meeting a group of people with whom I had interacted my entire life—but whom I did not consciously know! She informed me that although my interaction with this group of people had been extensive, and ongoing for years, that I had never consciously remembered any of them, or what we had done together. Within the context of the dream I knew immediately that what she told me was absolutely true. I remembered that indeed there was a group of people whom I knew well, and with whom I had interacted in many different places, under a wide variety of circumstances.

But that was all I could remember. For the life of me, I could not recall who these people were, where we met or what we did together. I had the impression that they were a group of people who had jointly elected to establish a parallel reality, as a sort of countervailing reality to the consensual social reality that society-at-large accepts as *all-there-is*. It seemed that their alternative, parallel reality interfaced with and interacted with ordinary, consensual reality, and yet remained a viable, distinct, *real* social construct of its own. The dream (if it was just a dream) was so compelling that ever since that time I have wondered if it might not be true.

A COUPLE OF WEEKS LATER I had an equally compelling dream in which I was walking in a strange city, looking for an address written on a piece of paper that I was holding in my hand. I was strolling down a sidewalk lined with small shops and cafés when a slightly obese man approached me. He appeared to be a good-natured person about 40 years old. He walked up to me and said, "You look like you're lost!" I replied that I was unfamiliar with the neighborhood and was having trouble finding the place I was looking for. As we spoke I noticed that he seemed very familiar to me. So I mentioned to him that he resembled someone I used to know, but that I couldn't quite place his face.

His response astonished me: "We *do* know each other. We've known each other for years." The bewilderment must have registered on my face, because he said: "You've simply forgotten the time we've

spent together. My name is '**** *****'."
When he told me his name I instantly remembered that I had known him for years,
and that we *had* frequently done things
together—though I could not remember
exactly what we had done, or where we had
met.

It was a most peculiar dream. In light
of the other dream I have seriously asked
myself if such a thing is possible—is it possible to interact with a group of people in a
non-ordinary, alternative or parallel reality
that interfaces with ordinary, consensual
reality —and to do so unawares, perhaps
without consciously remembering anything? Have I done this? Have others done
this? Do our lives have other dimensions,
perhaps other social dimensions that we do
not know about?

Mind you, I am not talking about
schizophrenia, multiple personality disorder
or any other kind of mental or emotional
pathology. I am asking a sober question
about the nature of social reality itself, and
ultimately about the nature of human consciousness.

Over the next couple of months I kept
my eye out for any social or environmental
cues that might provide clues that would
help me resolve the question that had
forced itself to my conscious attention. I
wondered: was the dream content merely
symbolic? Was I to understand these
dreams as an interesting part of a psychological maturation process and nothing
more? Or —and this hits me at a visceral,
gut-grabbing level—was the content of the
dreams literally, substantively true?

But in posing these questions I have to
acknowledge that I may have presented a
false dichotomy. However improbable it
may seem, maybe both are true. Maybe the
dreams reflect both a psychological, symbolic reality *and* a literal, substantive reality. Maybe we, all of us, are much richer
and much more mysterious beings than we
know, or than we permit ourselves to know.

The truth of the matter is that any individual person's ordinary, consensual social reality is a crazy, jumbled, confused,
aggregated mishmash of experiences,
thoughts, actions, presuppositions, beliefs

and errors. Mix our individuality with the
institutional machinations of governments,
religions, educational institutions, large
corporations, the mass media, secretive fra-
ternal organizations, criminal syndicates
and who-knows-what-other-groups with
unknown agendas that may not even have
names—and you have one complex, intricate, hard-to-understand "stew" that we call
ordinary, consensual reality.

But a moment of quiet reflection will
show that that there is nothing remotely
ordinary about so-called everyday social
reality. Not at all. It is exceedingly complex,
with several billion interacting individuals
and groups, innumerable nuances and an
infinite number of incessantly changing
facets.

Even without positing paranormal realities it is possible to carefully create an
alternate social reality in which people be-
long to the same group, interact with one
another under a wide variety of circumstances and yet are not aware of other
members of the group. Consequently, it is
possible for one or more members of such a
group to not consciously know they are part
of such a group and that they have interacted with other members of the group.

In fact, intelligence agencies for major
governments use a method of operation that
is very similar to the scenario I have just
described. Intelligence agencies routinely
compartmentalize their operations into mu-
tually exclusive "cells" of agents that are
insulated from each other. They also distribute information about projects on a
strict need-to-know basis. Need-to-know
simply means that if someone needs to
know about a particular aspect of an operation in order to carry out his/her assignment
then they are given the requisite information. If such information is not a requisite
for their assignment it is not divulged to
them.

As a consequence, the information flow
in an operation is carefully controlled. In
this way, it can sometimes happen that
agents who work for the same agency, and
who are working on the same project, perhaps in the same city, may never be told of
each other's existence. The agents may even

know each other. But because of strict secrecy oaths, and because of rigid compartmentalization and need-to-know procedures they may remain ignorant of the true dimensions of the meta-reality *behind* the outward reality in which they carry out their assignments. In a case like that, an intelligence agency has constructed an alternative, parallel, non-ordinary social reality.

Have I (and others) been caught up into something like this—perhaps by a very secretive agency or group that has pursued its own agenda unbeknownst to me and others? Let me state here that I have never worked for an intelligence agency, that I do not presently work for an intelligence agency, and that I do not desire or plan to work for any intelligence agency. But the question persists: during the course of my life have I been caught up unawares in the operations of such a group? (Such a group need not be working either *for* or *against* any government or other organization in the constellation of consensual reality. In fact, such a hypothetical group could easily have an agenda and *modus operandi* that completely defy the understanding of conventional reality!)

I confess that I do not have the answer to my own question—it might be yes or no. But the simple fact that I have arrived at the point where it occurs to me to ask it makes me wonder if the answer might not be *yes*.

What might the evidence be that I am the subject of such a group's attention? Well, there are the dreams of the summer of 1997 that I have already mentioned. It seems that they may have been triggered, at least in part, by my visits to the 33° Masonic Temple in Washington, DC and to the George Washington National Masonic Memorial in Alexandria, Virginia. I do not mean to imply that I am the victim of a Masonic plot; I am simply suggesting that something about those visits seemed to have tripped an interior switch inside me. I do not know what that 'something' might have been.

SEVERAL YEARS AGO, before I fully understood that the Monroe Institute was associated with military intelligence activities, I visited the Institute for a special session in their special exploration facility. This facility was in a building set apart from the main training building. I was greeted at the main office and accompanied down the road and into the special exploration facility by an elderly male and a 40-ish female affiliated with the institute. No one else was in the special exploration facility.

When I entered the special isolation booth these two remained behind to monitor my exploration session. The goal was simply to try to consciously enter non-ordinary states of reality and report back to them what I was experiencing. The session lasted the better part of an hour and was very similar in structure to what occurs on many of the tapes offered for sale by the Monroe Institute. I was so nervous that nothing unusual happened at all. Mercifully, the time was finally up and I exited the booth. When I rejoined the man and woman who had been monitoring the session I saw that they had been joined by a young, crew-cut man who had not been there when I began the session. They introduced him to me and informed me that he would be securing the electronic equipment and the recorded tape of my session. The young man was not in uniform, but he had a military bearing. So on a whim I asked him if he were in the Army. He said that he was. I asked if he were on active duty. He said that he was. I then asked what he was doing at the Monroe Institute if he was in the Army. He replied that he was on leave and was just at the Institute for a short period of time. He continued fiddling with the racks of electronic equipment and the tape that had been made of my time in the booth. I subsequently left the building in the company of the elderly man and the 40-ish woman.

I now suspect that the Monroe Institute lied to me and that that young soldier was in reality one of the unknown number of psychic military spies that matriculated there over the last 20 years. I concede the possibility that the Monroe Institute may have delivered that tape to Army Intelligence (or maybe to the CIA or NSA), since I last saw it in the hands of a man who told me he was on active duty in the Army. Who knows whether this may have happened with other people who innocently attended sessions at the Monroe Institute? Army Intelligence is a spy organization. Spies spy. That is axiomatic. And these particular spies have had a cozy relationship with the Monroe Institute for many years.

THEN THERE IS THE MATTER of the unexplained voice in the night, during the Holidays in 1992. "The underground bases are *real* ..." How well I remember lying there in the dark, listening to the quiet monologue. Someone, or something, specifically targeted my mind for a transmission of information.

Who is back there in the shadows-lurking at the fringes of my perception?

It makes me uncomfortable to say it, but I have the feeling of being watched, of being observed—and I believe it has nothing to do paranoia. Of course, we *are* all watched, observed and monitored regularly. We call a company or a government agency on the phone and a recorded voice, often a soothing female voice, tells us that our conversation may be monitored at any time for "training" purposes. Or you walk into the bank, or the pharmacy, or the shopping mall, or the convenience store, or a government agency—and you notice the ubiqui-tous surveillance cameras. You make a purchase with your credit card and your name, what you bought and when and where you bought it, and other information, is electronically entered in mammoth computerized databases that are available to anyone who wants to know all about you and your life. You withdraw money from a banking machine and a camera films you. Electronic surveillance and monitoring of individuals is pervasive in our society. We are all being watched every day.

But my feeling of being watched goes beyond a feeling of being observed by the rapidly expanding background level of surveillance that is pervasive. There were the unexplained (as of this writing) encounters with the men in the hovering helicopters in the early 1970s in Virginia. There was the unexplained interrogation by a United States Navy officer at the Kings Bay Naval Submarine Base in Georgia in the mid-1980s ("Mr. Sauder, do you know who I am? Have we ever met before? Are you sure you don't know who I am?"). And I strongly suspect surveillance by Army Intelligence at the Monroe Institute, as well.

What do you think—the musings of a man who is losing his mind? Or the sobering reflection of a man who is on the verge of getting his true social and mental bearings and *finding* his mind?

I prefer the latter view.

Thirty One

PERHAPS MY QUESTION in the previous chapter should be more inclusive: who is back there in the shadows, lurking at the fringes of perception of *lots* of us?

Permit me to explain what I mean. A big part of my initial motivation for writing this book was to gain an understanding of some of the numerous anomalous incidents in my own life. I felt that writing about the many mysterious and puzzling events in my life would be cathartic.

Things have happened to me over the years—many of which I have discussed here—that have mystified me and sometimes troubled me. I thought that the very act of thinking about and committing my experiences to paper would help me come to grips with those events and their effect on my personal life.

But as I have gone along, setting down my experiences and memories, many of them from long ago, I have continually bumped up against evidence from other sources and from other people that indicates to me that there may be a very dark agenda of social, psychological and spiritual control that shadowy military agencies such as Army Intelligence, the Office of Naval Intelligence (ONI), the National Security Agency (NSA), the Central Intelligence Agency (CIA), the Defense Intelligence Agency (DIA) and other unknown agencies are perpetrating against a wide array of mind-control victims. The clear implication of the available evidence —ref. U.S. Patents discussed in this chapter —is that these agencies are working to perfect sophisticated, electronic means of controlling the thoughts and actions of human beings.

Unfortunately, their plans may be well advanced. A cursory search of some of the existing United States patents for mind control applications reveals a whole suite of electronic devices and technologies that alter brain waves, transmit audible sounds into the brain, enable remote monitoring of brain waves, and permit desired states of consciousness to be artificially induced in the human mind.[35] I have no doubt at all that intelligence agencies are well aware of these sorts of devices and patents. I will cite just a few of them.

For example, consider the abstract from United States Patent No. 4,858,612—*Hearing Device*:

ABSTRACT

A method and apparatus for simulation of hearing in mammals by introduction of a plurality of microwaves into the region of the auditory cortex... A microphone is used to transform sound signals into electrical signals which are in turn analyzed and processed to provide controls for generating a plurality of microwave signals at different frequencies. The multifrequency microwaves are then applied to the brain in the region of the auditory cortex. By this method sounds are perceived by the mammal which are representative of the original sound perceived by the microphone.

You will not find a better description of the means by which voices can be electronically transmitted into a human mind. Although the text of the patent presents the invention as a therapeutic aid for individuals who have hearing impairments, the potential mind control applications of the device are

---

[35] See the following World Wide Web page for a listing of many patents with mind-control applications: http://www.trufax.org/menu/patents.html, 1997. The United States Patent and Trademark Office web page at http://patents.uspto.gov/, 1998 permits an online search by patent number and by key word. Also, all federal depository libraries have United States Patent collections on microfilm. The patent collections can be searched electronically by key words. These libraries are commonly found at large, research universities. Call the library at the nearest large university to find a U.S. Patent collection in your region.

obvious. (See the appendix at the end of the book for the complete patent.)

But why stop at the mere electronic transmission of voices into the human brain? Why not electronically alter the brain waves themselves by means of radio transmissions? Consider, for example, United States Patent No. 3,951,134 – *Apparatus and Method for Remotely Monitoring and Altering Brain Waves*. The abstract says:

ABSTRACT

Apparatus for and method of sensing brain waves at a position remote from a subject whereby electromagnetic signals of different frequencies are simultaneously transmitted to the brain of the subject in which the signals interfere with one another to yield a waveform which is modulated by the subject's brain waves. The interference waveform which is representative of the brain wave activity is re-transmitted by the brain to a receiver where it is demodulated and amplified. The demodulated waveform is then displayed for visual viewing and routed to a computer for further processing and analysis. The demodulated waveform also can be used to produce a compensating signal which is transmitted back to the brain to effect a desired change in electrical activity therein.

Quoting again from the text of the patent:

SUMMARY OF THE INVENTION

The present invention relates to apparatus and a method for monitoring brain waves wherein all components of the apparatus employed are remote from the test subject. More specifically, high frequency transmitters are operated to radiate electromagnetic energy of different frequencies through antennas which are capable of scanning the entire brain of the test subject or any desired region thereof. The signals of different frequencies penetrate the skull of the subject and impinge upon the brain where they mix to yield an interference wave modulated by radiations from the brain's natural electrical activity. The modulated interference wave is re-transmitted by the brain and received by an antenna at a remote station

where it is demodulated, and processed to provide a profile of the subject's brain waves. In addition to passively monitoring his brain waves, the subject's neurological processes may be affected by transmitting to his brain, through a transmitter, compensating signals. The latter signals can be derived from the received and processed brain waves.

The import of the invention could not be clearer. This patent spells out, in black and white, an electronic method and apparatus for remotely monitoring and altering the brain waves of human beings, by use of radio transmitters and computers. The subject's brain waves are electronically monitored, received, routed to a computer, modified, and then transmitted back to his/her brain, with the stated intention of altering the "electrical activity" of the subject's brain. As the patent states:

... the subject's neurological processes may be affected by transmitting to his brain, through a transmitter, compensating signals. The latter signals can be derived from the received and processed brain waves.

The potential for electronic mind control is transparent. (See the appendix at the end of the book for the complete patent.)

Thanks to modern electronic technology the electrical activity of the human brain can be precisely monitored and displayed. The subtle electromagnetic fields and accompanying electrical activity in the brain can be electronically monitored and recorded in real time. United States Patent No. 4,951,674—*Biomagnetic Analytical System Using Fiber-Optic Magnetic Sensors* describes one such method and apparatus:

ABSTRACT

A biomagnetic analytical system for sensing and indicating minute magnetic fields emanating from the brain or from any other tissue region of interest in a subject under study. The system includes a magnetic pickup device constituted by an array of fiber-optic magnetic sensors mounted at positions distributed throughout the inner confines of a magnetic shield configured to conform generally to the head of the subject or whatever other body region is of interest. Each sensor yields a light beam whose phase or other parameter is modulated in accordance with the magnetic field emanating from the related site in the region. The modulated beam from each sensor is compared in an interferometer with a reference light beam to yield an output signal that is a function of the magnetic field being emitted at the related site. The output signals from the interferometer are processed to provide a display or recording exhibiting the pattern or map of magnetic fields resulting from emanations at the multitude of sites encompassed by the region.

This device makes possible the mapping of the brain's biomagnetic activity. The data can be displayed visually, on a CRT monitor (as on a computer screen), permitting a specialist to electronically peer into a person's head and to:

> ..."see" a functional image of the brain on a CRT, ... the image will be a profile of the electromganetically "active" portions of the brain, as shown by the magnetic pattern derived from data reduction...

The data can also be digitized for subsequent storage and manipulation. In the words of the patent:

> The data can also be directed to a storage medium for the purpose of recording the digitized biomagnetic data for archiving and later retrieval and processing.

Patent No. 4,951,674 goes on to say that during the data processing stage, data from:

> ... modalities such as EEG, EKG, MRI and X-ray ... can be combined with the biomagnetic data ...

In other words, the practitioner can reconcile the biomagnetic data with an individual's EEG pattern. This means a specific pattern of biomagnetic activity can be correlated with a particular pattern of electrical activity in the brain. (See the appendix at the end of the book for the complete patent. Look at illustrations 1 to 3. Note the special helmet with the magnetic sensors that fits around the head of the person whose brain's biomagnetic activity is being monitored and digitally recorded.)

United States Patent No. 4,408,616, *Brain Electrical Activity Mapping*, provides further information on how the human brain can be electronically monitored. (See the appendix at the end of the book for the complete patent.) The patent abstract says, in part:

> Topographic displays of brain electrical activity are produced from matrices of data derived from evoked potential (EP) and steady-state responses of skull transducers ... the rate of data sampling is sufficient to capture rapid transient events ...

In other words, the transition from one mental state to another can be observed and electronically mapped. The text of the patent explains how this is done:

> Twenty electrodes (e.g., Grass gold cup) are attached to subject's skull ... Twenty leads from electrodes are connected through switch to conventional 24-channel polygraph ...

The patent succinctly explains how electrodes are attached to a person's skull and connected to a polygraph machine to record the electrical activity of their brain in real time, as it responds to various stimuli. It neatly sums up:

> ... (T)he brain electrical activity mapping system creates color topographic displays reflecting brain electrical activity using, as input, continuous electrical waveforms recorded from a number of points on the skull.

The data are then converted to digital form. Data are stored in individual files or combined with others into "group" files, so that a group profile of brain electrical activity in response to a variety of stimuli can be constructed. The stimulus may be a flashing light or something more complex, like being asked to distinguish between two similar, but slightly different, spoken words.

Over time, a library of digitized data (data that can be stored and analyzed by computer) about the electrical activity of the brains of individual people and groups of people is built up. This is precisely the type of data that can be used to modulate a radio wave that is transmitted into a target subject's brain to alter his/her brainwaves. In principle, by using averaged data derived from group files of brain electrical activity, it should be possible to modulate radio broadcasts to affect the brain electrical activity of large numbers of a target population.

When I recently became aware of the existence of this sort of technology I immediately realized that it may have some relevance to the many strange experiences that I have had over the years.

I also recognized that the stories that many alleged mind-control victims tell may well be true. The Mind Control Forum (on the World Wide Web at http://www.mk.net/~mcf/index.htm) carries many stories from people who insist that they have had electronic implants surgically implanted in their brains or who have been otherwise terrorized by intrusive, torturous, apparently electronic transmissions to their minds. Many of these people have experienced tremendous suffering and personal turmoil. In some cases, the origins of these transmissions are not known.

In other cases it appears military agencies, the CIA, the FBI, the NSA and similar organizations are behind these hellish experiments.

FOR A LISTING of various mind control programs carried out by the "alphabet soup" of covert agencies see the World Wide Web at http://www.trufax.org/research/projects.html. In many cases people's minds and brains have been tampered with and altered without their informed consent. Psychoactive drugs, microwaves, hypnosis, brain washing and electronic implants are some of the ways in which mind control victims have been attacked by these shadowy agencies.

Electronic and psychotronic mind control technologies are absolutely antithetical to the fundamental exercise of human freedom. Unfortunately, the patents and technologies described here are real. It is time for us all to wake up and see things as they are. A particularly insidious slavery is mental enslavement, accomplished by electronically or psychotronically altering people's thoughts, such that their very thoughts are not their own, but are ones that their self-appointed masters would have them to think.

Thirty Two

AS A RESULT OF MY OWN personal experience it is clear to me that great discernment is required to differentiate between two general classes, or varieties, of altered states of consciousness and their causes. The principal division is between naturally occurring altered states and artificially induced altered states. In many cases, naturally occurring altered states and artificially induced altered states can be difficult to differentiate—even for the practiced experiencer. Telling the difference takes a lot of time, maturity, study and self-knowledge. Above all, it is not wise to leap to conclusions about the cause of any given altered state of consciousness. What appears to be a simple matter at first may be something else entirely upon closer inspection.

For example, the out-of-body-experience (OOBE) can often be naturally induced by meditation, relaxation exercises, or lucid dreaming practices—it can even happen spontaneously. At the same time, psychotronic technology exists to artificially facilitate or induce OOBEs, exemplified by the binaural beat, audio technology developed and sold by Robert Monroe. (See the appendix at the end of the book for Robert Monroe's brain entrainment patents.) The problem is that I now know that electronic technology exists that has the capability to alter brain waves and to broadcast electronic transmissions right into the brain. Using myself as an example, what assurance can I have that the OOBEs in which I heard the voice of Robert Monroe were naturally occurring altered states, as opposed to artificially induced states using electronic or psychotronic technology that might be at the disposal of the Monroe Institute and United States military intelligence operatives? In fact, I now realize that I have precious little assurance that my experiences with Robert Monroe were naturally occurring altered states. At the time,

however, I was positively persuaded that those particular out-of-body experiences were natural events.

Similarly, an unknowing individual who hears a disembodied voice announce, seemingly inside his/her inner ear, that: *"The underground bases are real..."* might be tempted to ascribe such a voice to an angel, or to a demon, or to an extraterrestrial, or to higher consciousness. I did hear exactly such a voice in my ear. But I now know that the technology exists to electronically broadcast a voice right into the inner ear or auditory cortex of the human brain (See U.S. Patent No. 4,858,612—*Hearing Device* in the appendix at the end of the book). Thus, I realize that I may quite possibly have heard the voice of a perfectly ordinary human being, speaking through the microphone of an electronic device that broadcast his unusual message directly to my brain. So it is that an unusual event that could easily have been perceived as a supernatural, or spiritual event, may in actuality have really been a covert electronic broadcast from a military intelligence agency—and nothing more.

I even concede that a couple of my kundalini experiences may have been artificially induced. For instance, the one where a voice told me to "Party hearty!" is suspect to me. Not because of the words, "party hearty" (the kundalini can, after all, be a lot of fun), but because of the way the voice sounded. It lacked the kind of depth, the resonance, the timbre that voices in a genuine mystical or naturally occurring altered state have. The voices that come from deep inside, from the mystical and spiritual depths of universal being, have a vital, authoritative quality that you feel in an integral, comprehensive way with your living core. They strike a resonant chord that vibrates way down inside—they have texture and rich nuances that resonate with the marrow, bone and sinew of your very being. By way of contrast, the voice that said, "Party hearty!" seemed somewhat on the tinny side, a bit shallow, flat, one-dimensional, kind of forced, and slightly unnatural, somehow out of the natural flow of things.

I can best illustrate the other kind of voice, what might be called a vitally arche-typal voice, with an anecdote.

ONE MORNING, just before I awoke, I had the following dream: my Father was build-ing a huge house for me, beside a large lake. I was taking a tour of this enormous house, going by myself from room to room. The house had been framed, and roofed, but the sheet-rock between rooms had not yet been nailed onto the two-by-fours. So I was able to see easily from room to room as I walked alone through the place. Anyone who has walked around in a house under construc-tion should be able to visualize exactly what I mean. As I neared the back of the house my attention was drawn to a dock behind the house, where boats could come and go across the lake. I was looking though the unfinished back wall of the house at the dock when I suddenly heard a noise behind me. Thinking I was alone in the house, I whirled, startled, and saw a gleaming white, conical shape standing about 15 feet away from me. It stood about 6 feet tall. This shape, which strongly resembled the nose cone of a missile, addressed me in the most singular manner I have ever heard. It said, "I AM NEMOS." The voice spoke at a normal conversational volume, but it was hardly a normal voice. It sounded as if thousands, perhaps millions of people, were speaking the same phrase, at just the same time, and somehow uttering the words through this entity **NEMOS**. I sensed great gravity and singleness of purpose in the words. How can the teeming multitudes be one? And how can they speak as one? What does that mean? And yet it was clear that many, perhaps many *thousands* or *millions* of people, were speaking as one through **NEMOS**. As the voice spoke, I came quickly and briefly into an altered state of con-sciousness. The utterance was positively

charged with energy and significance. Within seconds I was wide, wide awake. Not drowsy at all, but really wide awake. The words were ringing in my mind and ears—I could practically hear that voice—the great **I AM**.

But who is **NEMOS**? In view of the re-semblance to a missile nose cone I initially thought that the allusion was surely to nu-clear missiles, representing the nemesis of the human race. And perhaps that was the meaning. Maybe **NEMOS** does represent the nuclear nemesis we have contrived for ourselves. Maybe **NEMOS** appeared and spoke to me to remind me of the seriousness of what we have already done and of the nuclear horror we may yet unleash, if we are not careful.

On the other hand, when I examined the dictionary definition for nemesis I no-ticed that the word below nemesis, nemo-phila, contains the root word of nemos. Ac-cording to my dictionary, the Greek word nemos means "a wooded pasture, originally a wooded valley."[36] So maybe the meaning of **I AM NEMOS** is really something like this: "**I AM** the life force of the wooded vale, of the peaceful valley throbbing with vital-ity; **I AM** the spirit of the meadow, the living trees and the animals that graze beneath their shade; **I AM** that natural life force, that force of creation in the trees, grass, animals and soil that you have twisted into nuclear warheads and fashioned into a nu-clear nemesis that holds the world in its harsh thrall. Gaze on me and hear my voice(s) speaking as one from the very core of *our* collective being. Lo! I set myself be-fore you in gleaming battle array. Do ye choose, and well, between the awful, dread shining of my nuclear sun-burst and the soul refreshing silence of my sacred, ancient grove!"

---

36 *Webster's New World Dictionary of the American Lan-guage, Second College Edition,* Editor in Chief, David B. Guralnik (New York: William Collins and World Publishing Co., Inc, 1974).

Thirty Three

DURING THE EARLY 1980's I was an anti-nuclear activist. I repeatedly expressed my opposition to preparation for nuclear war by demonstrating at Navy bases and climbing over Air Force security fences and onto the launch lids of inter-continental ballistic missiles (ICBMs). As a direct result of these activities I was repeatedly jailed and harassed by the government.

My philosophy at the time was simple: the world's problems must be confronted and dealt with on a personal level, within the context of each individual life. I remember well the question a deputy U.S. Marshal asked me one day, after I had been tried and convicted of petty misdemeanor trespass in Federal Court in Little Rock for demonstrating on a Titan II missile silo:

"Sauder, why do you go out on the missile silos?"

"Someone has to do it," I replied.

"Yes," he remonstrated. "But why this particular Titan II silo?"

"Because it's the closest one to my house," I answered.

He turned away perplexed, misunderstanding and incomprehension written all over his face. A short while later he handcuffed and chained me and took me away to jail.

That was not the first time I was tried, and it was not the only time I was jailed. In fact, the previous two years had been an excruciating civics lesson in what kind of rigid control the military and the "Just-us" system exert over this society.

Here is how part of those years transpired: in early April 1982 I made the decision to climb over the fence and onto the launch lid of a Minuteman ICBM silo, at Whiteman Air Force Base, in western Missouri. At that time I was a practicing Catholic (I am no longer a communicant) and living in Kansas City. I informed the editor of the *National Catholic Reporter*, Tom Fox, of my plans. He assigned a young reporter, Penni Crabtree, to tag along and report on what happened.

Early on the morning of 13 April 1982 I drove out to the silo, with Crabtree following behind in her own car. The silo was out in the rural Missouri countryside, in a farmer's field. I parked my car in front of the entrance gate, walked up to the silo compound and climbed over the security fence. The time was 5:55 a.m. A little over an hour and a half passed before Air Force MPs arrived to discover me standing on the missile's launch lid. In the interim, I walked around and looked at things inside the one acre compound. In addition to the thick, reinforced concrete launch lid, there were a few posts with electronic devices attached to them and a large hatch that provided access to the missile and the underground works.

I watched a farmer tend to his herd of cattle pastured in the field across the road. Little birds came and perched on the silo's security fence, twittering perkily. An occasional farmer passed down the road in his pick-up truck.

At about 7:30 a.m. the Air Force police arrived. Two MPs crept over the brow of a nearby hill in a small patrol truck and crunched to a stop on the gravel road. I watched them get out their M-16s and ammo clips, and put on their flak jackets and helmets. They got back in the truck and drove slowly up to Crabtree, along the side of the road. They ordered her to put her hands behind her head and kneel on the ground. One airman remained guarding her while the other trotted cumbersomely towards me. He unlocked the gate to the site and ordered me to put my hands behind my head and walk slowly out the gate. As I drew near him I told him that I would not harm him. He said, "Shut up!"

I was escorted to the side of Crabtree and ordered to the ground. We were held there at gunpoint until more Air Force personnel arrived. In the interim we were treated to the military chatter over the air. "Uh, roger, Whiteman, this is Red Rover. That's affirmative on the negatory. We'll be changing channels now and we'll, uh, be moving to Whiskey Bravo 4 now, over." Whiteman: "Roger, Red Rover. That's affirmative. Over."

More men arrived. An officer began strutting around, barking orders, a little beret cocked jauntily on the side of his head. "I want this site secured, everything, fence posts, all of it! *I mean by the numbers!!* " The veins stood out in his neck.

"Yes, sir!"

Much trotting around with M-16s. The officer disappeared underground with some of his men. They opened the hatch on the silo, handed their rifles below and climbed inside.

We were held at gun point for a couple of hours, spread-eagled against a barbed wire fence. Crabtree told the Air Force she was a reporter. She was told to be quiet. The Air Force confiscated her notebook and camera.

Finally, we were frisked and taken in handcuffs to the Johnson County jail. The jailor there was very talkative. He said that his former employer was the Air Force Office of Special Investigations. According to him, I was not shot because I was on American soil. In general, he said that the military would be much quicker to kill an intruder on foreign soil.

Three hours later two deputy U.S. Marshals picked us up and transported us, siren wailing, to the Federal building in downtown Kansas City. Charges were not brought against Crabtree and after half an hour of detention in a holding cell she was released. I was taken before

a U.S. Magistrate and arraigned. He charged me with trespassing, a petty misdemeanor, and set my bail at $75,000. He ordered me held in the Jackson County jail.

But how to convey the horror of the Jackson County jail? Words can scarcely do justice to the stark realities of an overcrowded, dirty, aging, violent, inner city prison.

Like a faded lithograph of someone else's nightmare memory the images come flooding up: Steve, the 18 year old Black man in the next cell, being taken away in the middle of the night to serve three and-a-half years in the state penitentiary at Jefferson City. Orphaned by a broken marriage, raised in White foster homes and graduated to the streets, barely able to read and write, puzzling out verses from the New Testament syllable by syllable. Fond of dope and one-arm push-ups, never had a job and apprehensive about prison. He spent a month in a padded cell, usually reserved for wackos and extremely violent anti-social prisoners, because he refused to submit to a command by a guard to bend over and spread his buttocks during a strip search. There was a story in the paper one day about a 16-year-old girl who had been found in a parking lot downtown. She had been strangled to death and was nude, except for her socks. Steve heard some other inmates talking about it and wanted me to read him the story. I asked why. He said that she had been a girl friend of his and had asked him to be her pimp when she was 14, because she liked him and didn't want to work for someone else.

Then there was Noah Moses, who named himself after biblical characters for reasons known only to himself, who spent hours upon hours, week after week, talking loudly to himself, rehashing his failed marriages and bouts of alcoholism and mental illness, who was alternately defiantly proud of and bashful about his Native American ancestry, who passionately despised Nazis, having fought them as an infantryman in WW

II, and who despised Jews equally as passionately, because they were ruining Kansas City, conspiring to take control of the whole town, and who was fiercely defensive about having been beaten by a group of younger inmates at a local mental hospital, which incident was known to another inmate on the tier and occasioned much foul, raucous heckling.

In the cell on the other side was Sam, at one and the same time a violent, raving psychotic and also (by very brief spells) a sensitive, intelligent, semi-literate 22-year-old. He was an incoherent mishmash of the prophet Muhammed (blessed be his name) and Jesus Christ, salted with fierce hatred of Whites, confusion over his mixed Native American-Black ancestry, devotion and adoration of his mother and simultaneous deep anger at her for having abused him as a child, an absolute, total homicidal schizophrenic who once shot a man during a hold-up because he had no money. As he explained it, if the man had given him even a couple of dollars he would have let him live, but since he had no money he killed him. He would spend hours on hours drumming out complex, intricately syncopated rhythms on his toilet bowel; would piss on the floor of the corridor through his cell door; would threaten my life in graphic terms and then apologize to me with real conviction just a few minutes later; once threw fire in my cell while I was resting on my bunk in an abortive attempt to kill me; was madly in love with a young woman in the projects whom he was going to shoot to death after his release because she was so fine and to keep her from being unfaithful, even though he had never so much as "kissed her on the jaw", only maybe he would marry her instead and have a baby, but he was going to go see her, and never wanted to see his mother again, because when he was a little boy she had beat him *so* bad. And on and on, shouting and drumming, invoking the Muslim credo, yelling crude, graphic homosexual taunts and invitations and repeatedly

cursing the infidel peckerwoods (Whites), occasionally being sexually serviced through his cell door by a homosexual whom the guards would let out to come around and masturbate him so that he would shut up for a few hours. On and on, day after day, night after long night. Hours on end. And then his sentence expired and he was released.

Then there were the drugs: trays of pills carried through the tier twice a day. Men staggered about listlessly with the thorazine shuffle. Suffusing it all was the homosexuality, men incessantly shouting at each other, calling each other "bitch", "girl", and "whore".

There was an inmate named Al, 40 years old and looking 65. Al was deeply depressed and heavily sedated to restrain his violent tendencies. As the drugs wore off and he got more violent he would bellow crude, obscene taunts for hours on end at the top of his lungs. One day he broke down completely and cried bitterly, like a mortally wounded animal, in great, gasping sobs, over having spent "most of my life in a goddamned, fucking cage!!" He was quickly silenced by a medical orderly the guards summoned to administer an intravenous tranquilizer. He fell back on his bunk within seconds, snoring loudly.

I VIVIDLY REMEMBER another inmate who was placed in the cell next to mine. I had seen him being booked while out of my cell to confer with my attorney. I first noticed him because he was in a wheelchair. I had spoken to him without getting a reply. Initially, he was brought up onto the tier and placed in a cell down the corridor from me. Five minutes after the guard left the other inmates began yelling frantically. The supposed invalid had climbed up on his sink, knotted a sheet around his neck, tied the other end to his ceiling lattice and proceeded to hang himself. But the guards got to him in the nick of time. They rushed in and dragged him over to the cell next to mine. He was stripped to his shorts and his sheet was taken away.

He spent the night rolling on the floor moaning and cackling in a howling falsetto about Vietnam. The next morning I was let out of my cell for a short walk along the corridor. He was lying on the floor, rolling back and forth, holding his head in his hands and moaning softly, "Lord have mercy! Oh Lord, have mercy! Please have mercy!"

I asked him if his head hurt.

"Oh yes," he said. "Lord, yes, my head hurts. Oh Lord, have *mercy!*"

And that was virtually all I could get out of him. I could see freshly healed bullet holes in his back. (The other inmates said that he had been involved in a shoot-out with the police and had been in the hospital for a few weeks to allow the bullet wounds to heal before being transferred to the county jail.) He was a young man, in his early thirties, almost skeletal. When he was served a tray of food he would dump it on the floor and lap it up like a dog. The bread he would rinse in his toilet bowl before eating. He would pass hours peering intently at the wall, wriggling his fingers like a hypnotist or a magician weaving a spell. His trance would break abruptly with frantic, staccato outbursts on Vietnam. He would continue ranting at the top of his lungs until he lapsed into exhaustion, voice cracked and shrill, throat parched and rasping: "Vietnam! Vietnam! Vietnam! Vietnam! Vietnam! Vietnam! Vietnam! Vietnam! Vietnam! Vietnam! Vietnam! Vietnam! Vietnam! Vietnam! Vietnam!" Followed by: "V-V-V-V-V-VV-V-V-V-V-V ... " (imitative of automatic weapons fire); followed by: "Get down! Get down! Get down! Get down! Get *down*, I say! I said, 'Get *down!*' I don't wanna shoot! Get down! I said, 'Get *down!*' Vietnam! Vietnam! Vietnam! Vietnam! Vietnam! Vietnam! Vietnam! Vietnam! Vietnam! Vietnam! Vietnam! Vietnam! ... " over and over, until, his mouth dry and cottony, he would resume with, "V-V-V-V-V-V-V-V-V ... " (indefinitely) and recommence rolling on

the floor with his head in his hands moaning, "Oh Lord, have *mercy!*"

Another inmate was a merchant marine named Joe. The FBI arrested him for allegedly mailing hundreds of supposedly libelous postcards about his estranged wife to people in his hometown. The only problem (according to him) was that the cards were postmarked on days when he was in mid-ocean. It was an unusual case, but not half as strange as the man himself. He spent his days laboriously creating mystical diagrams for his pre-school son. They were meticulously sketched out and painstakingly filled in with different colored drawing pencils—moons, suns, circles, rays, rings, triangles, angles, degrees, and other symbology—all quite dexterously arranged. The inspiration for his artwork was no less than God the Father, God the Son and God the Holy Spirit, incarnate in the form of his son and him, who were all three at the same time. God revealed all of this directly to him in the form of visions (though it never seemed to have occurred to him to wonder why, if *he* were God, he had to show visions to *himself*). In fact, through divine instruction he had been taught to speak ancient Egyptian and given the name of *Ra*, the Sun God. It was all very arcane. Upon request he would spout off in a strange language that he claimed was the vernacular of the Pharaohs.

How had God granted this singular boon? Simple: he merely requested enlightenment and — presto! — the visions commenced.

The rude clamor of an inmate being stabbed on the other side of the wall, in the next section, intruded on my cell early one morning. There was a lot of violent noise, muffled cursing and hate-filled hollering, the thud of something impacting on flesh, the metallic clanging of cell doors as guards hurriedly entered the tank to lock up the inmates, the scuffling and thumping of two men locked in a furious struggle. This is one of my last memories of the Jackson County Jail.

DURING THE TIME I WAS IN JAIL in Kansas City I went to trial in Federal Court. I appeared *pro se* with the assistance of my attorneys, and called two expert witnesses, one a local medical doctor and medical school professor, the other an international law expert from the University of Illinois. The doctor showed a few slides that graphically depicted the impact of an average nuclear warhead. The law professor attempted to testify to the illegality of nuclear war and preparations for it, from the standpoint of international law. But his testimony was not allowed, on grounds of irrelevance. For the purposes of the appellate record I made an offer of proof of several international treaties and agreements to which the United States government is signatory. The Magistrate accepted the offer of proof and dismissed the international law expert from the bench area.

Several Air Force men were in attendance to testify against me. I had little contact with them, but they took a great deal of interest in the whole proceeding. They craned their necks to see better when slides were shown illustrating the effects on Kansas City of the detonation of a one megaton nuclear warhead.

I called myself as a witness and gave my own summation before the verdict was rendered. I spoke of the history of the United States and noted that the same genocidal mind-set that led to the slaughter of Indians and theft of their lands also resulted in Black slavery, and that this same violent impulse finds expression today in massive preparations to wage planet-wide, thermonuclear warfare. I spoke of the Nazi missile program during WW II and of the Nazi V-2 rockets brought to the American Southwest by the United States Army, there to be perfected as the prototype for today's nuclear missiles. I observed that the United States had appropriated Nazi military technology as its own.

As I made these remarks I noticed the prosecuting attorney make a move to get to his feet to register an objection, but it was my summation and he thought better of it and sank back into his chair.

The Magistrate recessed for a few minutes to ponder the verdict. When he returned he pronounced me guilty of criminal trespass and ordered the U.S. Marshal to return me to jail, pending sentencing.

Several days later I was returned for sentencing. His beet-red face contrasting sharply with his jet-black robe, the Magistrate gave me the maximum 5 months and 29 days and ordered me confined in the Buchanan County jail, in St. Joseph, Missouri. As he pronounced the sentence he angrily observed that: (1) I was a threat to society; (2) I had needlessly endangered other people's lives (he explained that the arresting officers might have had a wreck while speeding to arrest me and might have hurt themselves and others); (3) I needed to be rehabilitated; (4) I needed to be incarcerated in a jail type institution for the maximum period of time permitted by federal law for the offense with which I was charged; in order to (5) discourage others who sympathized with what I had done from also demonstrating on nuclear missile silos.

Several days later I was transferred from Jackson County to the Buchanan County jail. If the jail in Jackson County was old and shabby, the one in Buchanan County was far worse. To make matters worse, when I arrived I discovered that the Buchanan County jail was under Federal Court order for civil rights violations against its inmates.

My first two days in the Buchanan County jail were spent in a foul, brick walled, dungeon-like cell with 7 other men. It was small and cramped and we were double bunked. Little of the outside world was visible—just bars and bricks. Three times a day the guard would open a metal trap door in the thick brick wall and the trustee would shove our food in. The trap door would clang shut, and with it, our precious cross ventilation. There was one naked light bulb overhead. Live wiring snaked out of the wall and the toilet leaked and stunk. Eight men, most of them violent, locked in a steel and brick *huis clos* to rival anything that Sartre contrived.

It was a relief to be released to a larger tank on the second day. I went on to pass the next 4 and 1/2 months on the 5th and 6th tiers of the Buchanan County jail, and to hear and see many terrible things. It was by spells boring, oppressive, fatiguing, violent, depressing, and always instructive. It was certainly not an intellectual experience.

One of the depressing things about jail and prison is the large number of young people there, many of them under 25, many of them under 20, some as young as 17, 16, 15 and even 14. Most are there, no matter their age, due to circumstances that somehow involve either alcohol or drugs, or both. But of course, alcohol and the other drugs are only symptoms that show up because of other problems in life, whether they are of an individual or societal nature. Drugs filter into jail. I saw young prisoners popping pills, smoking dope— teenagers, a wasteland inside, bored with life, bored with jail, angry at each other, angry at the police, confused, bitter, frightened, poorly educated, violent.

THE VIOLENCE CAN BE very intense in jail. I was kept awake for a long time one night by the other men on my tier who for some reason began to yell over and over, "We want to kill a nigger! We want to kill a nigger! Bring us a nigger up here! We want to kill a nigger!" They shouted hysterically for a couple of hours, whipping themselves into a murderous frenzy. And let the reader understand this well: they were not joking. I lay back on my bunk, my thoughts racing, emotions turbulent inside, so many powerful, conflicting feelings. I wanted to cry out, to bellow my defiance, but dared not, lest they fall on me and kill *me*. I began to hate my fellow prisoners for their ignorance and hatred, only to realize with despair that I was falling

into the same ugly trap as them. I made an effort to mentally block out their shouting but could not. It rang in my ears, on and on and on ... They yelled and cursed and hollered and rattled the bars like men possessed of howling demons—as indeed they were. The tier resounded and shook with their hate filled cries and the slamming of cell doors. Finally their fury subsided; their own rage exhausted them and they lapsed into silence.

There was a young marine in that jail who had gone AWOL. While AWOL he had stolen a couple of packs of cigarettes from a convenience store. He was apprehended and brought to jail. Since he was destitute and his family was quite poor he had no money to bond out. So he was locked up, to await his trial.

He was put on another tier, below me. One of the other inmates, a thickly muscled, violent man, began putting pressure on him to rape him. The outcome of it all was that the AWOL marine was unable to physically beat off the other man and in desperation, in order to preserve his honor, tried to hang himself. But he didn't succeed. The deputies cut him down, still alive, and sent him to the Missouri state mental hospital, only several blocks away. He remained there for a couple of weeks undergoing treatment and then was returned to jail, to the same tier, where he was once again homosexually harassed by the same inmate.

Another man, younger than I, and not long married, had narrowly avoided beating his wife to death with a curtain rod. It was a savage crime and he was a seriously disturbed young man, violence smoldering beneath the surface. He was also quite sensitive in other ways and gifted as an artist. In a rare pensive mood he told me a little of his childhood. His father was a hard drinking riverboat man and his mother raised him virtually by herself. One night his father came home late, in a drunken stupor, and his mother refused to let him in the house.

Outraged, his father slammed his body repeatedly against the door as it bulged inward and rattled noisily under the blows. Unable to break the door down, he smashed his fist through a door panel and jammed his forearm in the splintered wreckage. Stunned by the pain, he attempted to jerk it back and gashed himself badly. Blood spurted down the inside of the door. The preschool child watched in horror as his father ripped his bleeding arm out of the door. Half crazed with alcohol, pain and loss of blood he stumbled to his truck and fell in. There then ensued a hurried midnight drive to the hospital, his mother at the wheel, and an anxious wait as doctors administered emergency treatment to the arm. A few years later, the father left, never to return. But his legacy of alcoholism and violence lived on in his son, to surface brutally 20 years later.

The Buchanan County jail had an exercise yard surrounded by a security fence that was available for the prisoners to use. But weeks and months would go by without the men being allowed off the tiers to exercise. The jail itself was chronically understaffed and overcrowded. The holding tank was not fit for human habitation. No provision was made to separate violent prisoners from the nonviolent majority of inmates. The diet was deficient—never any fresh milk or fruit juice, only an occasional apple or banana—and very heavy on noodles, spaghetti, potatoes, white bread, toast and pancakes. Most of the plumbing did not work properly. And in mid-summer, when temperatures ranged into the 90's and higher on the tiers, the guards would cut off the water for hours at a time. One hot day, an elderly man in the sweltering holding tank had a heart attack and nearly died. The other inmates began shouting. He was taken by ambulance to the hospital and revived. When he recovered sufficiently he was returned to jail and put back in the same holding tank.

ON ONE OF THE OCCASIONS when we prisoners were permitted in the exercise yard I severely sprained my ankle going after a basketball rebound. I did not walk again for about a month. During that time I was not permitted to have crutches and received virtually no medical care. I was begrudgingly given an ice pack a few times, to reduce the considerable swelling. My foot ballooned to twice its normal size. An angry reddish-purple, yellow-and-black discoloration extended from mid-calf to my toes. The pain was intense.

Immediately after I sprained the ankle I asked the guards to be taken to the hospital for treatment. After about 6 hours they granted my request, but not before I first underwent an examination at the jail by a man whom I had not seen before.

A deputy brought me hopping on my good leg down three flights of stairs to the visiting room and told me to wait there. A man came in, in civilian clothes, and asked to see my foot. I showed him the foot and he examined it expertly, probing deftly here and there, seemingly very knowledgeable about fractures, sprains and the like. I asked if he were a medical doctor. He said, "Yes, you could say that." I asked him what that meant. He said that he was not an M.D., but that he had quite a bit of medical training. I then requested to see some professional identification. He opened his wallet and gave me a card that identified him as a United States Army officer, stationed at a base in West Germany. I remember his name as Major Gerald Dunham. I asked him if he was on active duty. He said that he was. I asked him why he was at the county jail in St. Joseph, Missouri. He replied that he and six other Army personnel were on a special mission there. (I saw him occasionally from that time on, when he would come up on the tier at meal time. He said very little and had a humorless, icy demeanor. One of the other guards was also an Army officer. It was a very strange arrangement for a shabby county jail.)

I renewed my demand to be taken to the hospital after Major Dunham finished his examination of my foot. So a guard handcuffed my hands behind my back and forced me to hop to a waiting patrol car. At the hospital I was forced to hop through the parking lot, into the hospital and down a corridor to the waiting room. At no time did the doctors or nurses who stood by offer me the use of a wheelchair or crutches.

My handcuffs were removed and x-rays were taken of the foot. When I asked the doctor to see the x-rays he became angry and refused to show them to me. He became belligerent. The deputy guarding me physically forced me down on the bed when the doctor left and handcuffed my hands behind the back again. When I protested his use of force he warned me sternly that he would do worse than that if I didn't learn to show some respect for the doctor. He made me hop to the patrol car. The doctors and nurses lined up to watch me. They were sullen to a person. There were several wheelchairs parked in the lobby, but they never offered me the use of one.

The doctor's parting words rang in my ears: "Now be sure to use crutches for this until it heals, O.K.?" Yet he did nothing at all to alleviate my pain or discomfort. Indeed, he was among those who stood in the lobby and watched stone faced as I hobbled painfully out of the hospital, handcuffed and under armed guard.

During the summer months I became increasingly concerned about conditions for the prisoners. I circulated a petition on Tiers 5 and 6 soliciting signatures from other prisoners for redress of grievances and mailed copies to the local newspaper and to the Federal Court in Kansas City. The local paper printed the petition and signatures. It also printed our crimes (or alleged crimes, for those who had not yet been tried and convicted) and length of our sentences. The petition created a small stir of local con-

cern over conditions at the jail. The quality of our food improved slightly for a couple of weeks. The jailors provided us with a medicinal salve with which we deloused ourselves. Our cracked and filthy bedding was replaced with new mats. Those who had no bedding to begin with were provided with bedding, so that they no longer had to sleep on bare concrete or bare steel racks. Violent prisoners were put on a separate tier. Our exercise schedule became more regular for a few weeks.

And then conditions began to deteriorate once again.

In the meantime, the Federal Court in Kansas City appointed a lawyer to investigate our complaints. The attorney's name was Claudia York. She visited the jail and interviewed me extensively one day. We went into the exercise room and had a long talk. On the basis of that conversation and the record of noncompliance on the part of Buchanan County, Missouri with an earlier court order mandating changes at the jail, she recommended that the county be found in contempt of court.

I never heard what the outcome of the contempt of court recommendation was, because I was transferred back to the Jackson County jail in Kansas City in the first week of October, to await extradition to the eastern District of Arkansas for a probation revocation hearing. I spent 6 days in jail in Kansas City and then was shipped to the Federal Penitentiary at Springfield, Missouri along with 5 other convicts. We were individually handcuffed and shackled, hand and foot, then chained together as a group and locked into a government van under armed guard for the trip down.

When we arrived I was put into administrative detention as a hold-over. The prison at Springfield, Missouri is a medical center for the Federal prison system. In addition to the resident prison population who do the kitchen work, maintenance and laundry and other jobs inside, there are also many men there for illnesses and medical conditions of various sorts, some physical, some mental.

The guards put me in a cell by myself. There was a toilet and a sink, a bare shelf and a double bunk. Nothing else.

That evening I was taken to see a "counselor". He began to interrogate me in an insulting manner and berate me for my "crimes". I attempted to explain to him why I demonstrated against nuclear weapons, but the effort fell on deaf ears.

I asked him why I was in the penitentiary, when I had not yet had a probation hearing, and my sentence for the demonstration at the missile silo in Missouri had expired. I asked if it was normal to imprison people in the penitentiary before they had been to court. He became defensive and testily explained that I was not facing reality, that I had to understand that I had committed a crime and was being punished for it.

I responded that the question of my guilt or innocence was a matter for a court of law to determine and not an employee of the Bureau of Prisons. He would have none of it, however, and continued to attempt to get me to see that I was a criminal.

I asked him how long I would be at Springfield. He gave no answer, said that he did not know. I asked him when I would be going to court. He pled ignorance on my court date, as well.

I asked to make a phone call that evening and was denied permission, though I was permitted to place one call to my family the following day. The counselor requested that I fill out a visiting card. I had been led to believe that I was a hold-over, on my way to trial, so the request puzzled me. Nevertheless, I filled out the card. I put down the names of 8 or 9 people that I knew in Arkansas and Kansas City. All but two were priests or nuns. Only my brother (in Virginia) was approved to see me. I was told none of the priests or nuns would be permitted to visit me.

A guard returned me to my cell for the night. I slept fitfully.

Before dawn the door to my cell was suddenly flung open. Two guards stood in the doorway and told me that I needed to be x-rayed. I protested that I did not need to be x-rayed. "No matter," they said. "You need to be x-rayed anyway." But I insisted that not only had I not asked to be x-rayed, I neither needed nor wanted x-rays.

"So," they said. "You are refusing your x-rays?"

"Yes. I haven't asked for any and I'm not going to have any."

"But everyone that comes here *must* have them." They were adamant.

"But *I* am not going to have any." I was equally adamant.

They left. Banged shut the door and disappeared.

Late in the second afternoon I was there they brought an older man and put him in the cell with me. He was very evasive about his reasons for being in my cell. He told me repeatedly, in coarse terms, that *they* were trying to brainwash me. He would say, "They're trying to fuck with your mind. Hey, you're not going anywhere, you're in the penitentiary now, brother. See that razor wire and that fence? And those gun towers? You're not going anywhere; they got you now! You won't leave here! They got you!"

"But no," I would remonstrate. "I haven't even been to court yet!"

And he would chuckle dryly. He told me that he had spent over half his adult life in prison and that he had children older than me. His vocation was bank robbery.

I remembered what the booking officer had said when I came into R&D. He looked at my papers and said, "I don't understand what you're doing here. I don't have anything on you. You're not supposed to be here."

A few days later I was let out in the exercise yard with some other prisoners. We were permitted to be outside for one hour. I was playing basketball when a guard came to the gate and called my name. I went over to see what he wanted. He handed me a medical history form through the bars and asked me to fill it out. I gave it back to him. He looked puzzled and asked me why I wouldn't fill it out. I said I hadn't *asked* to fill it out.

"But everyone here *has* to fill it out," he said.

"That may be," I replied. "But *I* am not going to fill it out."

"So you refuse to give us your medical history?"

'That's right."

"O.K., then," he said. "I'll have to get you to sign this form saying that you're refusing a medical exam.

He handed me a Bureau of Prisons form that specified that the signer was refusing a medical exam. I signed it.

"And then," he continued, "I'll have to get you to sign *this* form stating that you signed the *other* form stating that you refused to take a medical examination."

He shoved another form through the bars and handed me his pen. I signed on the indicated line. He pocketed the pen, clutched the papers in his hand, turned on his heel and went away. I never saw him again.

After six days I began to despair of leaving anytime soon. None of the guards were able or willing to answer my questions.

THE CATHOLIC CHAPLAIN was less than no help. I put in a request to see him shortly after my arrival. He came to my cell four days later. He didn't have time to hear my confession, as he explained, because he was running late and was in a hurry because his day off was the following day. I had not asked him to confess me, but he went on abruptly without inquiring why I had asked to see him. He told me that he could give me a blanket absolution without hearing my confession. He asked if I was sorry for my sins. I replied that I was. He reeled off a short and perfunctory prayer so

fast that it was unintelligible. He held out a wafer for me to take communion, and speedily muttered another utterly incomprehensible prayer. I attempted to explain to him why I was there. His eyes glazed over. He was distracted. I had the distinct impression that he would more gladly have heard a confession of murder. It was clear that he held me and my ideas in utter disregard. He hastened away after a rapid, "Father, Son and Holy Spirit."

Phone calls were forbidden, except to defense counsel. But I had no lawyer in Springfield, or anywhere else for that matter. Neither could I afford to hire an attorney. The government is required by law to appoint an attorney for those who cannot afford to retain legal counsel; however, I had not yet been arraigned on the probation revocation charge and so had no one to represent me.

I decided to tell a little lie to the guards. I told them I wanted to call my lawyer. Within a matter of minutes they brought a phone to my cell, reeled off a long cord the length of the corridor and plugged it into a jack in the wall. They handed the phone to me through the chuck hole and I called Dawn Gibeau, the managing editor of the *National Catholic Reporter*, in Kansas City. I explained the circumstances of my imprisonment and the harassment by prison officials. She was sympathetic and suggested that I find an attorney as soon as possible.

I can only surmise that prison authorities were eavesdropping on the call, because within minutes two guards came to my cell and escorted me to R&D. Less than two hours later I had been processed out of the penitentiary and was headed south to Arkansas, handcuffed and chained, in the company of two U.S. Marshals.

They delivered me to the local jail in Jacksonville, Arkansas where I spent 2 weeks being shuffled from cell to cell. The cells were designed for one man, but two men were routinely imprisoned in them, due to a shortage of cells.

After the formality of a probation revocation hearing in Little Rock (for a previous demonstration on a Titan II missile silo in Arkansas), Federal Magistrate Faulkner sentenced me to 5 more months and 29 days in prison. The U.S. Marshal's service transferred me to the Sebastian County jail in Fort Smith, Arkansas, right on the Oklahoma border. I spent the four-day Thansgiving day weekend there, locked in a small cell with 5 other men. The Sebastian County facility was a cramped, old, crumbling, dingy, dirty, maximum security type of jail. There was no law library of any kind, no access to reading material, no recreational or educational opportunities of any sort. The food was very bad and meager. A roll and some coffee for breakfast; and a skimpy meal in mid-afternoon. The portions were small and poorly prepared. As a federal prisoner in transit I was informed I could have no visitors.

Conditions in the Jackson and Buchanan County jails in Missouri were very bad. Conditions at the Sebastian County jail, in Fort Smith, Arkansas were much worse yet. On a Sunday afternoon I was transferred to the minimum security Federal Prison Camp in Texarkana, Texas.

It was a welcome change. There were no bars and the prisoners there are permitted to walk around outside during the daylight hours, within precise limits. The food was much better than it had been in jail and there were several recreational outlets. A small library and chapel provided quiet spaces for meditation and reflection. On the whole it was a big improvement on being in jail.

A FEW DAYS AFTER ARRIVING at Texarkana I was called out to take a physical examination and supply a medical history at the prison hospital. I refused to do so on principle, on the grounds that I was not sick, had not asked for a doctor, and that my medical history was none of the Bureau of Prison's business.

The M.D. in charge of the hospital called me into his office. He lectured me briefly and harshly, then picked up the phone on his desk and called the guards to come and lock me up for refusing a program assignment. Two guards escorted me into a cell block and locked me into an administrative segregation cell. Unbelievably, the prison psychologist showed up at my cell within three or four *minutes*. He wanted to know what was wrong with me. I told him I was fine, other than being confined against my will.

"If you are fine," he wanted to know, "then why not take a physical examination?"

"Because," I said, "I have no need of one." I repeated to him what I had told the prison doctor. I would gladly supply them with urine and blood specimens so they could ascertain for themselves that I was not a carrier of an infectious disease that might harm the other inmates. But I would not submit to the rest of the physical, including the chest x-rays.

The prison psychologist then wanted to know if there was anything he could do to help me with any problems I might have. I said yes, there was one thing. He wanted to know what it was. I told him that he could order the guards to release me from the lock-up.

He rolled his eyes and explained to me in an exasperated tone of voice that that was out of his hands entirely: I was the only one who could do anything about that.

I maintained that I was being held against my will and that there was absolutely no reason to confine a man because he would not submit to a physical exam. He, for his part, maintained that I was a threat to the orderly running of the institution and should change my attitude.

Incredibly, immediately after the prison psychologist left, the assistant warden also came to my cell. He, too, told me that I was myself responsible for being locked up. I had forced the guards to lock me up. They were but unwilling pawns of my uncooperative behavior. I held the key to my own fate and until I changed my mind, his hands were tied. He could do nothing to help me.

And so I spent three weeks in administrative detention and segregation (the hole).

I appeared before the institution disciplinary committee for adjudication of my "offense" and was treated with sneering ridicule and galling scorn. The proceeding was deathly serious. Never have I encountered men with such cold and violent intent—they were machine-like, rigid, unfeeling automatons lacking normal human emotions. I was summarily found guilty, stripped of my good time, and sentenced to the hole.

Several of the other men in the hole were sociopaths. I was threatened repeatedly with rape and murder. And yet, even among men with few moral scruples of any sort, there are still occasional flashes of human feeling. One evening one of the men was recounting in grisly detail how he and his accomplice had robbed an elderly Oriental couple in their home at gun-point. The old man refused to divulge the combination to his wall safe, so in retaliation the robbers took a hammer and nailed his wife's foot to the floor, doused her in a flammable liquid and set her on fire. Only then did the husband reveal the safe's combination.

Upon hearing of this wanton barbarism, one of the other inmates, a man with a lengthy criminal record, remarked with disgust that nailing the old woman to the floor and setting her on fire was an inexcusable and gratuitous act of violence. Still, the one who told the story was visibly treated with more deference from then on. He was a young man, in his early twenties.

After three weeks I was released back to the minimum security camp. In late March, after having spent nearly a year in various jails and prisons, I was handed 90 dollars, a voucher good for a one-way bus ticket to Kansas City, and released.

SHORTLY AFTER THAT I returned to my home state of Virginia, where I soon made the acquaintance of Sister Eileen Heaps, a Benedictine nun. After talking together all summer we decided to stage a respectful and cordial trespass in opposition to the nuclear weaponry stored at the Yorktown Naval Weapons Station, just off the Colonial Parkway in Yorktown, Virginia.

The week after the 20th Anniversary Martin Luther King March in Washington, DC we drove to Yorktown and walked through the rear gate and onto the base. We remained just inside the base for 2½ hours while an exasperated succession of base officials tried to talk us into leaving.

The Director of Base Security came to see us. A lifelong Catholic, he was distressed almost to the point of tears at seeing a serene, middle aged nun in a habit politely refusing his requests to leave the premises. In the throes of a genuine, heartfelt anguish he admonished her to leave: "But Sister, just think. You're here in a habit. You represent the Church. People will look at what you do and make a judgment based on that. You have to think of what kind of impact what you're doing can *have!*"

Her response only intensified his already considerable distress: "I know. That's why I'm here. I've thought and prayed a long time about doing this and I'm sure that this is the right thing to do." He was devastated. A whole system of cherished beliefs, stretching back to childhood and firmly rooted in sweet, innocent and pure Mary, the Virgin Mother of God, as eternally embodied in the chaste, loyal, and unquestioning obedience of the daughter Sisters of the Holy Roman Church, was brought crashing to the ground in one fell swoop, irretrievably dashed to pieces beyond any hope of repair. Unabashed sacrilege—and from a *nun*, at that! It was evident that he was in pronounced inner turmoil. He wrung his hands and begged and implored her to leave. But she quietly stood her ground.

He was not the first to talk to us. Before him, separately, and then together, were the Protestant and Catholic chaplains. A curious couple. One Black, one White. They cajoled; they threatened (mildly); they reasoned (subtly); they pled ignorance of the base's nuclear arsenal; and they upheld their patriotic duty to the Navy. They pulled clever sophistries and syllogisms out of their verbal bag of theological tricks. According to them there is no contradiction at all between Jesus' message of universal brotherhood and the Pentagon's nuclear preparations to incinerate tens or even hundreds of millions of people in order to defend the American "way of life." It was quite a theological education to hear the Gospel of the Prince of Peace according to the nuclear Navy. They were very unctuous, those two.

Others spoke with us. An officer was chauffeured out to look us over from the distance, his dress whites gleaming impeccably in the midday sun.

Finally we were hand delivered personally signed letters from the base commander, one Captain John F. Fox, informing us that we were going to be arrested.

But we were not arrested. Instead, two of the largest policeman I have ever seen were dispatched to physically eject us from the base. They took hold of our arms, force marched us outside the perimeter fence, and told us not to come back. At that point we left, not wishing to provoke a violent incident.

There were a couple of articles and photographs in the local newspapers and in the diocesan newspaper, but no charges were ever filed. The Navy does not like to arrest smiling nuns and haul them handcuffed and chained into Federal Court to discuss its preparations for Armageddon.

Afterword

THE ENCHANTING PLAY of the kundalini is never ending. The kundalini works its magic in all beings, everywhere, for all eternity. I cannot tell you where it comes from and where it goes. I only know that it is real, stupendously powerful and enticing beyond description.

For me, the kundalini represents a supremely free and creative aspect of universal consciousness. Accordingly, I regard it with delight and wonder. Unfortunately, there are those who feel personally threatened by the kundalini and the creative impulses that it engenders. Instead of consciously freeing life energy to marvel at the wonder of life, to express beauty and create joy, there are those who actively seek to rigidly control the minds and bodies of others, even to the point of destroying their minds and bodies.

The carnage and suffering wrought by such people are visible on every hand—the horror of the abortion clinics, where unborn children are cruelly murdered in their own mother's wombs; the ghastly preparations for biological, chemical and nuclear warfare in country after country; the genocide in Turkey and Germany earlier in the Twentieth Century; the ethnic "cleansing" in Central Africa and the Balkans in more recent years; the African slave trade and mass slaughter of Native Americans of the 18th and 19th centuries; the international narcotics trafficking of the CIA and the drug cartels; and the decades-long "Third-World War," waged by the former Soviet Union and the United States as they jockeyed for global geopolitical advantage, which has claimed untold millions of lives in conflicts all over the world —in Southeast Asia, in Central America, in numerous armed conflicts in Africa, in Afghanistan and in Iraq.

Mind control technology is yet one more avenue of control that those who fear the kundalini employ. The kundalini represents the basic, creative force that engenders life. Those who fear life energy the most react aggressively, oftentimes violently, against the creative expression of life by others. So great is their fear, so great the urge to control, that they endeavor to clamp the very minds of their victims into electronic straitjackets. And so they create mind control victims. Not content to enslave only the body, there are those who work for the CIA, the Pentagon, and other violent, shadowy organizations who aim to imprison the human mind itself with their treacherous electronic technologies.

The great mental and physical violence that pervades human culture in the late 20th century manifests in myriad ways — in dysfunctional family life, with all manner of physical, emotional and sexual abuse, in epidemic warfare and abortion, in "religious" excuses and justifications for war, and in an incessant mass media barrage of wanton material-consumerism, driven by the insatiable appetites of banks, corporations and the world's military forces for more money, more profits, more resources, more power, more consumers and more victims.

In the end, every man and every woman decides for himself or herself whether, and how, to be free. Those who desire true freedom will search diligently within themselves for the golden keys of consciousness that will unshackle the locks and chains that bind their bodies and minds. I am firmly persuaded that those keys do exist. Indeed, based on my own experience I believe that the kundalini is one such golden key of consciousness. I believe that anyone who approaches the kundalini with reverence, and sincerity of heart and purpose, can reap a rich reward.

Appendixes

〜〜〜

The following pages contain facsimile reproductions of patents that have been granted by the Patent Office of the United States of America for the purposes of mental monitoring and mind alteration:

⫽ *Hearing Device*—United States Patent 4,858,612.

⫽ *Apparatus and Method for remotely Monitoring and Altering Brain Waves*
  —United States Patent 3,951,134.

⫽ *Biomagnetic Analytical System Using Fiber-Optic Magnetic Sensors*
  —United States Patent 4,951,674.

⫽ *Brain Electrical Activity Mapping*—United States Patent 4,408,616.

⫽ *Method of Inducing Mental, Emotional and Physical States of Consciousness, Including Specific Mental Activity, in Human Beings*
  —United States Patent 5,213,562.

⫽ *Method of and Apparatus for Inducing Desired States of Consciousness*
  —United States Patent 5,356,368.

United States Patent [19]

Stocklin

[11] **Patent Number:**   **4,858,612**

[45] **Date of Patent:**   **Aug. 22, 1989**

[54] **HEARING DEVICE**

[76] Inventor: **Philip L. Stocklin,** P.O. Box 2111,
       Satellite Beach, Fla. 32937

[21] Appl. No.: **562,742**

[22] Filed: **Dec. 19, 1983**

[51] Int. Cl.⁴ A61N 1/36
[52] U.S. Cl. .... **128/422;** 178/419 S
[58] Field of Search .... 128/419 R, 419 S, 422,
       128/653, 771, 732, 741, 746, 791, 804; 340/407

[56]   **References Cited**

U.S. PATENT DOCUMENTS

3,490,458	1/1970	Allison	128/421
3,751,605	8/1973	Michelson	128/1 R
3,951,134	4/1976	Malech	128/131
4,428,377	1/1984	Zollner et al.	128/419 R

FOREIGN PATENT DOCUMENTS

893311	2/1972	Canada	128/422
2811120	9/1978	Fed. Rep. of Germany	128/419 R
591196	1/1978	U.S.S.R.	128/419 R

OTHER PUBLICATIONS

Gerkin, G., "Electroencephalography & Clinical Neurophysiology", vol. 135, No. 6, Dec. 1973, pp. 652–653.
Frye et al., "Science", vol. 181, Jul. 27, 1973, pp. 356–358.
Bise, William, "Low Power Radio–Frequency and Microwave Effects on Human Electroencephalogram and Behavior", Physiol. Chem. & Physics 10 (1978).

Primary Examiner—William E. Kamm
Attorney, Agent, or Firm—Wegner & Bretschneider

[57]   **ABSTRACT**

A method and apparatus for simulation of hearing in mammals by introduction of a plurality of microwaves into the region of the auditory cortex is shown and described. A microphone is used to transform sound signals into electrical signals which are in turn analyzed and processed to provide controls for generating a plurality of microwave signals at different frequencies. The multifrequency microwaves are then applied to the brain in the region of the auditory cortex. By this method sounds are perceived by the mammal which are representative of the original sound received by the microphone.

29 Claims, 7 Drawing Sheets

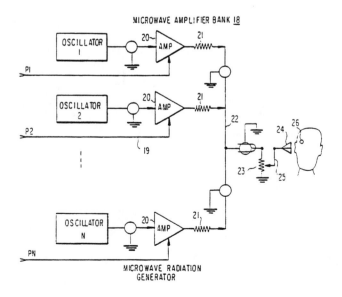

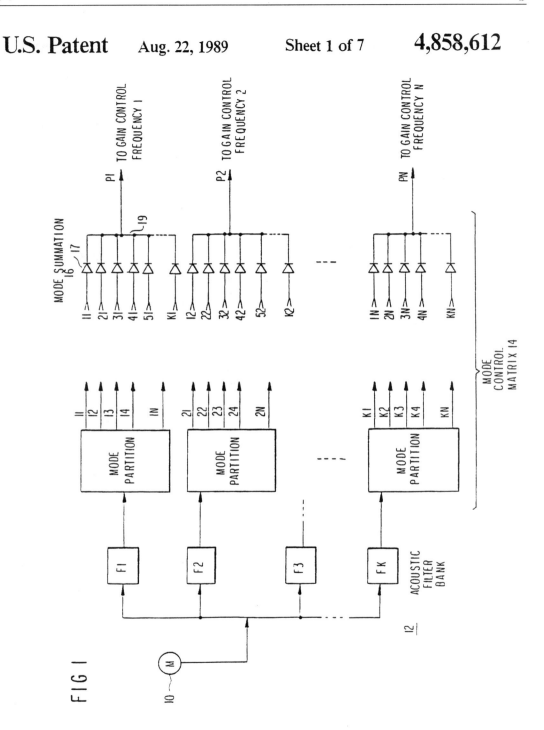

FIG 1

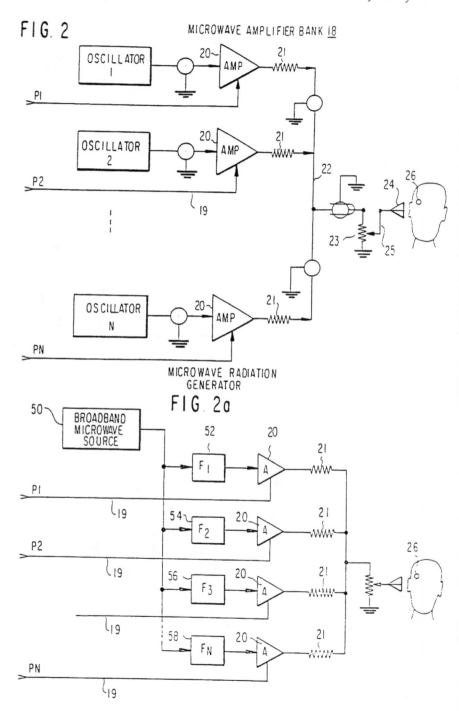

FIG. 2

MICROWAVE AMPLIFIER BANK 18

MICROWAVE RADIATION
GENERATOR

FIG. 2a

U.S. Patent   Aug. 22, 1989   Sheet 3 of 7   **4,858,612**

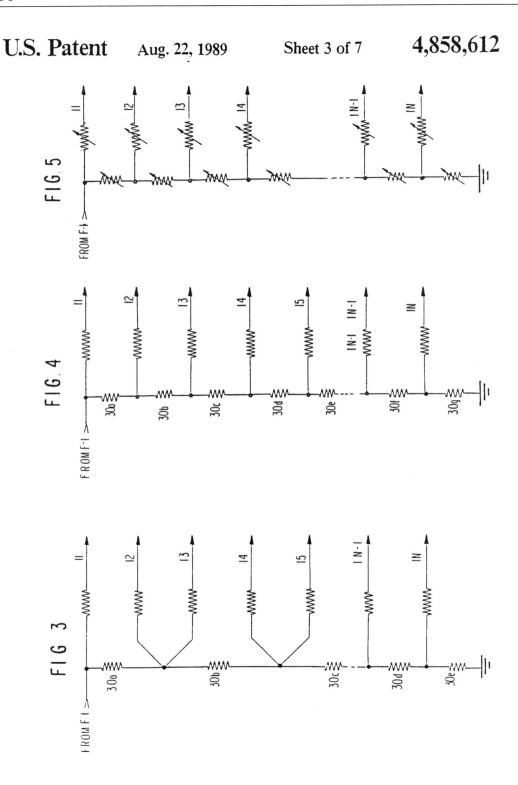

FIG. 6

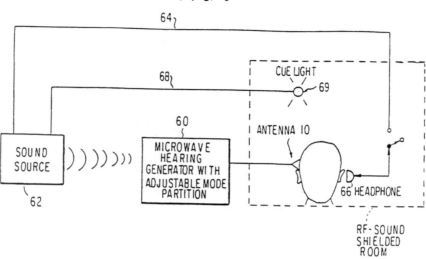

FIG. 7

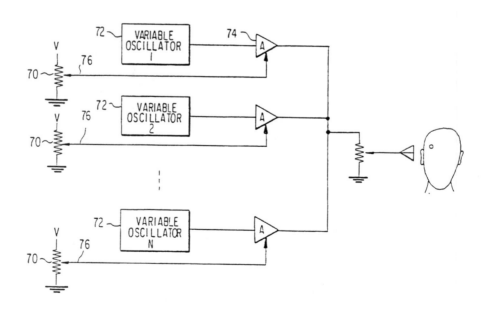

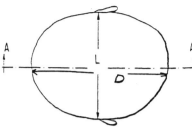

FIG.8

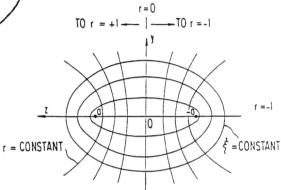

FIG.9

ξ, r, AND $\emptyset$ RELATED TO CARTESIAN COORDINATES x, y, z

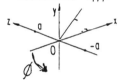

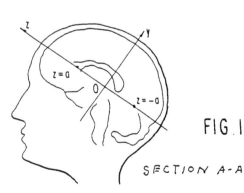

FIG.10

SECTION A-A

TRANSFORMATION EQUATIONS

$$x = a(\xi^2 - 1)^{1/2}(1 - r^2)^{1/2}\cos\emptyset$$

$$y = -a(\xi^2 - 1)^{1/2}(1 - r^2)^{1/2}\sin\emptyset$$

$$z = a\,\xi\,r$$

$1 \leq \xi \leq$

$-1 \leq \emptyset \leq +1$

$0 \leq \emptyset \leq 2\pi$

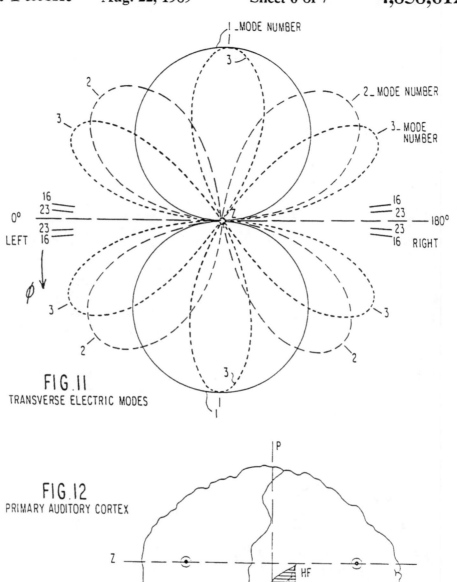

FIG.11
TRANSVERSE ELECTRIC MODES

FIG.12
PRIMARY AUDITORY CORTEX

U.S. Patent   Aug. 22, 1989   Sheet 7 of 7   4,858,612

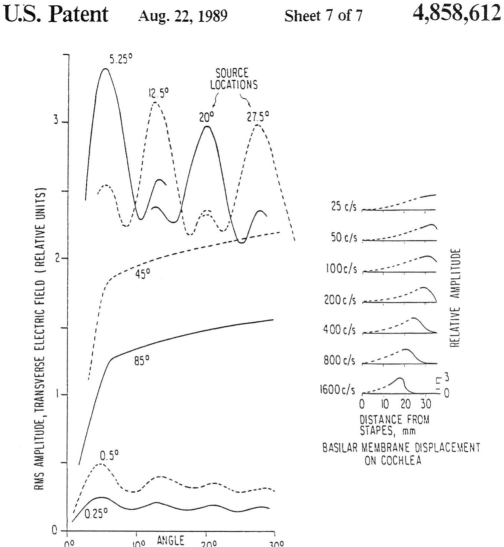

FIG. 13

4,858,612

1

HEARING DEVICE

BACKGROUND OF THE INVENTION

1. Field of the Invention

This invention relates to devices for aiding of hearing in mammals. The invention is based upon the perception of sounds which is experienced in the brain when the brain is subjected to certain microwave radiation signals.

2. Description of the Prior Art

In prior art hearing devices for human beings, it is well known to amplify sounds to be heard and to apply the amplified sound signal to the ear of the person wearing the hearing aid. Hearing devices of this type are however limited to hearing disfunctions where there is no damage to the auditory nerve or to the auditory cortex. In the prior art, if there is damage to the auditory cortex or the auditory nerve, it cannot be corrected by the use of a hearing aid.

During World War II, individuals in the radiation path of certain radar installations observed clicks and buzzing sounds in response to the microwave radiation. It was through this early observation that it became known to the art that microwaves could cause a direct perception of sound within a human brain. These buzzing or clicking sounds however were not meaningful, and were not perception of sounds which could otherwise be heard by the receiver. This type of microwave radiation was not representative of any intelligible sound to be perceived. In such radar installations, there was never a sound which was generated which resulted in subsequent generation of microwave signals representative of that sound.

Since the early perception of buzzing and clicking, further research has been conducted into the microwave reaction of the brain. In an article entitled "Possible Microwave Mechanisms of the Mammalian Nervous System" by Philip L. Stocklin and Brain F. Stocklin, published in the TIT Journal of Life Sciences, Tower International Technomedical Institute, Inc. P.O. Box 4594, Philadelphia, Pa. (1979) there is disclosed a hypothesis that the mammalian brain generates and uses electro magnetic waves in the lower microwave frequency region as an integral part of the functioning of the central and peripheral nervous systems. This analysis is based primarily upon the potential energy of a protein integral in the neural membrane.

In an article by W. Bise entitled "Low Power Radio-Frequency and Microwave Effects On Human Electro-encephalogram and Behavior", Physiol. Chemistry Phys. 10, 387 (1978), it is reported that there are significant effects upon the alert human EEG during radiation by low intensity CW microwave electromagnetic energy. Bise observed significant repeatable EEG effects for a subject during radiation at specific microwave frequencies.

SUMMARY OF THE INVENTION

Results of theoretical analysis of the physics of brain tissue and the brain/skull cavity, combined with experimentally-determined electromagnetic properties of mammalian brain tissue, indicate the physical necessity for the existence of electromagnetic standing waves, called modes in the living mammalian brain. The mode characteristics may be determined by two geometric properties of the brain; these are the cephalic index of the brain (its shape in prolate spheroidal coordinates)

2

and the semifocal distance of the brain (a measure of its size). It was concluded that estimation of brain cephalic index and semifocal distance using external skull measurements on subjects permits estimation of the subject's characteristic mode frequencies, which in turn will permit a mode by mode treatment of the data to simulate hearing.

This invention provides for sound perception by individuals who have impaired hearing resulting from ear damage, auditory nerve damage, and damage to the auditory cortex. This invention provides for simulation of microwave radiation which is normally produced by the auditory cortex. The simulated brain waves are introduced into the region of the auditory cortex and provide for perceived sounds on the part of the subject.

BRIEF DESCRIPTION OF THE DRAWINGS

FIG. 1 shows the acoustic filter bank and mode control matrix portions of the hearing device of this invention.

FIG. 2 shows the microwave generation and antenna portion of the hearing device of this invention.

FIG. 3 shows a typical voltage divider network which may be used to provide mode partition.

FIG. 4 shows another voltage divider device which may be used to provide mode partition.

FIG. 5 shows a voltage divider to be used as a mode partition wherein each of the resistors is variable in order to provide adjustment of the voltage outputs.

FIG. 6 shows a modified hearing device which includes adjustable mode partitioning, and which is used to provide initial calibration of the hearing device.

FIG. 7 shows a group of variable oscillators and variable gain controls which are used to determine hearing characteristics of a particular subject.

FIG. 8 shows a top view of a human skull showing the lateral dimension.

FIG. 9 shows the relationship of the prolate spherical coordinate system to the cartesian system.

FIG. 10 shows a side view of a skull showing the medial plane of the head, section A—A.

FIG. 11 shows a plot of the transverse electric field amplitude versus primary mode number M.

FIG. 12 shows a left side view of the brain and auditory cortex.

FIG. 13 shows the total modal field versus angle for source location.

DETAILED DESCRIPTION OF THE PREFERRED EMBODIMENT

This invention is based upon observations of the physical mechanism the mammalian brain uses to perceive acoustic vibrations. This observation is based in part upon neuro anatomical and other experimental evidence which relates to microwave brain stimulation and the perception of sounds.

It is has been observed that monochromatic acoustic stimuli (acoustic tones, or single tones) of different frequencies uniquely stimulate different regions of the cochlea. It has also been observed that there is a corresponding one to one relationship between the frequency of a monochromatic acoustic stimulus and the region of the auditory cortex neurally stimulated by the cochlear nerve under the physiologically normal conditions (tonotopicity).

It is has been observed that for an acoustic tone of a frequency which is at the lower end of the entire acous-

4,858,612

3

tical range perceivable by a person, that a thin lateral region ("Line") parallel to the medial axis of the brain and toward the inferior portion of the primary auditory cortex is stimulated. For an acoustic tone whose frequency is toward the high end of the entire perceivable acoustic range, a thin lateral region parallel to the medial axis and toward the superior portion of the primary auditory cortex is stimulated.

Neural stimulation results in the generation of a broad band of microwave photons by the change in rotational energy state of protons integral to the neuron membrane of the auditory cortex. The physical size and shape of the brain/skull cavity, together with the (semiconductor) properties (conductivity and dielectric constant) of the brain tissue provide an electromagnetic resonant cavity. Specific single frequencies are constructively reinforced so that a number of standing electromagnetic waves, each at its own single electromagnetic frequency in the microwave frequency region, are generated in the brain. Each such standing electromagnetic wave is called a characteristic mode of the brain/skull cavity.

Analysis in terms of prolate spheroidal wave functions indicates that transverse electric field components of these modes have maxima in the region of the auditory cortex. This analysis further shows that transverse electric field possess a variation of amplitude with angle in the angular plane (along the vertical dimension of the auditory cortex) and that is dependent only upon the primary mode number.

The auditory cortex in the normally functioning mammalian brain is a source of microwave modes. The auditory cortex generates these modes in accordance with the neural stimulation of the auditory cortex by the cochlear nerve. Mode weighting for any one acoustic tone stimulus is given by the amplitude of each mode along the line region of the auditory cortex which is neurally stimulated by that acoustic tone stimulus. A listing of mode weighting versus frequency of acoustic stimulus is called the mode matrix.

In this invention, the functions of the ear, the cochlear nerve, and the auditory cortex are simulated. Microwaves simulating the mode matrix are inserted directly into the region of the auditory cortex. By this insertion of simulated microwave modes, the normal operation of the entire natural hearing mechanism is simulated.

Referring now to FIG. 1 and FIG. 2 there is shown an apparatus which provides for induced perception of sound into a mammalian brain. This hearing device includes a microphone 10 which receives sounds, an acoustic filter bank 12 which separates the signals from the microphone into component frequencies, and a mode control matrix 14 which generates the mode signals which are used to control the intensity of microwave radiations which are injected into the skull cavity in the region of the auditory cortex.

The acoustic filter bank 12 consists of a bank of acoustic filters F1 through Fk which span the audible acoustic spectrum. These filters may be built from standard resistance, inductance, and capacitance components in accordance with well established practice. In the preferred embodiment there are 24 filters which correspond to the observed critical bandwidths of the human ear. In this preferred embodiment a typical list of filter parameters is given by Table 1 below:

4

TABLE I

Filter No.	Center Frequency (Hz)	Bandwidth (Hz)
1	50	less than 100
2	150	100
3	250	100
4	350	100
5	450	110
6	570	120
7	700	140
8	840	150
9	1,000	160
10	1,170	190
11	1,370	210
12	1,600	240
13	1,850	280
14	2,150	320
15	2,500	380
16	2,900	450
17	3,400	550
18	4,000	700
19	4,800	900
20	5,800	1,100
21	7,000	1,300
22	8,500	1,800
23	10,500	2,500
24	13,500	3,500

The rectifier outputs one through K are feed to K mode partition devices. The mode partitioning devices each have N outputs wherein N is the number of microwave oscillators used to generate the microwave radiation. The outputs 1 through N of each mode partition device is applied respectively to the inputs of each gain controlled amplifier of the microwave radiation generator. The function of the mode control matrix 14 is the control of the microwave amplifiers in the microwave amplifier bank 18. In the preferred embodiment thus will be 24 outputs and 24 microwave frequency oscillators.

Connected to each microwave amplifier gain control line is a mode simulation device 16 which receives weighted mode signals from the mode partition devices 14. Each mode simulation device consists of one through k lines and diodes 17 which are each connected to summing junction 19. The diodes 17 provide for isolation from one mode partition device to the next. The diodes 17 prevent signals from one mode partition device from returning to the other mode partition devices which are also connected to the same summing junction of the mode summation device 16. The diodes also serve a second function which is the rectification of the signals received from the acoustic filter bank by way of the mode partition devices. In this way each mode partition device output is rectified to produce a varying DC voltage with major frequency components of the order of 15 milliseconds or less. The voltage at the summation junction 19 is thus a slowly varying DC voltage.

The example mode partition devices are shown in greater detail in FIGS. 3, 4, and 5. The mode partition devices are merely resistance networks which produce 1 through N output voltages which are predetermined divisions of the input signal from the acoustic filter associated with the mode partition device. FIG. 3 shows a mode partitioning device wherein several outputs are associated with each series resistor 30. In the embodiment depicted in FIG. 4 there is an output associated with each series resistor only, and thus there are N series resistors, or the same number of series resistors as there are outputs. The values of the resistors in the mode partition resistor network are determined in ac-

4,858,612

5   6

cordance with the magnitudes of the frequency component from the acoustic filter bank 12 which is required at the summation point 19 or the gain control line for amplifiers 20.

The microwave amplifier bank 18 consists of a plurality of microwave oscillators 1 through N each of which is connected to an amplifier 20. Since the amplifiers 20 are gain controlled by the signals at summation junction 19, the magnitude of the microwave output is controlled by the mode control matrix outputs F1 through F_n. In the preferred embodiment there are 24 amplifiers.

The leads from the microwave oscillators 1 through N to the amplifiers 20 are shielded to prevent cross talk from one oscillator to the next, and to prevent stray signals from reaching the user of the hearing device. The output impedance of amplifiers 20 should be 1000 ohms and this is indicated by resistor 21. The outputs of amplifiers 20 are all connected to a summing junction 22. The summing junction 22 is connected to a summing impedance 23 which is approximately 50 ohms. The relatively high amplifier output impedance 21 as compared to the relatively low summing impedance 23 provides minimization of cross talk between the amplifiers. Since the amplitude of the microwave signal needed at the antenna 24 is relatively small, there is no need to match the antenna and summing junction impedances to the amplifier 20 output impedances. Efficiency of the amplifiers 20 is not critical.

Level control of the signal at antenna 24 is controlled by pick off 25 which is connected to the summing impedance 23. In this manner, the signal at antenna 24 can be varied from 0 (ground) to a value which is acceptable to the individual.

The antenna 24 is placed next to the subject's head and in the region of the subject's auditory cortex 26. By placement of the antenna 24 in the region of the auditory cortex 26, the microwave field which is generated simulates the microwave field which would be generated if the acoustic sounds were perceived with normal hearing and the auditory cortex was functioning normally.

In FIG. 2A there is shown a second embodiment of the microwave radiation and generator portion of the hearing device. In this embodiment a broad band microwave source 50 generates microwave signals which are feed to filters 52 through 58 which select from the broad band radiation particular frequencies to be transmitted to the person. As in FIG. 2, the amplifiers 20 receive signals on lines 19 from the mode control matrix. The signals on lines 19 provide the gain control for amplifiers 20.

In FIG. 6 there is shown a modified microwave hearing generator 60 which includes a mode partition resistor divider network as depicted in FIG. 5. Each of the mode partition voltage divider networks in this embodiment are individually adjustable for all of the resistances in the resistance network. FIG. 5 depicts a voltage division system wherein adjustment of the voltage partition resistors is provided for.

In FIG. 6, the sound source 62 generates audible sounds which are received by the microphone of the microwave hearing generator 60. In accordance with the operation described with respect to FIGS. 1 and 2, microwave signals are generated at the antenna 10 in accordance with the redistribution provided by the mode control matrix as set forth in FIG. 5.

The sound source 62 also produces a signal on line 64 which is received by a head phone 66. The apparatus depicted in FIG. 6 is used to calibrate or fit a microwave hearing generator to a particular individual. Once the hearing generator is adjusted to the particular individual by adjustment of the variable resistors in the adjustable mode partition portion of the hearing generator, a second generator may be built using fixed value resistors in accordance with the adjusted values achieved in fitting the device to the particular subject. The sound produced by headphone 66 should be the same as a sound from the sound source 62 which is received by the microphone 10 in the microwave hearing generator 60. In this way, the subject can make comparisons between the perceived sound from the hearing generator 60, and the sound which is heard from headphone 66. Sound source 62 also produces a signal on 68 which is feed to cue light 69. Cue light 69 comes on whenever a sound is emitted from sound source 62 to the microwave generator 60. In this manner, if the subject hears nothing, he will still be informed that a sound has been omitted and hence that he is indeed perceiving no sound from the microwave hearing generator 60.

In FIG. 7 there is shown a modified microwave hearing generator which may be used to determine a subject's microwave mode frequencies. In this device, the acoustic filter bank and the mode control matrix have been removed and replaced by voltage level signal generated by potentiometers 70. Also included are a plurality of variable frequency oscillators 72 which feed microwave amplifiers 74 which are gain controlled from the signal generated by potentiometers 70 and pick off arm 76.

This modified microwave hearing generator is used to provide signals using one oscillator at a time. When an oscillator is turned on, the frequency is varied about the estimated value until a maximum acoustic perception by the subject is perceived. This perception however may consist of a buzzing or hissing sound rather than a tone because only one microwave frequency is being received. The first test of perception is to determine the subject's lowest modal frequency for audition ($M = 1$). Once this modal frequency is obtained, the process is repeated for several higher modal frequencies and continued until no maximum acoustic perception occurs.

Another method of determination of a subject's modal frequencies is through anatomical estimation. This procedure is by measurement of the subject's cephalic index and the lateral dimensions of the skull. In this method, the shape is determined in prolate spheroidal coordinance.

Purely anatomical estimation of subject's modal frequencies is performed by first measuring the maximum lateral dimension (breadth) L FIG. 8, of the subject's head together with the maximum dimension D (anterior to posterior) in the medial plane of the subject's head. D is the distance along Z axis as shown in FIG. 10. The ratio L/D, called in anthropology the cephalic index, is monotonically related to the boundary value ξ_o defining the ellipsoidal surface approximating the interface between the brain and the skull in the prolate spheroidal coordinate system. ξ_o defines the shape of this interface; ξ_o and D together give an estimate of a, the semi-focal distance of the defining ellipsoid. Using ξ_o and a, together with known values of the conductivity and dielectric constants of brain tissue, those wavelengths are found f   which the radial component of the electric   es the boundary condition that it is zero at ξ_o.

4,858,612

7 | 8

These wavelengths are the wavelengths associated with the standing waves or modes; the corresponding frequencies are found by dividing the phase velocity of microwaves in brain tissue by each of the wavelengths.

A subject's microwave modal frequencies may also be determined by observing the effect of external microwave radiation upon the EEG. The frequency of the M equal 1 mode may then be used as a base point to estimate all other modal frequencies.

A typical example of such an estimation is where the subject is laterally irradiated with a monochromatic microwave field simultaneous with EEG measurement and the microwave frequency altered until a significant change occurs in the EEG, the lowest such frequency causing a significant EEG change is found. This is identified as the frequency of the M=1 mode, the lowest mode of importance in auditory perception. The purely anatomical estimation procedure (FIGS. 8, 9, 10) is then performed and the ratio of each modal frequency to the M=1 modal frequency obtained. These ratios together with the experimentally-determined M=1 frequency are then used to estimate the frequencies of the mode numbers higher than 1. The prolate spheroidal coordinate system is shown in FIG. 9. Along the lateral plane containing the x and y coordinates of FIG. 9, the prolate spheroidal coordinate variable φ (angle) lies FIGS. 9 and 10. Plots of the transverse electric field amplitude versus primary mode number m are shown in FIG. 11. The equation is

$$E_{transverse}(m, \phi) = E_o \sin(m \phi)$$

The "elevation view" FIG. 12, of the brain from the left side, shows the primary auditory cortex 10. The isotone lines and the high frequency region are toward the top of 100 and the low frequency region toward the bottom of 100.

The formula I, set forth below is the formula for combining modes from an iso-tone line at φ=φj being excited to obtain the total modal field at some other angular location φ. For this formula, if we let J=1 (just one iso-tone single frequency acoustic stimulus line), then it can be shown that ALL modes (in general) must be used for any ONE tone.

FORMULA I
RMS TRANSVERSE ELECTRIC
FIELD IN ANGULAR PLANE, f(0)

$$f(0) = \left[\sum_{m=1}^{M} \left\{ \sin(m0) \cdot \sum_{j=1}^{J} e^{-(0-0j)/\Delta 0 m} \sin(m0j) \right\}^2 \right]^{\frac{1}{2}}$$

φ = ANGLE (0° LATERAL)
φj = LOCATION OF j-TH SOURCE (TOTAL NUMBER J)
Δφm = ATTENUATION LENGTH (IN ANGLE) OF m-TH MODE
m = PRIMARY MODE NUMBER (HIGHEST MODE M)

FIG. 13 shows the resulting total modal field versus angle φ for source location φ at 5.25°, 12.5°, etc. With reference to the set of curves at the left top of this figure. A spacing of approximately 7.25° in φ corresponds to a tonal difference of about 1 octave. This conclusion is based on the side-lobes of pattern coming from φ=5.25°, etc. The total filed (value on y-axis) falls considerably below the top curves for source locations well below 5.25° (toward the high acoustic stimulus end) and

also as the source of frequency goes well above 30° (low frequency end). φ is plotted positive downward from 0° at lateral location as indicates in FIG. 11.

Resistor weightings are obtained from the |sin (m[φ−φj])|, Formula I. The scale between acoustic frequency and φ must be set or estimated from experiment. Approximately 5.25±1° corresponds to a tonal stimulus at about 2 kHz (the most sensitive region of the ear) since this source location gives the highest electric field amplitude.

The apparatus of FIG. 7 may also be used to determine values for a hearing device which are required for a particular subject. Once the modal frequencies have been estimated, the device of FIG. 7 which includes variable microwave oscillators may be used to determine values for the oscillators which match the subject, and to determine resistance values associated with the mode partition devices of the mode control matrix.

In FIG. 7 manual control of the amplifier gain is achieved by potentiometers 76. In this manner the amplifier gains are varied about the estimated settings for an acoustic tone stimulus in the region of two thousand Hertz (2 kHz) until maximum acoustic perception and a purest tone are achieved together. The term purest tone may also be described as the most pleasing acoustic perception by the subject. This process may be repeated at selected frequencies above and below 2 kHz. The selected frequencies correspond to regions of other acoustic filter center frequencies of the subject. When modal frequency (oscillator frequency) and gain set values (setting a potentiometer 76) are noted, it is then possible to calculate fixed oscillator frequencies and control resistor values for the adjusted hearing device for this particular subject.

In the event the subject has no prior acoustic experience, that is deaf from birth, estimated resistor values must be used. Also, a complex acoustic stimulation test including language articulation and pairs of harmonically related tones may be developed to maximize the match of the hearing device parameters for those of this particular subject.

Typical components for use in this invention include commercially available high fidelity microphones which have a range of 50 Hz to 15 kHz with plus or minus 3 dB variation.

The audio filters to be used with the acoustic filter bank 12 are constructed in a conventional manner, and have Q values of about 6. The filters may also be designed with 3 dB down points (½ the bandwidth away from the center frequency) occurring at adjacent center frequency locations.

The diodes 17 in the mode control matrix which provide isolation between the mode partition circuits are commercially available diodes in the audio range.

The microwave oscillators 1 through N and the microwave amplifiers 20 are constructed with available microwave transistors which can be configured either as oscillators or amplifiers. Examples of the transistors are GaAsFET field effect transistors by Hewlitt Packard known as the HFET series or silicone bipolar transistors by Hewlitt Packard known as the HXTR series.

All the cable between the oscillators, the microwave amplifiers, and the antenna should be constructed with either single or double shielded coaxial cable.

The antenna 24 for directing microwave signals to the audio cortex 26 should be approximately the size of the auditory cortex. A typical size would be one and

4,858,612

9

one half CM high and one half to one CM wide. The antenna as shown is located over the left auditory cortex, but the right may also be used. Since the characteristic impedance of the brain tissue at these microwave frequencies is close to 50 ohms, efficient transmission by 5 commercially available standard 50 ohm coax is possible.

The invention has been described in reference to the preferred embodiments. It is, however, to be understood that other advantages, features, and embodiments 10 may be within the scope of this invention as defined in the appended claims.

What is claimed is:

1. A sound perception device for providing induced perception of sound into a mammalian brain comprising 15 in combination:

    means for generating microwave radiation which is representative of a sound to be perceived, said means for generating including means for generating a simultaneous plurality of microwave radia- 20 tion frequencies and means for adjusting the amplitude of said microwave radiation frequencies in accordance with the sound to be perceived; and

    antenna means located in the region of the auditory cortex of said mammalian brain for transmitting 25 said microwave energy into the auditory cortex region of said brain.

2. A hearing device for perception of sounds comprising in combination:

    means for generating a signal representative of 30 sounds;

    means for analyzing said signal representative of said sounds having an output;

    means for generating a plurality of microwave signals having different frequencies having a input con- 35 nected to said output of said means for analyzing said signals, having an output;

    means for applying said plurality of microwave signals to the head of a subject, and

    whereby the subject perceives sounds which are rep- 40 resentative of said sounds.

3. The apparatus in accordance with claim 2 wherein said means for generating a signal is a microphone for detecting sound waves.

4. The apparatus in accordance with claim 2 wherein 45 said means for applying said plurality of microwave signals is an antenna.

5. The apparatus in accordance with claim 4 wherein said antenna is placed in the region of the auditory cortex of the subject. 50

6. The apparatus in accordance with claim 2 wherein the subject is a human being.

7. The apparatus in accordance with claim 2 wherein said means for analyzing said signal comprises:

    an acoustic filter bank for dividing said sounds into a 55 plurality of component frequencies; and

    a mode control matrix means for providing control signals which are weighted in accordance with said plurality of component frequencies, having an output connected to said means for generating a plu- 60 rality of microwave signal inputs.

8. The apparatus in accordance with claim 7 wherein said acoustic filter bank includes a plurality of audio frequency filters.

9. The apparatus in accordance with claim 8 wherein 65 said audio frequency filters provide a plurality of output frequencies having amplitudes which are a function of said signal representative of sounds.

10

10. The apparatus in accordance with claim 9 wherein said amplitudes are the weighted in accordance with transform function of the signal representative of sounds.

11. The apparatus in accordance with claim 7 wherein said mode control matrix device includes a voltage divider connected to each of said plurality of said audio frequency filters.

12. The apparatus in accordance with claim 11 wherein each of said voltage dividers has a plurality of outputs which are connected in circuit to said means for generating a plurality of microwave signals.

13. The apparatus in accordance with claim 2 wherein said means for generating a plurality of microwave signals comprises a plurality of microwave generators each having a different frequency and means for controlling the output amplitude of each of said generators.

14. The apparatus in accordance with claims 2 wherein said means for generating a plurality of microwave signals comprises a broad band microwave source and a plurality of filters.

15. The apparatus in accordance with claim 13 wherein said generators each comprise a microwave signal source and a gain controlled microwave amplifier.

16. The apparatus in accordance with claim 13 wherein said means for analyzing output is connected to said means for controlling microwave amplifier output amplitudes.

17. The apparatus in accordance with claim 13 wherein analyzing includes K audio frequency filters.

18. The apparatus in accordance with claim 17 wherein there are N microwave generators.

19. The apparatus in accordance with claim 18 including a mode partitioning means which provides N outputs for each of said K audio frequency filters.

20. The apparatus in accordance with claim 19 wherein said N amplifiers each have K inputs from said mode partitioning means.

21. The apparatus in accordance with claim 20 wherein said N amplifiers have K inputs less the mode partitioning means outputs which are so small that they may be omitted.

22. The apparatus in accordance with claim 20 wherein said mode partitioning output device outputs each include a diode connected to each microwave amplifier gain control to provide isolation between all outputs.

23. The apparatus in accordance with claim 20 wherein said K audio frequency filters are chosen to correspond to the critical bandwidths of the human ear.

24. The apparatus in accordance with claim 20 wherein said N microwave generators are each adjustable in frequency output.

25. The apparatus in accordance with claim 18 wherein the frequency of each N microwave generators is determined by anatomical estimation.

26. The apparatus in accordance with claim 18 wherein the frequency of the lowest frequency microwave generator is chosen by determination of the effect of external microwave generation on the EEG of the subject.

27. The apparatus in accordance with claim 18 wherein the frequency of each of said N microwave generators corresponds to the subject's microwave modal frequencies.

4,858,612

11

28. The apparatus in accordance with claim 27 wherein the subject's modal frequencies are determined by measurement of the subject's cephalic index and the lateral dimensions of the skull.

29. The apparatus in accordance with claim 28 wherein the subject's lowest modal frequency is deter-

12

mined by varying the frequency of the lowest frequency microwave generator about the estimated value until a maximum acoustic perception is obtained by the subject.

*   *   *   *   *

United States Patent [19]

Malech

[11] **3,951,134**

[45] **Apr. 20, 1976**

[54] **APPARATUS AND METHOD FOR REMOTELY MONITORING AND ALTERING BRAIN WAVES**

[75] Inventor: **Robert G. Malech,** Plainview, N.Y.

[73] Assignee: **Dorne & Margolin Inc.,** Bohemia, N.Y.

[22] Filed: **Aug. 5, 1974**

[21] Appl. No.: **494,518**

[52] U.S. Cl. .... **128/2.1 B**
[51] Int. Cl.² **A61B 5/04**
[58] Field of Search .... 128/1 C, 1 R, 2.1 B, 128/2.1 R, 419 R, 422 R, 420, 404, 2 R, 2 S, 2.05 R, 2.05 V, 2.05 F, 2.06 R; 340/248 A, 258 A, 258 B, 258 D, 229

[56] **References Cited**
UNITED STATES PATENTS

2,860,627	11/1958	Harden et al.	128/2.1 B
3,096,768	7/1963	Griffith, Jr.	128/420
3,233,450	2/1966	Fry.....................................	128/2.1 R
3,483,860	12/1969	Namerow	128/2.05 F
3,495,596	2/1970	Condict...............................	128/1 C
3,555,529	1/1971	Brown et al......................	128/2.1 R
3,773,049	11/1973	Rabichev et al.	128/1 C
3,796,208	3/1974	Bloice.................................	128/2 S

Primary Examiner—William E. Kamm
Attorney, Agent, or Firm—Darby & Darby

[57] **ABSTRACT**

Apparatus for and method of sensing brain waves at a position remote from a subject whereby electromagnetic signals of different frequencies are simultaneously transmitted to the brain of the subject in which the signals interfere with one another to yield a waveform which is modulated by the subject's brain waves. The interference waveform which is representative of the brain wave activity is re-transmitted by the brain to a receiver where it is demodulated and amplified. The demodulated waveform is then displayed for visual viewing and routed to a computer for further processing and analysis. The demodulated waveform also can be used to produce a compensating signal which is transmitted back to the brain to effect a desired change in electrical activity therein.

11 Claims, 2 Drawing Figures

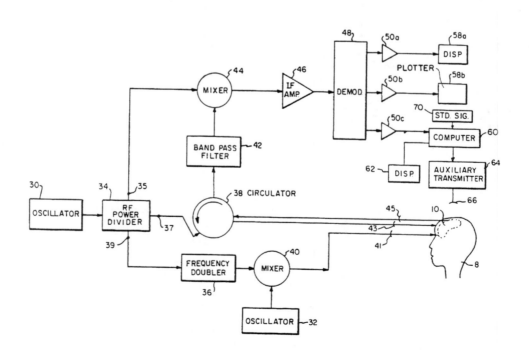

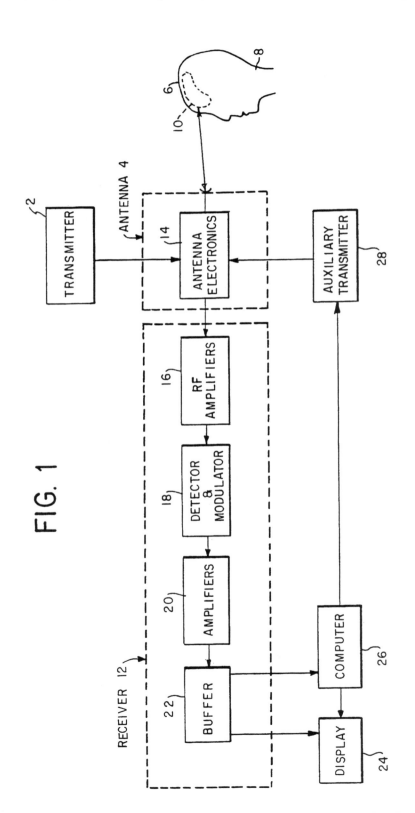

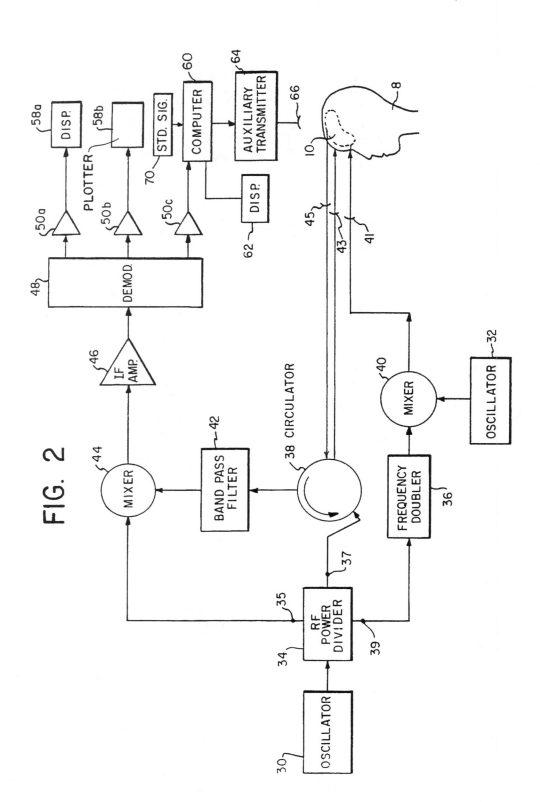

FIG. 2

3,951,134

1

APPARATUS AND METHOD FOR REMOTELY MONITORING AND ALTERING BRAIN WAVES

BACKGROUND OF THE INVENTION

Medical science has found brain waves to be a useful barometer of organic functions. Measurements of electrical activity in the brain have been instrumental in detecting physical and psychic disorder, measuring stress, determining sleep patterns, and monitoring body metabolism.

The present art for measurement of brain waves employs electroencephalographs including probes with sensors which are attached to the skull of the subject under study at points proximate to the regions of the brain being monitored. Electrical contact between the sensors and apparatus employed to process the detected brain waves is maintained by a plurality of wires extending from the sensors to the apparatus. The necessity for physically attaching the measuring apparatus to the subject imposes several limitations on the measurement process. The subject may experience discomfort, particulary if the measurements are to be made over extended periods of time. His bodily movements are restricted and he is generally confined to the immediate vicinity of the measuring apparatus. Furthermore, measurements cannot be made while the subject is conscious without his awareness. The comprehensiveness of the measurements is also limited since the finite number of probes employed to monitor local regions of brain wave activity do not permit observation of the total brain wave profile in a single test.

SUMMARY OF THE INVENTION

The present invention relates to apparatus and a method for monitoring brain waves wherein all components of the apparatus employed are remote from the test subject. More specifically, high frequency transmitters are operated to radiate electromagnetic energy of different frequencies through antennas which are capable of scanning the entire brain of the test subject or any desired region thereof. The signals of different frequencies penetrate the skull of the subject and impinge upon the brain where they mix to yield an interference wave modulated by radiations from the brain's natural electrical activity. The modulated interference wave is re-transmitted by the brain and received by an antenna at a remote station where it is demodulated, and processed to provide a profile of the suject's brain waves. In addition to passively monitoring his brain waves, the subject's neurological processes may be affected by transmitting to his brain, through a transmitter, compensating signals. The latter signals can be derived from the received and processed brain waves.

OBJECTS OF THE INVENTION

It is therefore an object of the invention to remotely monitor electrical activity in the entire brain or selected local regions thereof with a single measurement.

Another object is the monitoring of a subject's brain wave activity through transmission and reception of electromagnetic waves.

Still another object is to monitor brain wave activity from a position remote from the subject.

A further object is to provide a method and apparatus for affecting brain wave activity by transmitting electromagnetic signals thereto.

2

DESCRIPTION OF THE DRAWINGS

Other and further objects of the invention will appear from the following description and the accompanying drawings, which form part of the instant specification and which are to be read in conjunction therewith, and in which like reference numerals are used to indicate like parts in the various views;

FIG. 1 is a block diagram showing the interconnection of the components of the apparatus of the invention;

FIG. 2 is a block diagram showing signal flow in one embodiment of the apparatus.

DESCRIPTION OF THE PREFERRED EMBODIMENT

Referring to the drawings, specifically FIG. 1, a high frequency transmitter 2 produces and supplies two electromagnetic wave signals through suitable coupling means 14 to an antenna 4. The signals are directed by the antenna 4 to the skull 6 of the subject 8 being examined. The two signals from the antenna 4, which travel independently, penetrate the skull 6 and impinge upon the tissue of the brain 10.

Within the tissue of the brain 10, the signals combine, much in the manner of a conventional mixing process technique, with each section of the brain having a different modulating action. The resulting waveform of the two signals has its greatest amplitude when the two signals are in phase and thus reinforcing one another. When the signals are exactly 180° out of phase the combination produces a resultant waveform of minimum amplitude. If the amplitudes of the two signals transmitted to the subject are maintained at identical levels, the resultant interference waveform, absent influences of external radiation, may be expected to assume zero intensity when maximum interference occurs, the number of such points being equal to the difference in frequencies of the incident signals. However, interference by radiation from electrical activity within the brain 10 causes the waveform resulting from interference of the two transmitted signals to vary from the expected result, i.e., the interference waveform is modulated by the brain waves. It is believed that this is due to the fact that brain waves produce electric charges each of which has a component of electromagnetic radiation associated with it. The electromagnetic radiation produced by the brain waves in turn reacts with the signals transmitted to the brain from the external source.

The modulated interference waveform is re-transmitted from the brain 10, back through the skull 6. A quantity of energy is re-transmitted sufficient to enable it to be picked up by the antenna 4. This can be controlled, within limits, by adjusting the absolute and relative intensities of the signals, originally transmitted to the brain. Of course, the level of the transmitted energy should be kept below that which may be harmful to the subject.

The antenna passes the received signal to a receiver 12 through the antenna electronics 14. Within the receiver the wave is amplified by conventional RF amplifiers 16 and demodulated by conventional detector and modulator electronics 18. The demodulated wave, representing the intra-brain electrical activity, is amplified by amplifiers 20 and the resulting information in electronic form is stored in buffer circuitry 22. From the buffers 22 the information is fed to a suitable visual

3,951,134

3

display **24**, for example one employing a cathode ray tube, light emitting diodes, liquid crystals, or a mechanical plotter. The information may also be channeled to a computer **26** for further processing and analysis with the output of the computer displayed by heretofore mentioned suitable means.

In addition to channeling its information to display devices **24**, the computer **26** can also produce signals to control an auxiliary transmitter **28**. Transmitter **28** is used to produce a compensating signal which is transmitted to the brain **10** of the subject **8** by the antenna **4**. In a preferred embodiment of the invention, the compensating signal is derived as a function of the received brain wave signals, although it can be produced separately. The compensating signals affect electrical activity within the brain **10**.

Various configurations of suitable apparatus and electronic circuitry may be utilized to form the system generally shown in FIG. 1 and one of the many possible configurations is illustrated in FIG. 2. In the example shown therein, two signals, one of 100 MHz and the other of 210 MHz are transmitted simultaneously and combine in the brain **10** to form a resultant wave of frequency equal to the difference in frequencies of the incident signals, i.e., 110 MHz. The sum of the two incident frequencies is also available, but is discarded in subsequent filtering. The 100 MHz signal is obtained at the output **37** of an RF power divider **34** into which a 100 MHz signal generated by an oscillator **30** is injected. The oscillator **30** is of a conventional type employing either crystals for fixed frequency circuits or a tunable circuit set to oscillate at 100 MHz. It can be a pulse generator, square wave generator or sinusoidal wave generator. The RF power divider can be any conventional VHF, UHF or SHF frequency range device constructed to provide, at each of three outputs, a signal identical in frequency to that applied to its input.

The 210 MHz signal is derived from the same 100 MHz oscillator **30** and RF power divider **34** as the 100 MHz signal, operating in concert with a frequency doubler **36** and 10 MHz oscillator **32**. The frequency doubler can be any conventional device which provides at its output a signal with frequency equal to twice the frequency of a signal applied at its input. The 10 MHz oscillator can also be of conventional type similar to the 100 MHz oscillator herebefore described. A 100 MHz signal from the output **39** of the RF power divider **34** is fed through the frequency doubler **36** and the resulting 200 MHz signal is applied to a mixer **40**. The mixer **40** can be any conventional VHF, UHF or SHF frequency range device capable of accepting two input signals of differing frequencies and providing two output signals with frequencies equal to the sum and difference in frequencies respectively of the input signals. A 10 MHz signal from the oscillator **32** is also applied to the mixer **40**. The 200 MHz signal from the doubler **36** and the 10 MHz signal from the oscillator **32** combine in the mixer **40** to form a signal with a frequency of 210 MHz equal to the sum of the frequencies of the 200 MHz and 10 MHz signals.

The 210 MHz signal is one of the signals transmitted to the brain **10** of the subject being monitored. In the arrangement shown in FIG. 2, an antenna **41** is used to transmit the 210 MHz signal and another antenna **43** is used to transmit the 100 MHz signal. Of course, a single antenna capable of operating at 100 MHz and 210 MHz frequencies may be used to transmit both signals. The scan angle, direction and rate may be controlled

4

mechanically, e.g., by a reversing motor, or electronically, e.g., by energizing elements in the antenna in proper synchronization. Thus, the antenna(s) can be of either fixed or rotary conventional types.

A second 100 MHz signal derived from output terminal **37** of the three-way power divider **34** is applied to a circulator **38** and emerges therefrom with a desired phase shift. The circulator **38** can be of any conventional type wherein a signal applied to an input port emerges from an output port with an appropriate phase shift. The 100 MHz signal is then transmitted to the brain **10** of the subject being monitored via the antenna **43** as the second component of the dual signal transmission. The antenna **43** can be of conventional type similar to antenna **41** herebefore described. As previously noted, these two antennas may be combined in a single unit.

The transmitted 100 and 210 MHz signal components mix within the tissue in the brain **10** and interfere with one another yielding a signal of a frequency of 110 MHz, the difference in frequencies of the two incident components, modulated by electromagnetic emissions from the brain, i.e., the brain wave activity being monitored. This modulated 110 MHz signal is radiated into space.

The 110 MHz signal, modulated by brain wave activity, is picked up by an antenna **45** and channeled back through the circulator **38** where it undergoes an appropriate phase shift. The circulator **38** isolates the transmitted signals from the received signal. Any suitable diplexer or duplexer can be used. The antenna **45** can be of conventional type similar to antennas **41** and **43**. It can be combined with them in a single unit or it can be separate. The received modulated 110 MHz signal is then applied to a band pass filter **42**, to eliminate undesirable harmonics and extraneous noise, and the filtered 110 MHz signal is inserted into a mixer **44** into which has also been introduced a component of the 100 MHz signal from the source **30** distributed by the RF power divider **34**. The filter **42** can be any conventional band pass filter. The mixer **44** may also be of conventional type similar to the mixer **40** herebefore described.

The 100 MHz and 110 MHz signals combine in the mixer **44** to yield a signal of frequency equal to the difference in frequencies of the two component signals, i.e., 10 MHz still modulated by the monitored brain wave activity. The 10 MHz signal is amplified in an IF amplifier **46** and channeled to a demodulator **48**. The IF amplifier and demodulator **48** can both be of conventional types. The type of demodulator selected will depend on the characteristics of the signals transmitted to and received from the brain, and the information desired to be obtained. The brain may modulate the amplitude, frequency and/or phase of the interference waveform. Certain of these parameters will be more sensitive to corresponding brain wave characteristics than others. Selection of amplitude, frequency or phase demodulation means is governed by the choice of brain wave characteristic to be monitored. If desired, several different types of demodulators can be provided and used alternately or at the same time.

The demodulated signal which is representative of the monitored brain wave activity is passed through audio amplifiers **50** *a*, *b*, *c* which may be of conventional type where it is amplified and routed to displays **58** *a*, *b*, *c* and a computer **60**. The displays **58** *a*, *b*, *c* present the raw brain wave signals from the amplifiers

3,951,134

5

50 a, b, c. The computer **60** processes the amplified brain wave signals to derive information suitable for viewing, e.g., by suppressing, compressing, or expanding elements thereof, or combining them with other information-bearing signals and presents that information on a display **62**. The displays can be conventional ones such as the types herebefore mentioned employing electronic visual displays or mechanical plotters **58b**. The computer can also be of conventional type, either analog or digital, or a hybrid.

A profile of the entire brain wave emission pattern may be monitored or select areas of the brain may be observed in a single measurement simply by altering the scan angle and direction of the antennas. There is no physical contact between the subject and the monitoring apparatus. The computer **60** also can determine a compensating waveform for transmission to the brain **10** to alter the natural brain waves in a desired fashion. The closed loop compensating system permits instantaneous and continuous modification of the brain wave response pattern.

In performing the brain wave pattern modification function, the computer **60** can be furnished with an external standard signal from a source **70** representative of brain wave activity associated with a desired nuerological response. The region of the brain responsible for the response is monitored and the received signal, indicative of the brain wave activity therein, is compared with the standard signal. The computer **60** is programmed to determine a compensating signal, responsive to the difference between the standard signal and received signal. The compensating signal, when transmitted to the monitored region of the brain, modulates the natural brain wave activity therein toward a reproduction of the standard signal, thereby changing the neurological response of the subject.

The computer **60** controls an auxiliary transmitter **64** which transmits the compensating signal to the brain **10** of the subject via an antenna **66**. The transmitter **64** is of the high frequency type commonly used in radar applications. The antenna **66** can be similar to antennas **41**, **43** and **45** and can be combined with them. Through these means, brain wave activity may be altered and deviations from a desired norm may be compensated. Brain waves may be monitored and control signals transmitted to the brain from a remote station.

It is to be noted that the configuration described is one of many possibilities which may be formulated without departing from the spirit of my invention. The transmitters can be monostratic or bistatic. They also can be single, dual, or multiple frequency devices. The transmitted signal can be continuous wave, pulse, FM, or any combination of these as well as other transmission forms. Typical operating frequencies for the transmitters range from 1 MHz to 40 GHz but may be altered to suit the particular function being monitored and the characteristics of the specific subject.

The individual components of the system for monitoring and controlling brain wave activity may be of conventional type commonly employed in radar systems.

Various subassemblies of the brain wave monitoring and control apparatus may be added, substituted or combined. Thus, separate antennas or a single multimode antenna may be used for transmission and reception. Additional displays and computers may be added to present and analyze select components of the monitored brain waves.

6

Modulation of the interference signal retransmitted by the brain may be of amplitude, frequency and/or phase. Appropriate demodulators may be used to decipher the subject's brain activity and select components of his brain waves may be analyzed by computer to determine his mental state and monitor his thought processes.

As will be appreciated by those familiar with the art, apparatus and method of the subject invention has numerous uses. Persons in critical positions such as drivers and pilots can be continuously monitored with provision for activation of an emergency device in the event of human failure. Seizures, sleepiness and dreaming can be detected. Bodily functions such as pulse rate, heartbeat reqularity and others also can be monitored and occurrences of hallucinations can be detected. The system also permits medical diagnoses of patients, inaccessible to physicians, from remote stations.

What is claimed is:

1. Brain wave monitoring apparatus comprising means for producing a base frequency signal,
means for producing a first signal having a frequency related to that of the base frequency and at a predetermined phase related thereto,
means for transmitting both said base frequency and said first signals to the brain of the subject being monitored,
means for receiving a second signal transmitted by the brain of the subject being monitored in response to both said base frequency and said first signals,
mixing means for producing from said base frequency signal and said received second signal a response signal having a frequency related to that of the base frequency, and
means for interpreting said response signal.

2. Apparatus as in claim 1 where said receiving means comprises
means for isolating the transmitted signals from the received second signals.

3. Apparatus as in claim 2 further comprising a band pass filter with an input connected to said isolating means and an output connected to said mixing means.

4. Apparatus as in claim 1 further comprising means for amplifying said response signal.

5. Apparatus as in claim 4 further comprising means for demodulating said amplified response signal.

6. Apparatus as in claim 5 further comprising interpreting means connected to the output of said demodulator means.

7. Apparatus according to claim 1 further comprising means for producing an electromagnetic wave control signal dependent on said response signal, and
means for transmitting said control signal to the brain of said subject.

8. Apparatus as in claim 7 wherein said transmitting means comprises means for directing the electromagnetic wave control signal to a predetermined part of the brain.

9. A process for monitoring brain wave activity of a subject comprising the steps of
transmitting at least two electromagnetic energy signals of different frequencies to the brain of the subject being monitored,
receiving an electromagnetic energy signal resulting from the mixing of said two signals in the brain modulated by the brain wave activity and retrans-

3,951,134

7

mitted by the brain in response to said transmitted energy signals, and,

interpreting said received signal.

10. A process as in claim **9** further comprising the step of transmitting a further electromagnetic wave signal to the brain to vary the brain wave activity.

11. A process as in claim **10** wherein the step of transmitting the further signals comprises

obtaining a standard signal,

8

comparing said received electromagnetic energy signals with said standard signal,

producing a compensating signal corresponding to the comparison between said received electrogagnetic energy signals and the standard signal, and

transmitting the compensating signals to the brain of the subject being monitored.

* * * * *

5

10

15

20

25

30

35

40

45

50

55

60

65

United States Patent [19]

Zanakis et al.

[11] **Patent Number:** **4,951,674**

[45] **Date of Patent:** **Aug. 28, 1990**

[54] **BIOMAGNETIC ANALYTICAL SYSTEM USING FIBER-OPTIC MAGNETIC SENSORS**

[76] Inventors: **Michael F. Zanakis**, 60 Martin Rd., Livingston, N.J. 07039; **Philip A. Femano**, 69 Alexander Ave., Nutley, N.J. 07110

[21] Appl. No.: **325,942**

[22] Filed: **Mar. 20, 1989**

[51] Int. Cl.⁵ A61B 5/04
[52] U.S. Cl. .... 128/653 R; 128/731; 324/244.1
[58] Field of Search .... 324/244 OP; 128/653 R, 128/639, 630, 731, 732

[56] **References Cited**

U.S. PATENT DOCUMENTS

4,591,787 5/1986 Hoening 324/260
4,771,239 9/1988 Hoenig .... 128/653 R

OTHER PUBLICATIONS

"Introduction to Magnetoencephalography—A New Window on the Brain", Biomagnetic Technologies, Inc., San Diego, Calif., undated.
Kersey et al., Journal of Lightwave Technology, vol. LT–3, No. 4, Aug. 1985, pp. 836–840.
Enokiharae et al., Journal of Lightwave Technology, vol. LT–5, No. 11, Nov. 1987, pp. 1584–1590.
Mermelstein, Journal of Lightwave Technology, vol. LT–4, No. 9, Sep. 1986, pp. 1376–1380.
Koo et al., Journal of Lightwave Technology, vol. LT–5, No. 12, Dec. 1987, pp. 1680–1684.

Yariv et al., Optics Letters, vol. 5, No. 3, Mar. 1980, pp. 87–89.
Koo et al., Optics Letters, vol. 7, No. 7, Jul. 1982, pp. 334–336.
Koo et al., J. Lightwave Tech., vol. LT–1, No. 3, Sep. 1983, pp. 524–525.

Primary Examiner—Lee S. Cohen
Assistant Examiner—John C. Hanley
Attorney, Agent, or Firm—Michael Ebert

[57]   **ABSTRACT**

A biomagnetic analytical system for sensing and indicating minute magnetic fields emanating from the brain or from any other tissue region of interest in a subject under study. The system includes a magnetic pick-up device constituted by an array of fiber-optic magnetic sensors mounted at positions distributed throughout the inner confines of a magnetic shield configured to conform generally to the head of the subject or whatever other body region is of interest. Each sensor yields a light beam whose phase or other parameter is modulated in accordance with the magnetic field emanating from the related site in the region. The modulated beam from each sensor is compared in an interferometer with a reference light beam to yield an output signal that is a function of the magnetic field being emitted at the related site. The output signals from the interferometer are processed to provide a display or recording exhibiting the pattern or map of magnetic fields resulting from emanations at the multitude of sites encompassed by the region.

8 Claims, 2 Drawing Sheets

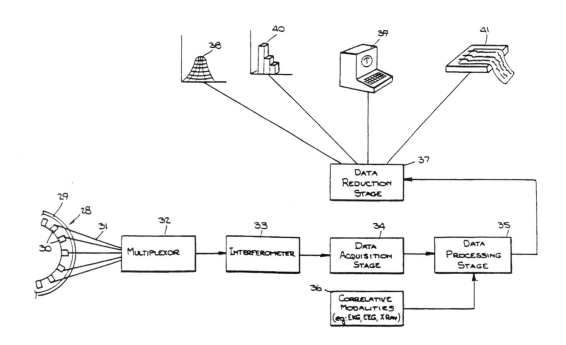

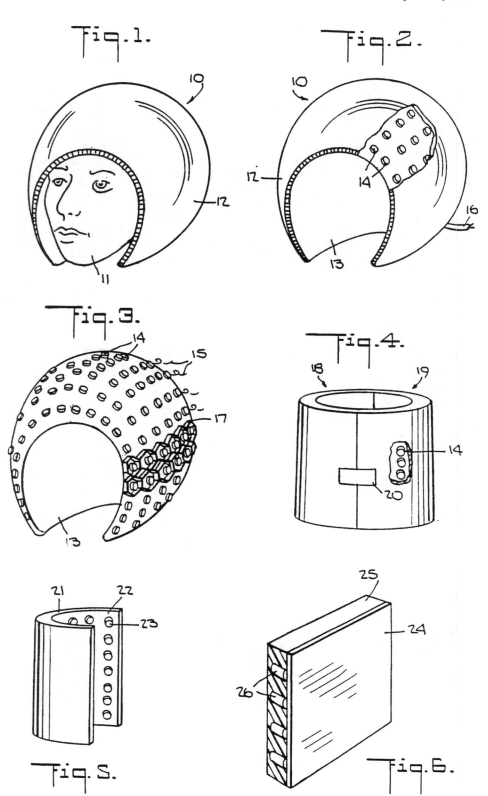

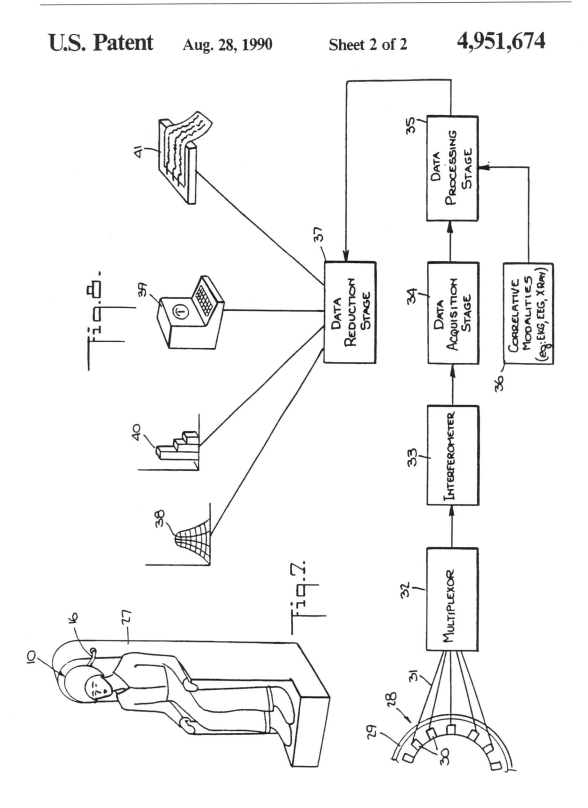

Fig.8.

Fig.7.

1

BIOMAGNETIC ANALYTICAL SYSTEM USING FIBER-OPTIC MAGNETIC SENSORS

BACKGROUND OF INVENTION

1. Field of Invention

This invention relates generally to biomagnetic analytic systems for sensing and indicating minute magnetic fields emanating from the brain and other tissue regions of the human body, and more particularly to a system using fiber-optic magnetic sensor pick-up devices for this purpose.

2. Status of Prior Art

Biomagnetic fields arise from three principal sources, the first being electric currents produced by the movement of ions. The second source is remanent magnetic movement of contaminants, and the third is paramagnetic or diamagnetic constituents of the body.

The first source is of primary significance in human brain activity in which the currents creating the magnetic fields result from signals generated by neurons as they communicate with each other and with sensory organs of the body. The intensity of extracranial magnetic field produced by such currents is extremely minute, having a strength no more than about a billionth of the magnetic field at the earth's surface. It is usually measured in terms of tesla (T) or gauss (G), one T being equal to 10^4 G.

The magnetic field arising from spontaneous brain activity (alpha waves) is about one picotesla ($IpT = 10^{-12}T$), whereas the magnetic field at the earth's surface is about $6 \times 10^{-5}T$. The magnetic field emanating from the brain has a strength much below that emitted by the heart. Hence monitoring of brain magnetic activity presents formidable difficulties.

A major concern of the present invention is magnetoencephalography (also commonly referred to as MEG). This is the recording of magnetic fields emanating from the brain resulting from neuronal electric currents, as distinguished from an electroencephalogram (EEG) in which electric potentials originating in the brain are recorded. With an EEG measurement, it is difficult to extract the three-dimensional distribution of electrically active brain sites from potentials developed at the scalp. While this difficulty can be overcome by inserting electrodes through apertures bored in the skull, this invasive technique is not feasible in the study of normal brain functions or to diagnose functional brain disorders or brain dysfunctions. Thus ionic currents associated with the production of electrically measurable epileptic seizures generate detectable extracranial magnetic fields, and these can be detected externally without invading the skull.

Non-invasive MEG procedures are currently used in epilepsy research to detect the magnetic field distribution over the surface of the head of a patient with a view to localizing the seizure foci and spread patterns. This analysis serves as a guide to surgical intervention for the control of intractable seizures. (See: "Magnetoencephalography and Epilepsy Research"—Rose et al.; Science—16 Oct. 1987—Volume 238, pp. 329-335.)

MEG procedures have been considered as a means to determine the origin of Parkinson's tremor, to differentiate at the earliest possible stage Alzheimer's disease from other dementias, and to localize the responsible cortical lesions in visual defects of neurological origin. MEG procedures are also of value in classifying active drugs in respect to their effects on specific brain structures, and to in this way predict their pharmaceutical efficacy. And with MEG, one can gain a better understanding of the recovery process in head trauma and strokes by observing the restoration of neurological functions at the affected site.

2

But while MEG holds great promise in the above-noted clinical and pharmaceutical applications, practical considerations, mainly centered on limitations inherent in magnetic sensors presently available for this purpose, have to a large degree inhibited these applications.

The characteristics of biomagnetic activity that are measurable are the strength of the field, the frequency domain and the nature of the field pattern outside of the body. In magnetoencephalography, measurement of all three of these components are important. Ideally, simultaneous measurement of three orthogonal components of the magnetic field provides a complete description of the field as a function of space and time. Coincident measurement of the magnetic field along the surface of the skull can provide a magnetic field map of the cortical and subcortical magnetic activity. With spontaneous activity, the brain emits magnetic fields of about 10^{-8} to 10^{-9} Gauss, compared with approximately 10^{-6} Gauss emitted by the heart. Thus, monitoring of the brain's magnetic activity places heavy demand upon the required hardware.

In brain activity, the current dipole or source is generated by the current flow associated within a neuron or group of neurons. Volume current is analogous to the extracellular component of the current source. In MEG, the net magnetic field measured depends on the magnetic field generated by the current dipole itself. The contribution from volume conduction is small in which approximations to spherical symmetry are made. However, there are tangential magnetic components originating from secondary sources representing perturbations of the pattern by the volume current at boundaries between regions of different conductivity. Contributions from these secondary sources to the tangential component of the field become relatively more pronounced with distance from the current dipole. But there is no interference from these secondary sources when measurement is confined to the magnetic fields perpendicular to the skull.

In biomagnetic analysis, three types of magnetic sensors are known to have adequate sensitivy and discrimination against ambient noise for this purpose. (See: "Magnetoencephalography"—Sato et al.—Journal of Clinical Neurophysiology—Vol. 2, No. 2—1985.) The first is the induction coil. But because of Nyquist noise associated with the resistance of the windings and its loss of sensitivity at frequencies below a few Herz, the induction coil is rarely used in MEG studies.

The second is the Fluxgate magnetometer; and while this has been used in geophysical studies, it has certain drawbacks when used in MEG applications. It is for this reason that the third type, the SQUID system, is presently used almost exclusively in MEG applications.

A SQUID (Superconducting QUantum Interference Device) comprises a superconducting loop incorporating a "weak link" highly sensitive to the magnetic field encompassed within the area of the loop. While the loop itself can act as a magnetic field sensor, use is made of a detection coil tightly coupled to the superconducting loop, the coil acting as a flux transformer. Both the coil and the loop are immersed in a bath of liquid helium contained within a dewar.

4,951,674

3

With the advent of so-called high-temperature superconductors operating at liquid nitrogen temperatures, a SQUID magnetometer has been developed using such superconductors. (See: "The Impact of High Temperature Superconductivity on SQUID Magnetometers"—Clarke et al.—Science—Vol. 242—14 Oct. 1988.)

In the booklet published by Biomagnetic Technologies, Inc., of San Diego, Calif., entitled "Introduction to Magnetoencephalography—A New Window on The Brain," there is disclosed a SQUID-type sensor for MEG studies. This SQUID is especially suited to measure magnetic fields in the frequency range from DC to 20 kHz, the magnetic field being converted into a signal that is amplified, filtered and displayed for subsequent analysis.

Because the brain's field falls off sharply with distance from the head, the dewar for the cryogenic liquid, which is inherently bulky, is provided with a tail section of reduced diameter to house the pick-up coil and to minimize the distance of the coil from the head of the patient being studied, thereby maximizing the detected field.

As pointed out in the above-identified booklet, in order to produce a contour map of the brain, the magnetic field must be measured simultaneously at a number of points outside the head. While it is possible with SQUIDS to sample the magnetic field emanating from the brain at one to seven points separated laterally from each other by several centimeters, a complete mapping of the field pattern at a given instant requires forty or more pick-up points. It is proposed, therefore, in the booklet to move SQUID sensors from one point to another to accumulate the required field data. But a measurement taken at a point X will not reveal magnetic brain activity taking place concurrently at a point Y if one has to physically shift the sensor from point X to point Y.

The booklet notes that the ultimate goal of MEG measurement is to simultaneously observe all areas of the brain to produce real-time activity maps responding instantaneously to changes as they occur. However, the booklet concedes that this goal has not yet been realized with SQUID sensors.

The present invention attains this goal by means of fiber-optic magnetometers (FOM). In a FOM sensor, a magnetostrictive alloy is interfaced with an optical fiber to produce a magnetometer whose principle of operation is based on the transference of strain from the magnetostrictive material to the core of the optical fiber via mechanical bonding. This results in modulation of the phase or other parameters of the light propagated in the fiber which is subsequently detected by a fiber-optic interferometer. Integrated fiber-optic magnetometers in which all components are fabricated on or around the optical fibers are now known.

FOM sensors of the type currently available are far less expensive to manufacture and maintain than SQUID sensors; they are considerably more compact, and they operate at room temperature. Their sensitivity to weak magnetic fields, which can be greater than that of a SQUID, renders them suitable for MEG and other applications.

The following publications disclose various forms of FOM sensors:

1. "Single-Mode Fiber-Optic Magnetometer with DC Bias Field Stabilization"—Kersey et al.—Journal of Lightwave Technology—Vol. LT-3, N° 4—August 1985.

4

2. "Fiber-Optic Polarimetric DC Magnetometer Utilizing a Composite Metallic Glass Resonator"—Mermelstein—Journal of Lightwave Technology, Vol. LT-4, No. 9—September 1986.

3. "Optical Fiber Sensors Using The Method of Polarization-Rotated Reflection"—Enokihara et al.—Journal of Lightwave Technology—Vol. LT-5—No. 11—November 1987.

4. "An Analysis of A Fiber-Optic Magnetometer with Magnetic Feedback"—Koo et al.—Journal of Lightwave Technology—Vol. LT-5—No. 12—December 1987.

The disclosures of these publications are incorporated herein by reference.

SUMMARY OF INVENTION

In view of the foregoing, the main object of this invention is to provide a biomagnetic analytical system which includes a pick-up device employing an array of fiber-optic magnetic (FOM) sensors for measuring and indicating minute magnetic fields emanating from a multitude of sites in the brain or in other tissue regions of interest in a subject being diagnosed.

A significant advantage of a fiber-optic magnetic sensor (FOM) over a SQUID is that the former is a solid-state device that is considerably smaller than the latter and requires no cryogenics, thereby making it possible to distribute a multitude of the sensors (i.e., in excess of forty) around the skull of the patient or about any other tissue region of interest to effect more accurate localization of magnetic activity, as well as a more precise determination of the physiological condition of the region being studied.

More particularly, an object of this invention is to provide a system of the above type for MEG analysis in which the FOM sensors are so distributed in a three-dimensional array as to pick up magnetic fields emanating from a multitude of brain sites simultaneously and to spatially localize the field signals.

Also an object of the invention is to provide a shielded magnetic pick-up device in which the FOM sensors in the array are magnetically shielded from each other to prevent magnetic interaction therebetween, as well as from magnetic fields extraneous to the region of interest, thereby obviating the need for a shielded room to conduct studies on biomagnetic activity.

Yet another object of the invention is to provide a biomagnetic system in which the outputs of the FOM sensors in the array are multiplexed, whereby a common interferometer can be used for the multitude of sensors in the array thereof.

Briefly stated, these objects are attained in a biomagnetic analytical system for sensing and indicating minute magnetic fields emanating from the brain or from any other tissue region of interest in a subject under study. The system includes a magnetic pick-up device constituted by an array of fiber-optic magnetic sensors mounted at positions distributed throughout the inner confines of a magnetic shield configured to conform generally to the head of the subject or whatever other body region is of interest.

Each sensor yields a light beam whose phase or other parameter is modulated in accordance with the magnetic field emanating from the related site in the region. The modulated beam from each sensor is compared in an interferometer with a reference light beam to yield an output signal that is a function of the magnetic field being emitted at the related site. The output signals

4,951,674

5

from the interferometer are processed to provide a display or recording exhibiting the pattern or map of magnetic fields resulting from emanations at the multitude of sites encompassed by the region.

BRIEF DESCRIPTION OF DRAWINGS

For a better understanding of the invention as well as other objects and further features thereof, reference is made to the following detailed description to be read in conjunction with the accompanying drawings, wherein:

FIG. 1 is a perspective view of a magnetic field pick-up device in the form of a helmet which is fitted over the head of a patient and which incorporates an array of FOM sensors for simultaneously detecting magnetic fields emanating from a multitude of sites in the brain;

FIG. 2 shows the helmet partially cut away to expose an inner insulating liner on which the sensors are mounted;

FIG. 3 is a separate view of the inner liner, illustrating the manner in which the FOM sensors are shielded from each other;

FIG. 4 illustrates, in perspective, a cylindrical magnetic pick-up device;

FIG. 5 shows a semi-cylindrical section of the pick-up device;

FIG. 6 shows a flat pick-up magnetic device;

FIG. 7 illustrates a unit for accommodating a patient undergoing a magnetoencepahlographic examination; and

FIG. 8 illustrates schematically a biomagnetic analytical system in accordance with the invention operating in conjunction with a pick-up device that is appropriate to the region being studied.

DETAILED DESCRIPTION OF INVENTION

FOM Pick-Up Devices

Referring now to FIGS. 1 to 3, there is shown one preferred embodiment of a pick-up device 10 in accordance with the invention, adapted to detect magnetic fields emanating from a multitude of sites on the brain of a patient for purposes of magnetoencelographic (MEG) examination.

Pick-up device 10 includes a generally spherical helmet 12 formed of ferromagnetic or superconductive shielding material, the helmet being configured to generally conform to the head of a patient 11 so that the brain therein lies within the confines of the helmet, and the weak magnetic fields emanating from the brain are confined within the helmet which acts to exclude extraneous magnetic fields, including those emanating from external electronic equipment associated with the pick-up device.

Helmet 12 is provided with a conforming inner liner 13 formed of electrical insulating material, such as in synthetic plastic material or an epoxy compound having good dielectric properties. Embedded in liner 13 or otherwise mounted thereon is a three-dimensional array of identical FOM sensors 14, each provided with a fiber-optic light conducting line 15 to supply light from a suitable laser beam source to the sensor and to conduct the light modulated by the sensor in response to the magnetic field detected thereby to an external interferometer. Lines 15 are bundled to form a cable 16 running from the pick-up device to external signal processing apparatus.

The FOM sensors 14 in the three-dimensional array are distributed uniformly throughout the inner confines

6

of helmet 12, so that each sensor acts to pick up a unique magnetic field emanating from the head.

As shown in FIG. 3, FOM sensors 14 are internally shielded from each other but not from the magnetic fields emanating from the brain by an open cell ferromagnetic honeycomb 17 so that there is no magnetic interaction between the sensors.

Fiber-optic magnetometers are well known, as evidenced by references (1) to (4), supra. The operation of FOM sensor is based on the transference of strain from the magnetostrictive material in response to a magnetic field to the core of the optical fiber via mechanical bonding, resulting in a phase modification of the propagated light beam. The modulated light from the sensor is subsequently processed in an interferometer which may take the form of a photodetector which compares the phase-modulated light beam with a reference light beam to provide an output signal that is a function of the phase displacement caused by the magnetic field to which the sensor is exposed.

FOM sensors are available in various configurations. In one such configuration, the optical fiber is bonded to a magnetostrictive element to form a waveguide strip that is then coiled into a spool so that the entire sensor is very small. For alternating-current measurements using, for example, metallic glasses as the sensing material, magnetic sensitivities of the order of 10^{-9} G/m of fiber core are obtainable.

Design improvements such as magnetic feedback nulling (Reference 4) can lead to improvements in the linear dynamic range, high suppression of magnetic hysteresis associated with the magnetic material, and improved long-term stability. Methods of improving fluctuations of the transmission characteristics of the fiber (induced by the surrounding environment) exist such as use of phase-sensitive transducers combined with a single polarization-maintaining fiber. Thus polarization-rotated reflection can be used to enhance the performance of the system.

Of the many configurations the magnetometer can take, all detect an externally-induced optical phase shift. The sensitivity of the system is proportional to the length of the fiber, until such time as the length approaches the point where other optical properties of the fiber interfere with the propagation of light. The measurement of the linear strain in length of the fiber which is bonded to (or coated by) the magnetostrictive material forms part of one arm of a fiber interferometer. Several types of interferometer designs have been employed, among which are the Fabra Perot, Mach Zender, Michelson and Sagnac types. Well designed interferometers can detect induced optical phase shifts below $10^{31\,6}$ rad over the frequency range of 10–10^4 Hz. Thus, very weak magnetic fields per meter of fiber can be detected.

The sensor configuration can be a fiber bonded to a magnetostrictive tube or mandrel, a metal film deposited on the fiber, a metallic glass strip bonded to fibers or a metallic glass cylinder. The magnetic materials which are sensitive in the range of DC to 50 kHz are nickel, iron-nickel alloys, cobalt-nickel, and metallic glasses. Piezoelectric activity in the jacket of the fiber can be achieved by the use of various types of polymer films.

Sensing of small AC magnetic fields at optimal DC
ʰⁱ ᵉᵗⁱᶜ fields for various frequencies can occur.
easuring technique enables the separation of
ic effect (at relatively higher frequencies)

4,951,674

7   **8**

from environmental effects (such as temperature or acoustics at lower frequencies) on the fiber interferometer. Thus, the fiber interferometer can be stabilized without losing sensitivity to magnetic fields.

To extend the AC measuring technique to measure DC bias magnetic fields, one can make use of the effect of DC bias magnetic fields to change the interferometer output due to a fixed AC magnetic field drive at a given frequency. In a sense, this technique utilizes an AC approach to measure DC magnetic fields, thereby overcoming both the environmental perturbation and the 1/f noise problem usually associated with low frequency measurements. It is the nonlinear response of the magnetostrictive material that allows the utilization of an AC technique to measure DC magnetic fields.

In the helmet-type pick-up device shown in FIGS. 1 to 3 which is adapted for MEG studies, each FOM sensor 14 in the three-dimensional array thereof is oriented so that the longitudinal axis of the optical waveguide coil or spool is substantially perpendicular to the surface of the skull of patient 11 wearing the helmet. This orientation makes it possible to dispose a multitude ·of sensors (forty or more) at positions distributed uniformly about the skull. The density of the coils in the array is limited by factors such as the physical diameter of each spool and induced noise from nearby spools such as eddy currents.

In biomagnetic measurements, sensitivity is limited by fluctuations in the ambient fields and not the intrinsic noise of the sensor. Such ambient fields are produced primarily by the sensor itself, motorized machinery and metallic structural components of buildings which distort the earth's geomagnetic field. The earth's geomagnetic field is uniform and steady. The problem arises when a sensing system vibrates, often in the 1–10 Hz range. Also, the subject may produce noise from normal physiological activity. In MEG, the head proper is the source of a significant amount of noise, produced primarily by the cortex. But because the array of sensors lies within a shield and each sensor occupies a position within a cell in a honeycomb shield, the sensors are isolated from ambient noise and magnetic interaction therebetween is prevented.

Each sensor acts as a gradiometer of predetermined order, any three of which can be used to localize biomagnetic sources at any brain site by the use of the computation techniques described hereinafter.

The pick-up device shown in FIGS. 1 to 3 is adapted to be placed over the head of a patient for MEG analysis. But in practice, the pick-up device can be customized to pick up magnetic field activity arising in other body regions of interest. Thus in measuring magnetic fields generated by the heart, the appropriate pick-up device, as shown in FIGS. 4 and 5, is in a cylindrical form composed of a pair of complementary semi-cylindrical sections 18 and 19 which are joined together by Velcro fasteners 20 or similar means which makes it possible to detach the sections from each other. In practice, for heart analysis, the cylinder is positioned around the thorax.

The cylinder is constituted by an outer shell 21 of shielding material having an inner liner 22 of insulating material in which are embedded a cylindrical array of FOM sensors 23. This cylindrical array of sensors surrounds the thorax, each sensor picking up the magnetic field emanating from a respective site in the heart.

The cylindrical pick-up device can also be configured to go around a limb to measure magnetic fields gener-

ated by the muscles therein. For other parts of the body, a flat pick-up device may be appropriate. This flat device, as shown in FIG. 6, is provided with an outer metal plate 24 of shielding material laminated to an inner block 25 of electrical insulating material in which a rectangular array of FOM sensors 26 is embedded.

In practice, the cylindrical pick-up device may be applied to any extremity; and a semi-cylindrical pick-up section can be used separately for measurement purposes. The flat pick-up device is useful for small surface measurements.

In practice, the pick-up device may be contoured to conform to any body region of interest. Thus the pick-up device can be used in a broad range of medical applications by making available to the practitioner a family of pick-up devices, each customized for a particular part of the body. The pick-up device is strapped or otherwise attached to the body part when a biomagnetic study is to be conducted.

For MEG procedures, as shown in FIG. 7, the helmet-type pick-up device 10 may be included as the headpiece of a support unit 27 which also provides a seat, a back rest and a foot platform for the patient whose head is received by the helmet. Housed in the unit is electronic equipment for processing the outputs of the FOM array contained in the helmet.

If one wishes to conduct biomagnetic studies on all portions of the body with a single pick-up device, the pick-up device for this purpose (not shown) may take the form of a sarcophagus-like magnetically shielded enclosure with suitable breathing vents, within which enclosure are disposed arrays of FOM sensors to pick up magnetic fields from different regions of the body. In practice, various standard electronic techniques can be used for noise reduction, either separately or in combination with physical shielding.

The Biomagnetic Analytical System

As shown in FIG. 8, one preferred embodiment of a biomagnetic analytical system in accordance with the invention includes a magnetic field pick-up device 28 in a configuration appropriate to the region under study. Device 28 includes an outer shield 29 within which is an array of FOM sensors 30, each coupled by a fiber-optic line 31 to the input of a multiplexer 32 whose output is applied to an interferometer 33.

Thus instead of having a separate interferometer channel for each FOM sensor which would be very costly, a common interferometer now serves sequentially to compare the modulated light beam derived from each sensor in the array with a reference light beam to produce an output signal. This output signal is a function of the sensed magnetic field emanating from the site related to the sensor.

In practice, multiplex transmission of the signals from the interferometer may be either optical or electrical; that is, by optical waveguides or by conductive wires in the case where the interferometer is of the type which applies the modulated light signal to a photodetector to be compared with the reference light beam.

The output signals from interferometer 33 representing the sensed magnetic fields is applied to a data acquisition stage 34.

The output of interferometer 33 is phase information related to the degree of phase rotation resulting from the detection of the incident vector of the magnetic field transient on the fiber optic sensor. This phase information can evolve over time as the biomagnetic

4,951,674

9   **10**

signal progresses, and it is of an analog nature. Therefore, it can be acquired, recorded, and processed in either the analog or digital form. For purposes of the present embodiment, reducing the data to, and processing the data in digital form will be discussed. However, the specific means of data handling is not important to the invention.

Time-varying phase information can be represented in the form of an evolving analog voltage which is proportional to the phase shift by a predetermined relationship. This signal can be converted to digital form through a conventional high speed sample-and-hold and analog-to-digital converter (ADC) means whereby the resulting bandwidth of the recorded signal can be limited to that which is determined by the sampling rate of this analog signal according to the Nyquist sampling theorem.

Since the signal from each sensor on the sensor array is time-multiplexed before entering data acquisition stage 34, a single ADC system is sufficient to digitize the signals from the entire sensor array. However, it should be noted that due to the signal bandwidth requirements and the size of the sensor array, it might be possible that the amount of data generated may result in a data rate which is high enough that the conversion rate of a single ADC might be exceeded and thus, a single ADC channel would not suffice. In this case, the multiplexed signal must then be de-multiplexed, the data from each sensor within the array then being directed to a respective ADC channel, there being one ADC channel per sensor, for example.

In practice, several electronic methods may be used to reduce noise, including the use of comb filters, subtracting a reference channel from a signal channel, adaptive filtering of analog or digital format or balancing of detectors. These can quite effectively reduce the ambient noise, even to the point where physical shielding may not be necessary.

The system lends itself to any number of data acquisition and processing means. For example, since the phase information in a magnetoencephalographic signal can be presented in optical form, the data is particularly suited to processing by optical computer technology.

The output of data acquisition stage 34 is applied to a data processing stage 35. Through the applications of standard spatial localization algorithms, such as are addressed by point source theory, a three-dimensional histogram map can be generated to represent the location and relative magnitude of each magnetic dipole source. The processing of the data will depend upon the configuration of the sensor array, since the proper 3-D mapping of the magnetic dipoles mandates a predetermined geometry of the plane of the array as well as the spacing between each sensor element within the array.

Once the data is acquired in digital form, it can be immediately processed by conventional digital computer means for the purposes of relating the data in various formats including those clinically relevant such as (a) time-varying analog and bandwidth information for each channel, and (b) the spatial localization, through the application of point source theory, of the magnetic dipoles which generated the magnetic field transients that were detected by the sensor array. The data can also be directed to a storage medium for the purpose of recording the digitized biomagnetic data for archiving and later retrieval and processing.

Additionally, other correlative modalities may be employed in conjunction with the biomagnetic data in order to obtain more complete information about a particular body tissue or system. Thus, modalities such as EEG, EKG, MRI and X-ray from a source 36 can be combined with the biomagnetic data in the data processing stage 35 and represented according to the particular need of the practitioner.

The output of data processing stage 35 is applied to a data reduction stage 37. The computational techniques necessary for resolution of the image and decoding it into a meaningful "image" for the clinician to interpret requires Fourier analysis of the affected light similar to the analyses utilized by the magnetic resonance imaging (MRI) technology. The FOM-based system in accordance with the invention allows for the detection of a large number of points simultaneously. This feature is most important, since clinicians have long sought a method of actually visualizing the physiological processes of the intact brain (especially deep brain structures) in various states of sleep and consciousness.

Two major problems encountered by the conventional SQUID-based system for MEG is that the resolution is not very good, and that the number of sensors that can be employed is quite limited, thereby limiting the sites in the brain that can be "scanned" for possible pathologies. These two cumbersome problems are overcome with the FOM-based system, making possible many more clinical applications.

With regard to the actual diagnosis of pathologies, the system is targeted toward the same professionals for whom the conventional SQUID-based system is designed. Primarily. these are radiologists, neurologists and surgeons. For example, the practitioner could "see" a functional image of the brain on a CRT, but the image will be a profile of the electromagnetically "active" portions of the brain, as shown by the magnetic pattern 38 derived from data reduction stage 37. The display plane can represent the location of each magnetic dipole source, and one pixel intensity can represent the magnetic dipole magnitude or phase with respect to a reference signal. What these active areas mean, and how they relate to pathologies is currently an area of intense interest in the basic and clinical neurosciences. Such areas of activity might signify anything from a soft-tissue pathology to abnormal behavioral patterns where no morphological or biochemical anomaly can be detected.

The format of data presentation can take the form of a static or time-varying uni- or multi-dimensional display.

Uni-dimensional display conforms to the current standards of SQUID-based magnetometry and of clinical electrophysiology. In this case, data is represented as linear time-varying representations of single detector elements. Multi-dimensional analysis can provide two- or three-dimensional graphic representations of the data. These multi-dimensional constructs are the result of applying the point source theory algorithms referred to above and can represent the dipole data spatially, or in terms of other dimensionalities, such as k-space in the Fourier domain.

Thus, the three-dimensional histogram map which can be representative of the location and relative magnitude of each magnetic dipole source can be rendered on a standard graphic workstation 39. Application-specific labelling must be applied to convey orientation and scaling of the 3-D data matrix. The display may take the graphical form 40 in which the level of each sensed field derived from the FOMs is represented by a column. Or

4,951,674

11

the levels may be separately indicated on a record chart **41**.

Advantages

The main advantages of the system are as follows:

I. Each FOM-based sensor is far smaller than a SQUID-based sensor. Thus, a multitude of FCM sensors can be placed over or around the region of interest by the magnetic pick-up device.

II. A system of gradiometers of predetermined order allows for a more accurate localizatior of biomagnetic activity, and a precise determination of the physiological condition.

III. The system affords more freedom to investigate several areas of the tissue region of interest simultaneously, since it provides a means to spatially localize the field signals.

IV. The biomagnetic analyzing system does not use expensive cryogens. The FOM-based pick-up device entails minimal installation time and service requirements.

V. The FOM sensor is relatively easy and inexpensive to construct, since only "solid-state" materials are required.

VI. The magnetic shielding needed for the FOM-based biomagnetic monitoring is limited to the area surrounding the region of interest, thereby eliminating the need for a specially shielded room.

VII. Even if a shielded room or enclosure is preferred for added noise reduction, the enclosure need not be larger than that required to placed the patient in comfortably.

VIII. Multiplexing the output from the sensing array makes it possible for more sensors to be monitored with fewer "decoding" devices at the "back end."

IX. The FOM-based pick-up device produces optical data that lends itself to optical computing available through the field of "photonics" involving optical processing technologies which can drastically decrease data processing times without compromising resolution.

While there has been shown and described a biomagnetic analytical system using various embodiments of FOM pick-up devices in accordance with the invention, it will be appreciated that many changes and modifications may be made therein, without, however, departing from the essential spirit thereof.

We claim:

12

1. A biomagnetic analytical system for sensing and indicating minute magnetic fields emanating from the brain or any other tissue region of interest in a subject being diagnosed, said system comprising:

(a) a magnetic pick-up device having an outer shell contoured to conform generally to the region of interest, said shell being formed of magnetic shielding material to exclude from its inner confines extraneous magnetic fields, whereby the emitted magnetic fields exist within the confines of the shell, and an array of fiber-optic magnetometer sensors which conforms to the contours of the shell, the sensors being mounted within the shell at positions distributed throughout the inner confines thereof, whereby each sensor is related to a site in the region and yields a light beam modulated in accordance with the magnetic field emanating from this site; and

(b) means including an interferometer to compare the modulated light beam yielded by each sensor in the array with a reference light beam to produce an output signal that is a function of the magnetic field emitted at the related site.

2. A system as set forth in claim 1, wherein said sensors are each disposed within a respective cell of a honeycomb shield supported within the shell to prevent magnetic interaction between the sensors.

3. A system as set forth in claim 1, wherein said sensors in the array are supported on an electrically insulating inner liner conforming to the inner contours of the shell.

4. A system as set forth in claim 1, wherein said shell is configured as a helmet to be worn by the subject for brain magnetic field diagnosis.

5. A system as set forth in claim 1, wherein said shell is configured as a cylinder for heart magnetic field diagnosis.

6. A system as set forth in claim 1, further including means coupled to the output of said interferometer to process the output signals from the interferometer to provide a display exhibiting the pattern of magnetic fields emanating from the sites encompassed by the region.

7. A system as set forth in claim 1, wherein said array has at least forty sensors.

8. A system as set forth in claim 1, wherein the modulated light beams from the sensors are applied sequentially to the interferometer through a multiplexer.

* * * * *

United States Patent [19]

Duffy et al.

[11] **4,408,616**

[45] **Oct. 11, 1983**

[54] **BRAIN ELECTRICAL ACTIVITY MAPPING**

[75] Inventors: **Frank H. Duffy**, Brookline, Mass.;
Norman D. Culver, Spotswood, N.J.

[73] Assignee: **The Children's Medical Center
Corporation**, Boston, Mass.

[21] Appl. No.: **264,043**

[22] Filed: **May 15, 1981**

[51] Int. Cl.³ **A61B 5/04**
[52] U.S. Cl. **128/731**
[58] Field of Search 128/731–733,
128/905

[56] **References Cited**

U.S. PATENT DOCUMENTS

2,928,189	3/1960	Molner et al.	35/22
3,696,808	10/1972	Roy et al.	128/2.1 B
3,705,297	12/1972	John	235/150.53
3,706,308	12/1972	John et al.	128/2.06 R
3,707,147	12/1972	Sellers	128/2.06 G
3,717,141	2/1973	Krohn et al.	128/2.66 R
3,780,724	12/1973	John	128/2.1 B
3,799,146	3/1974	John et al.	128/2.1 B
3,837,331	9/1974	Ross	128/732 X
3,901,215	8/1975	John	128/2.1 B
3,958,563	5/1976	Fernandez et al.	128/731
4,094,307	6/1978	Young	128/2.1 B
4,171,696	10/1979	John	128/731
4,201,224	5/1980	John	128/731
4,214,591	7/1980	Sato et al.	128/731

OTHER PUBLICATIONS

Duffy et al.; *Significance Probability Mapping: An Aid in the Topographic Analysis of Brain Electrical Activity;* EEG and Clin. and Neurophysiology, 1981; pp. 1–8.
Duffy et al.; "Quantification of Focal Abnormalities in Beam Data by Grid Sector Analysis".
Duffy et al.; "Dyslexia: Automated Diagnosis of Computerized Classif. of Brain Electrical Activity"; *Annals of Neur.,* vol. 7, No. 5, 5–1980, pp. 421–428.
Duffy et al.; "Dyslexia: Regional Diff. in Brain Electri-cal Activity by Topographic Mapping"; *Annals of Neur.,* vol. 7, No. 5, 5–1980, pp. 412–420.
Ueno et al., Topographic Computer Display of Abnormal EEG Activities in Patients with CNS Diseases, Memoirs of the Faculty of Engineering, Kyushu University, vol. 34, No. 3, (Feb., 1975) pp. 195–209.
Marguerite Zientara (CW Staff) Multiple Personalities 'Mapped' by Computer, Computer World Publication, Jan. 24, 1983, p. 14.
Duffy et al., "Brain Electrical Activity Mapping (BEAM): A Method for Extending the Clinical Utility of EEG and Evoked Potential Data," *Annals of Neurology,* vol. 5, No. 4 (Apr., 1979) pp. 309–321.

Primary Examiner—Lee S. Cohen
Assistant Examiner—Angela D. Sykes

[57] **ABSTRACT**

Topographic displays of brain electrical activity are produced from matrices of data derived from evoked potential (EP) and steady-state responses of skull transducers. In different aspects, EP responses are displayed at a variable frame rate, the rate of data sampling is sufficient to capture rapid transient events, difference matrices are derived as the difference between matrices corresponding to two different brain conditions, the baseline of the EP responses is zeroed based on the average prestimulus response, and the steady-state response is analyzed by Fourier transforms. In other aspects, statistical comparison matrices representing statistical differences between corresponding elements in two matrices are generated, a coefficient-of-variance matrix is generated, additional display matrices are temporally interpolated, response waveforms are previewed and tagged for elimination from further processing, the topographic maps are displayed on a video monitor with appropriate scaling of the data to the tones of the display, and additional display points are interpolated between the measured data points for display.

82 Claims, 32 Drawing Figures

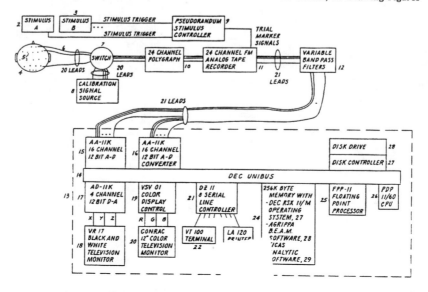

U.S. Patent   Oct. 11, 1983   Sheet 1 of 27   4,408,616

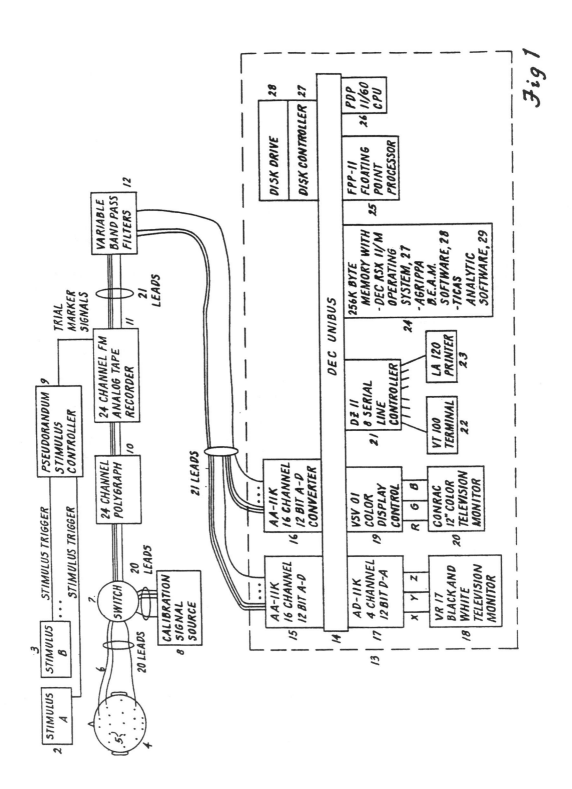

Fig 1

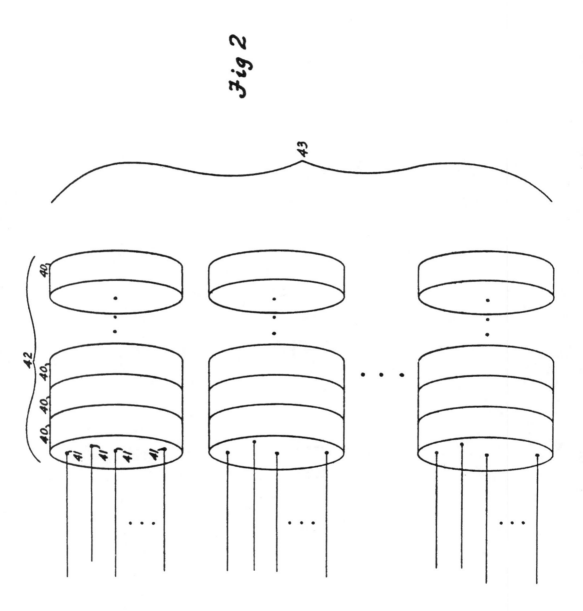

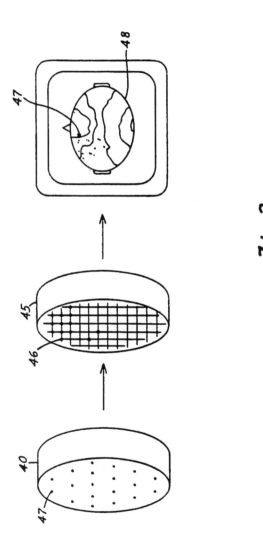

Fig 3

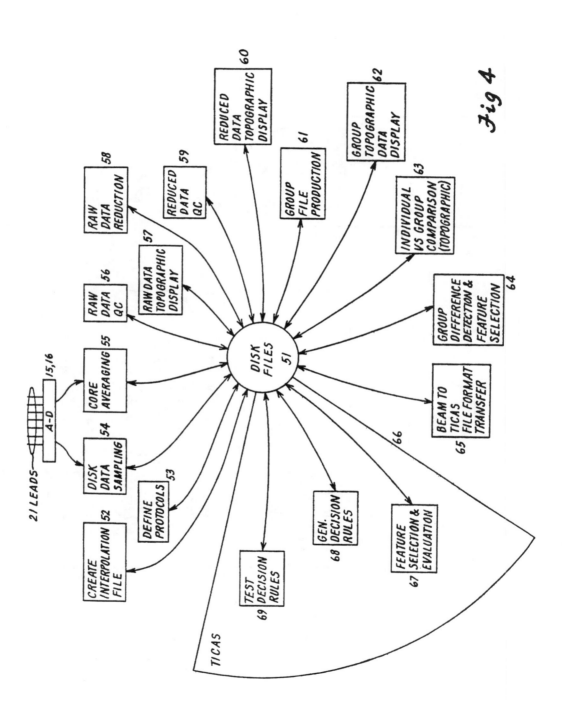

Fig 4

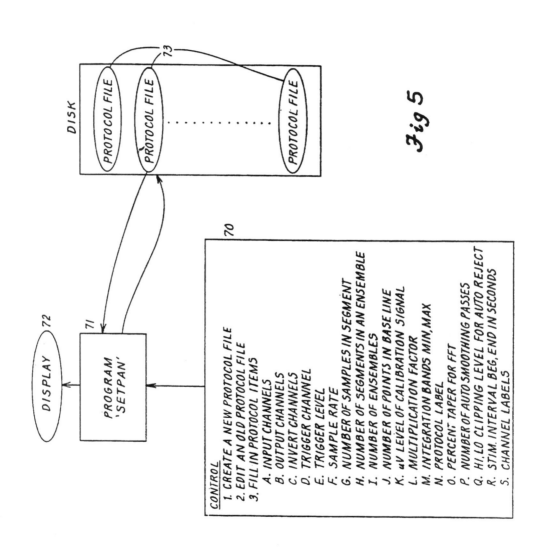

Fig 5

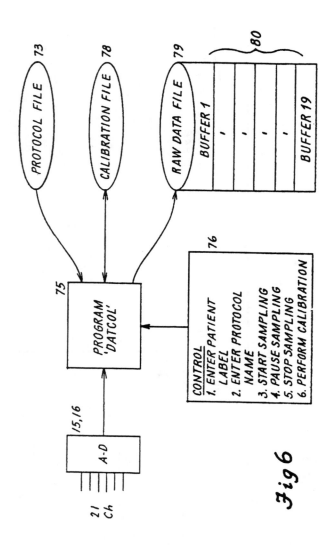

Fig 6

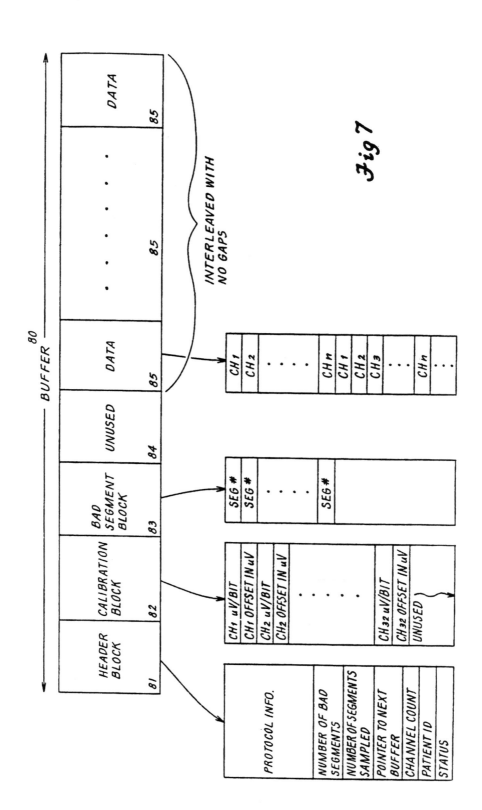

Fig 7

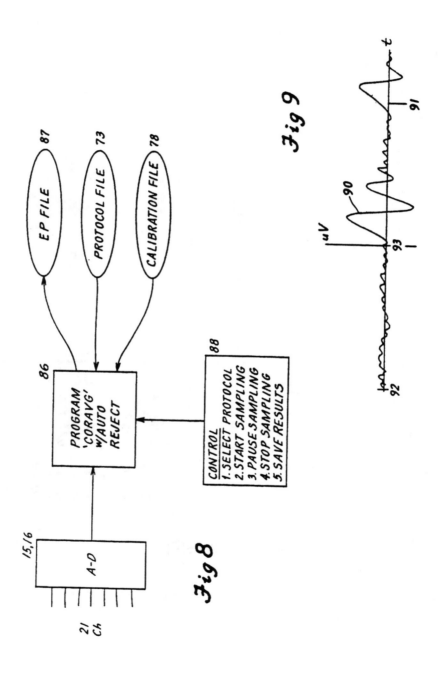

Fig 8

Fig 9

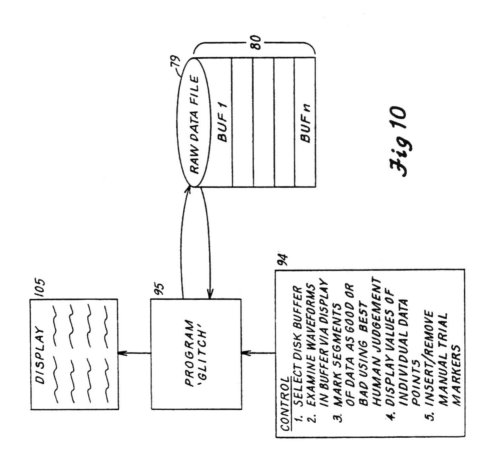

Fig 10

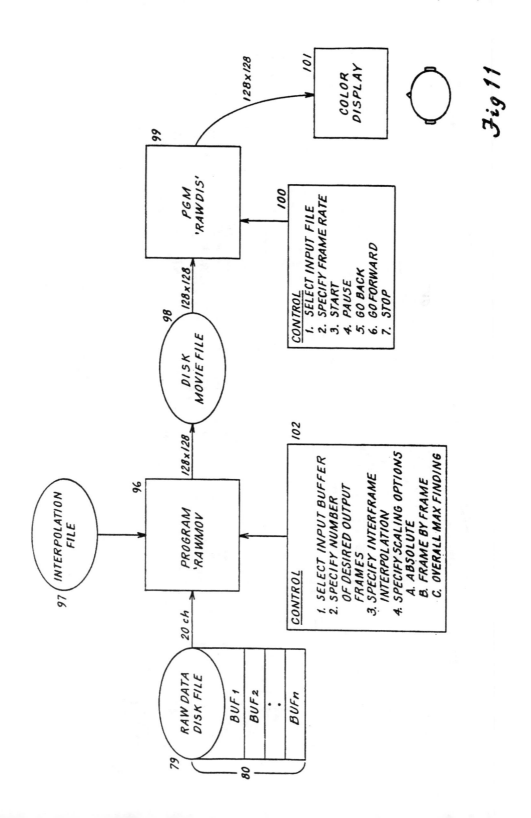

Fig 11

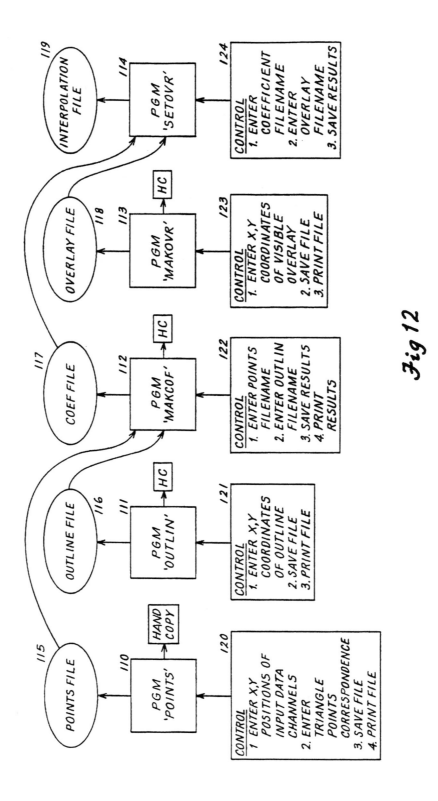

Fig 12

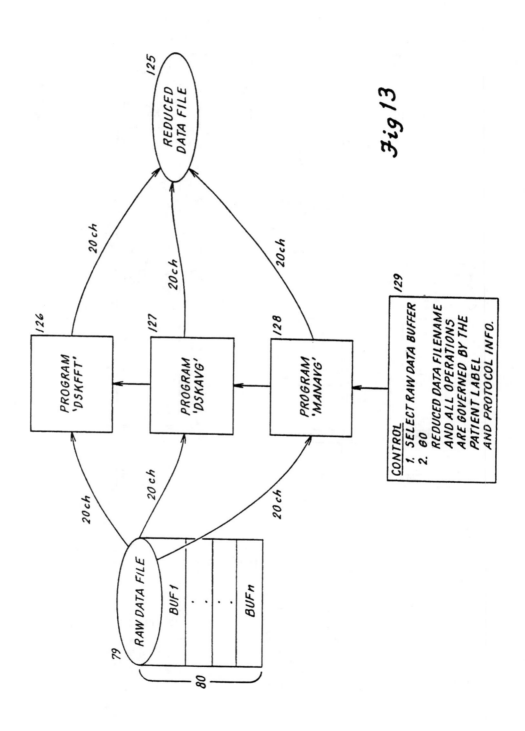

Fig 13

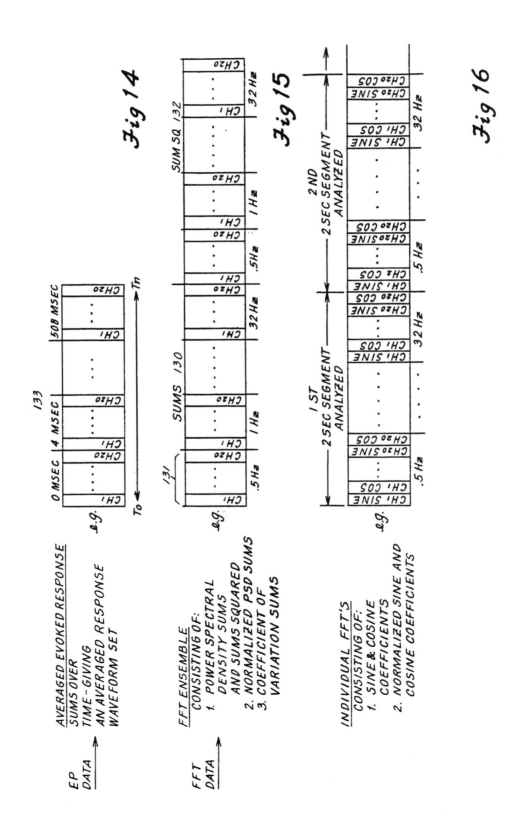

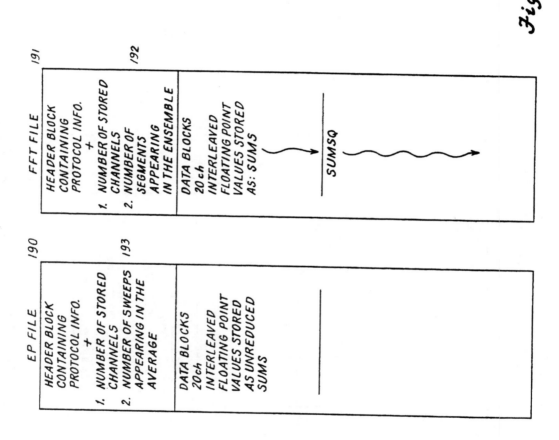

Fig 18

Fig 17

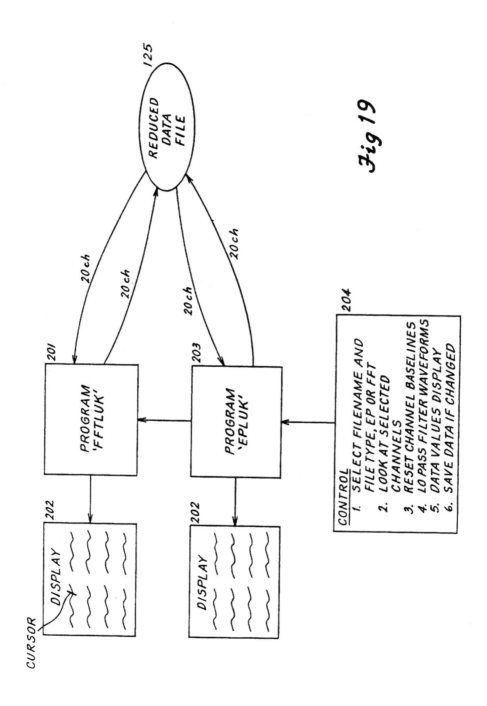

Fig 19

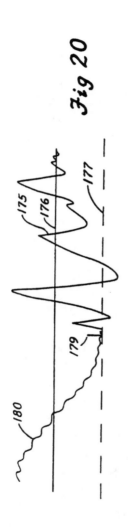

Fig 20

Fig 26

FRAME 1	FRAME n

| HEADER BLOCK CONTAINING: 1. NUMBER OF SAVED FRAMES 2. FOR EACH FRAME A. FFT BAND OR EP FRAME OR INTEGRATION INTERVAL B. PROTOCOL UNDER WHICH DATA WAS COLLECTED | 128×128 ARRAY OF FLOATING POINT t VALUES | | |

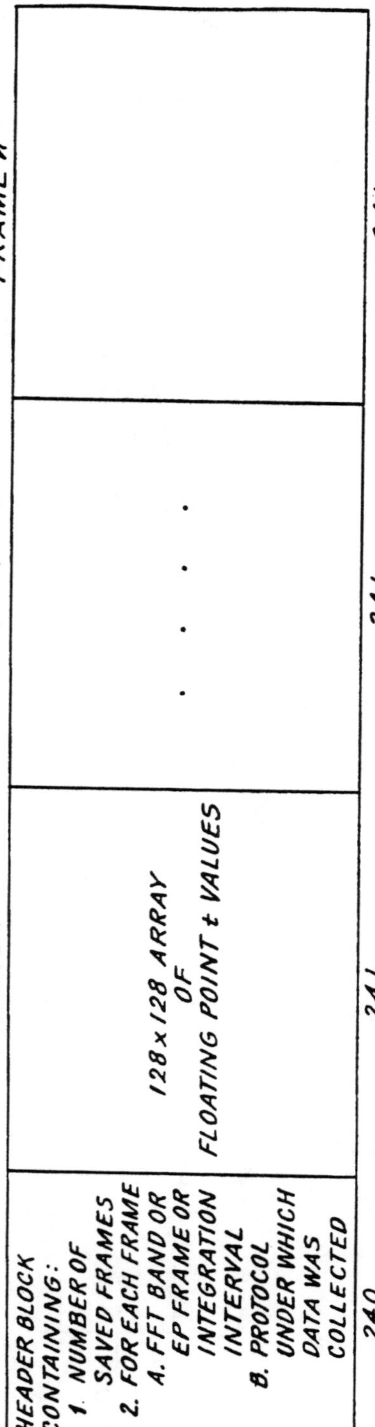

240   241   241 . . .   241

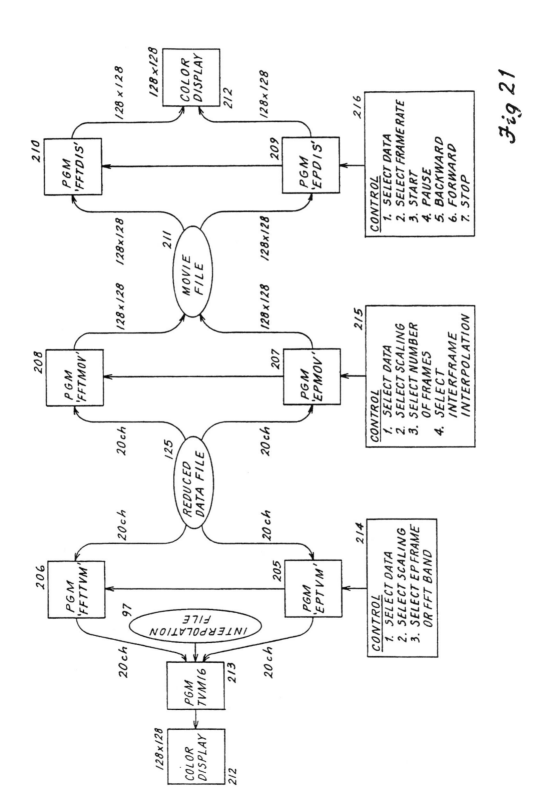

Fig 21

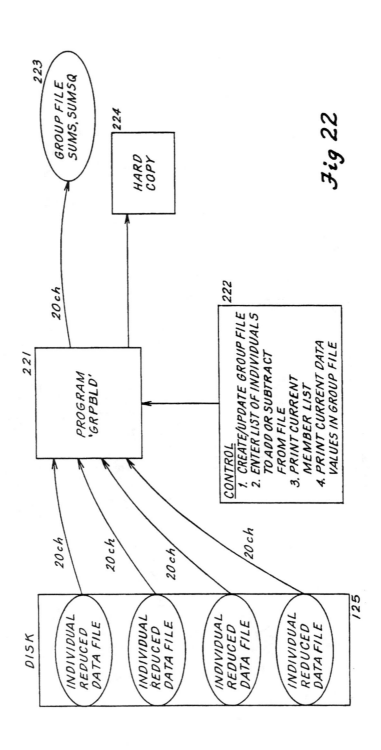

Fig 22

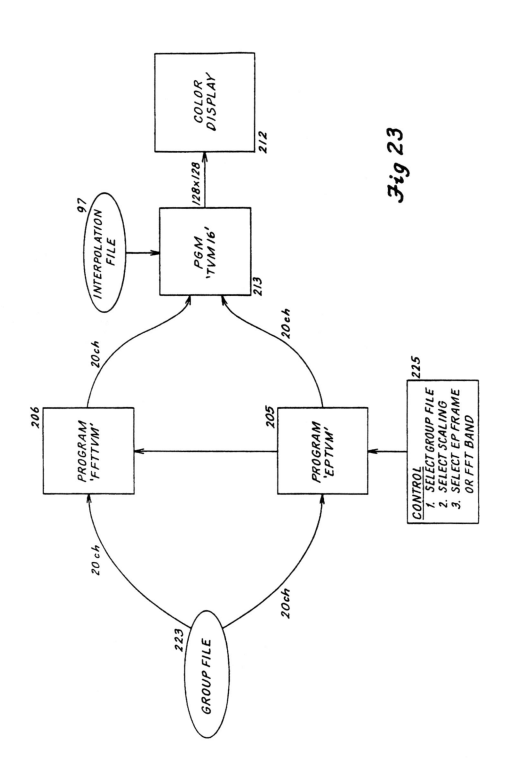

Fig 23

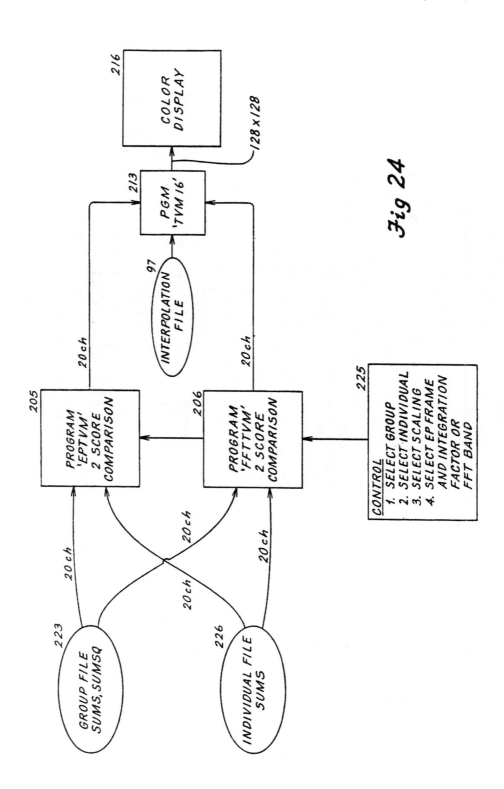

Fig 24

U.S. Patent   Oct. 11, 1983   Sheet 21 of 27   4,408,616

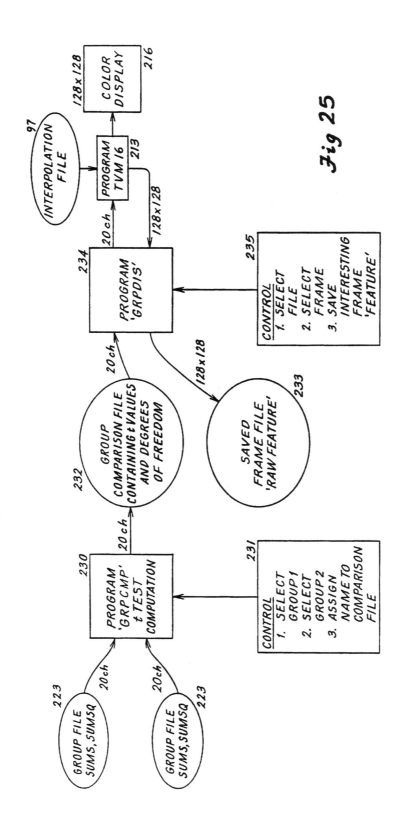

Fig 25

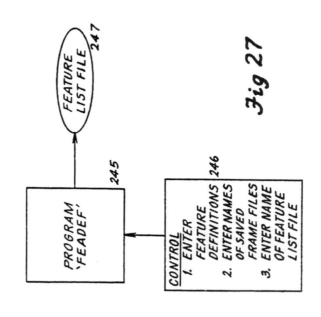

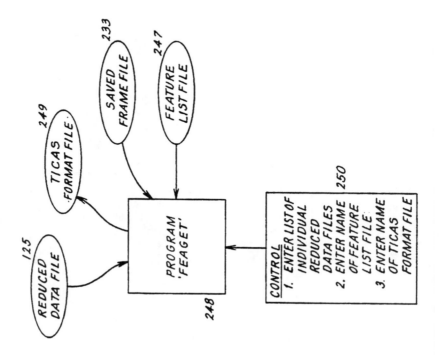

Fig 27

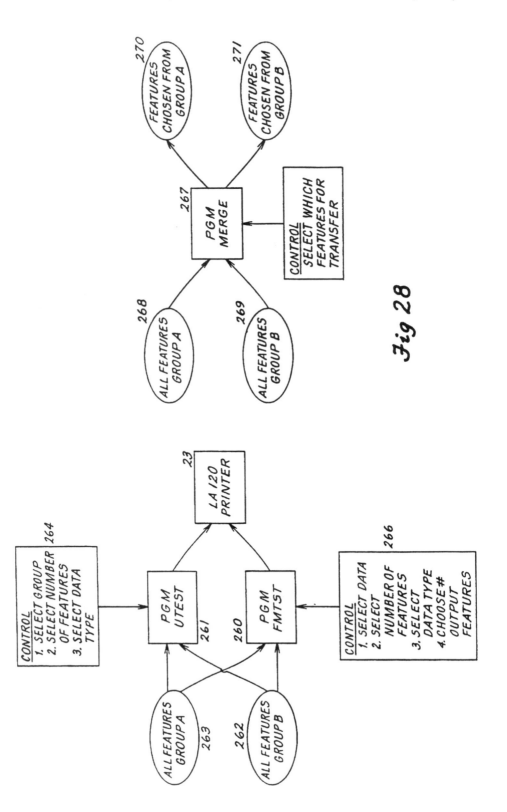

Fig 28

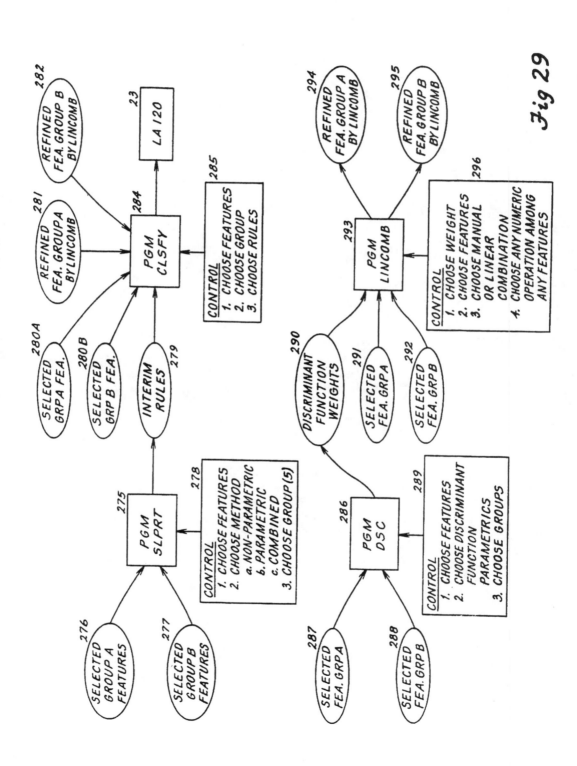

Fig 29

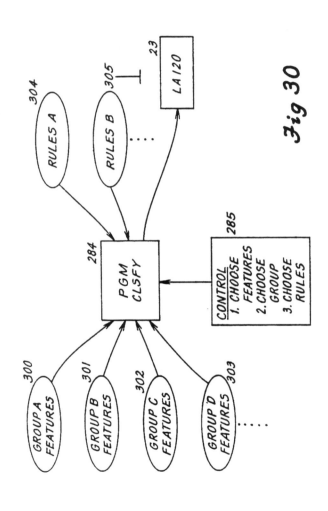

Fig 30

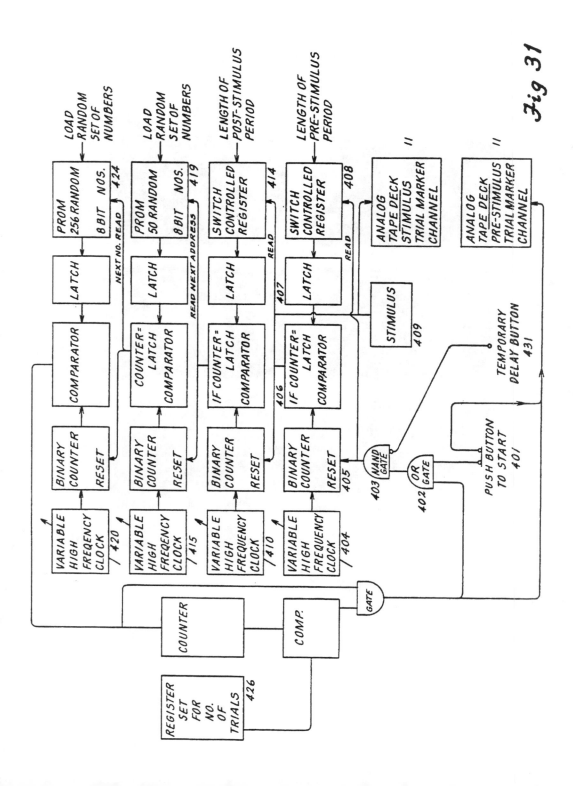

Fig 31

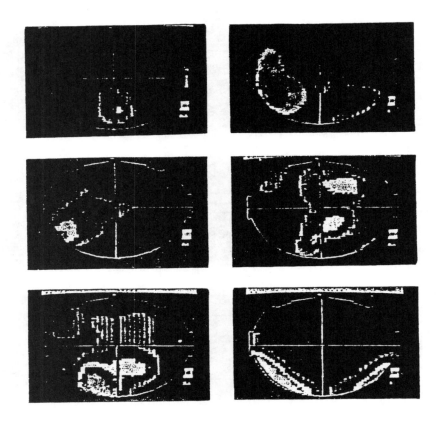

FIG. 32

4,408,616

1

BRAIN ELECTRICAL ACTIVITY MAPPING

The invention described herein was made in the course of work under a grant or award from the Department of Health and Human Services.

BACKGROUND OF THE INVENTION

This invention relates to analysis of brain electrical activity and diagnosis of brain disorders.

Traditional electro-encephalographic (EEG) techniques of analyzing brain electrical activity to diagnose brain dysfunction require the skilled neurophysiologist to observe and distinguish time and frequency related characteristics of many channels of voltage waveforms derived from an individual's brain and to determine, largely from memory, differences between that individual's waveforms and waveforms characteristic of a normalized population. The process necessarily fails to take account of many subtle but potentially useful pieces of information contained in the analyzed data.

Signal averaged sensory evoked potential (EP) transient responses have also been used as a source for brain electrical activity analysis, but large amounts of useful information contained in such transient response waveforms have traditionally been disregarded because of the difficulty of visualizing the inter-relationship over time of many channels of such information.

SUMMARY OF THE INVENTION

The invention features, in one aspect, displaying time sequences of topographic maps at a variable frame rate. In preferred embodiments, the rate can be selected to display protions of the EP response immediately following the stimulus at a slower rate than later portions; and in preferred embodiments the rate can be varied logarithmically. The variation of display rate permits the operator to give more emphasis to matrices which contain relatively more information, such as the earlier EP response matrices.

In another aspect, the invention features generating topographic displays of information on electrical activity of the brain produced at a plurality of transducers on the skull; generating a time sequence of matrices of electrical activity at successive points in time sufficient in number to capture the onset of a rapid transient event; and displaying the matrices as topographic maps in time sequence at a variable rate. In preferred embodiments, the processor is capable of generating 200 or more matrices for each second of real time. The ability to capture a large number of matrices in a short period of time permits the observation of short-term events such as epileptic spikes.

In another aspect, the invention features generating topographic displays of information on brain electrical activity produced at a plurality of skull transducers; storing the electrical activity of such transducers for two different brain conditions; generating matrices of elements representing electrical activity in the two conditions; forming a difference matrix between corresponding elements of the two matrices; and displaying the difference matrix as a topographic map. In preferred embodiments, the two brain conditions are attained by the use of a patterned light stimulus and a non-patterned light stimulus. The ability to form and display difference matrix enables the operator to identify parts of the brain involved in particular brain states or evoked responses.

2

In another aspect, the invention features generating topographic displays of information on brain electrical activity produced at a plurality of skull transducers; repeatedly triggering EP responses at the transducers, including pre-stimulus and post-stimulus responses; averaging the responses; setting as a baseline the mean level of the pre-stimulus response; generating matrices from such responses; and displaying topographic maps of the matrices. In preferred embodiments the time occurrence of each stimulus is stored and the response is divided into pre-stimulus and post-stimulus periods; the matrices generated are a set of time-sequenced frames during the response and are displayed as a sequence of topographic maps; the sequence can be displayed as an endless sequence of maps; the averaging process can be performed using digital words added into summing buffers; and the sampling, storing, response averaging, baseline calculation and subtraction can all be performed digitally; averaging of the pre-stimulus baseline can exclude selected portions of the response; the response can be reviewed to determine the appropriateness of the baseline; there can be calculated the V_{RMS} of the average pre-stimulus and post-stimulus responses and the V_{RMS} can be displayed with the responses, so that the user can determine whether the noise level for any transducer is unacceptably large; the operator can manually adjust the baseline up or down; high-frequency components can be filtered from the post-stimulus response by multipoint interpolation; and the baseline calculation can be repeated until the results are satisfactory. In general, these various features permit the operator to assemble, modify and adjust to an accurate zero level a set of EP responses so that the ultimate topographic display will be accurate and useful. The display of a time-sequence of frames permits the operator to visualize the movement of brain activity in the course of an EP response over the skull. The proper setting at the baseline improves the utility of each response when used in a topographic display, since the relative levels of response at different transducers is more accurately portrayed.

In another aspect, the invention features filtering to remove from the EEG responses frequency components outside the prominent frequency bands of electrical activity; determining, for each transducer, the Fourier transforms and the spectral energy in selected frequency bands, during a period when the brain activity remains in the same state; and processing the results into display matrices for the selected frequency bands. In preferred embodiments, the brain activity can be sampled, stored and Fourier transformed digitally; the filters can remove frequency components below 0.5 Hz and about 50 Hz; the samples can be taken at least 3 times as frequently as the highest frequency in the prominent frequency bands, and particularly at 4 to 5 times that highest frequency; the Fourier analysis can be limited to a period between marked starting and stopping points; the period during which electrical activity is sampled can be limited to avoid interruptions in the subject's brain state, and particularly can be limited to two second sampling periods; the number of samples can be between 20 and 2000; and the frequency bands analyzed can comprise the alpha, beta, delta and theta bands. Removal of irrelevant frequency bands, sampling at high rate, and limiting the sampling period all enable the operator to obtain accurate spectral analyses with minimum interference. The ability to analyze specific frequency bands of interest enables the operator to

4,408,616

3

review information which effectively corresponds to the electrical activity of the brain in various states.

In another aspect, the invention also features generating a statistical comparison matrix from two matrices, each element of the statistical comparison matrix representing a statistical difference between the corresponding elements in the two matrices; and displaying the statistical comparison matrix as a topographic map. In preferred embodiments, the statistical comparison matrix can be interpolated into a display matrix having additional display points; the statistical comparison can be made between two expanded matrices rather than between two unexpanded matrices; the statistical comparison can be a t-statistic analysis, or a z-statistic analysis; and quantitative features useful for diagnosis can be determined from regions of the maps. The ability to perform and topographically display statistical differences between groups and between an individual and a group offers a versatile and effective tool for visualizing brain areas which are connected to particular brain dysfunctions or to particular brain activities, and for neurophysiological diagnosis and research.

In another aspect, the invention also features generating a coefficient-of-variance matrix, each element of which represents the normalized standard deviation at one skull location; and displaying the coefficient-of-variance as a topographic map.

In another aspect, the invention also features temporally interpolating matrices which represent the response at time instants between other matrices; and displaying said interpolated matrices. The temporal interpolation provides a smoother visual transition between the original frames when a time-sequenced display is presented.

In another aspect, the invention also features previewing waveforms and tagging a waveform to indicate whether it should be used in later processing, eliminating a response from further processing, automatically eliminating a response from further processing if a portion of the response exceeds a predetermined threshhold, smoothing a response by eliminating undesired high-frequency components, for adjusting the zero baseline of a response, eliminating selected portions of a response from further processing, and displaying in numerical form the value of a response at a point in time selected by the operator. These waveform quality control procedures enable the operator to improve the quality and accuracy of the topographic displays.

In another aspect, the invention features generating a topographic display of information on the electrical activity produced at a plurality of skull transducers; sampling and storing the information as a series of matrices; viewing the data as a waveform; adjusting or eliminating portions of the data, processing the matrices into processed matrices; interpolating to expand the matrices for viewing; and displaying the matrices as topographic maps in a grey tone scale. In preferred embodiments, the data matrices, processed matrices and expanded matrices can be tagged and stored for later recall and processing; and the data matrix elements can be calibrated to stored calibration signals by calculating a DC offset and gain component for each transducer. The ability to store display matrices for later use enables the operator to accumulate a series of significant matrices derived from diagnostic or research work. The calibration assures that the topographic displays will be accurate.

4

In another aspect, the invention features generating a topographic display of electrical activity of the brain produced from a plurality of electrical transducers on the skull; generating matrices of elements representing the electrical activity at different points; using a video monitor to display said matrices, each element of which is represented by a discrete point having a gray tone of color lying within a range of gray tones; and scaling the elements to the tones. In preferred embodiments, scaling can be performed so that all elements are linearly interpolated between the maximum gray tone and the minimum gray tone, or between the maximum gray tone and a "zero" gray tone, or to an operator supplied gray one, or so that certain display elements are excluded from the scaling, or that elements falling outside the available gray tone range are assigned to the closest gray tone; the gray tones can be generated in two colors, which can be complementary colors, representing values on either side of a zero tone, the zero tone being an absence of color; the scaling can be performed either on a matrix by matrix basis, or for all matrices taken together; the data which forms the input to the scaling operation can be previewed to by selected lab for exclusion from the scaling operation. The ability to scale the display data to a range of gray tones in a variety of ways improves the utility and visual effect of the display. The variety of scaling options is suitable for the variety of data which may be displayed. The ability to eliminate very large values from the scaling operation assures the most effective scaling for a given set of data.

In another aspect, the invention features normalizing display matrix elements to a selected value which can be assigned to a selected gray tone for purposes of scaling. In preferred embodiments, the normalization can be to a matrix element representing a particular vertex transducer on the skull, or to the root mean square value of the background activity at the transducer being normalized, or to the average root mean square value of the background activity at all skull locations; normalization can be done in connection with apparatus for topographically displaying a sequence of matrices representing averaged EP responses to repeatedly provided stimuli; normalization can be done in connection with apparatus for displaying spectral band matrices derived by Fourier transform analysis of the electrical activity, the normalization being of each element of each spectral band to the total spectral energy at the corresponding transducer on the average total spectral energy at all transducers. The ability to normalize display elements improves the operator's ability to compare different sets of data by normalizing them to the same value.

In preferred embodiments, the invention features interpolating to form additional matrix elements between the transducer points; the interpolation can be three-point interpolation, particularly three-point linear interpolation to the values of the three closest transducers; the number of transducers can be in the range of 10 to 200; and the number of picture elements is at least 5 times the number of transducers. The expansion of a matrix of a small number of points to a display matrix of a large number of points significantly improves the smoothness, readability and utility of the resulting topographic displays.

BRIEF DESCRIPTION OF THE DRAWINGS

FIG. 1 is a block diagram of the BEAM system.

4,408,616

5 6

FIG. 2 is a representation of the organization of samples of data in the brain electrical activity mapping system.

FIG. 3 is a representation of the formation of a topographic display from a frame of data in the brain electrical activity mapping system.

FIG. 4 is a block diagram of the functions performed by the BEAM system.

FIG. 5 is block diagram of the define protocols operation.

FIG. 6 is a block diagram of the disk data sampling operation.

FIG. 7 is a data file format diagram of the raw data file.

FIG. 8 is a block diagram of the core averaging operation.

FIG. 9 is a graph of an average EP transient response waveform after automatic baseline zeroing.

FIG. 10 is a block diagram of the raw data quality control operation.

FIG. 11 is a block diagram of the raw data topographic display operation.

FIG. 12 is a block diagram of the create interpolation file operation.

FIG. 13 is a block diagram of the raw data reduction operation.

FIG. 14 is a data file format diagram of signal averaged EP data.

FIG. 15 is a data file format diagram of FFT ensemble data.

FIG. 16 is a data file format diagram of individual FFT data.

FIG. 17 is a data file format diagram of an EP file.

FIG. 18 is a data file format diagram of an FFT file.

FIG. 19 is a block diagram of the reduced data quality control operation.

FIG. 20 is a graph of an average EP transient response waveform after automatic baseline zeroing and after manual baseline readjustment.

FIG. 21 is a block diagram of the reduced data topographic operation

FIG. 22 is a block diagram of the group file production operation.

FIG. 23 is a block diagram of the group topographic display operation.

FIG. 24 is a block diagram of the individual vs. group comparison operation.

FIG. 25 is a block diagram of the group difference detection and feature selection operation.

FIG. 26 is a data file format diagram of a saved frame file.

FIG. 27 is a block diagram of the brain electrical activity mapping to TICAS file transfer operation.

FIG. 28 is a block diagram of the TICAS feature selection and evaluation operation.

FIG. 29 is a block diagram of TICAS generate decision rules operation.

FIG. 30 is a block diagram of TICAs test decision rules operation.

FIG. 31 is a block diagram of pseudorandom stimulus controller.

FIG. 32 is a sample of topographic displays generated by a brain electrical activity mapping system.

DESCRIPTION OF THE PREFERRED EMBODIMENT

We now turn to a description of the preferred embodiment.

System Organization and Software

FIG. 1 illustrates the components of a brain electrical activity mapping system. Twenty electrodes 5 (e.g., Grass gold cup) are attached to subject's skull 4 in a conventional international 10–20 format. Twenty leads 6 from electrodes 5 are connected through switch 7 to conventional 24-channel polygraph 10 (e.g., Grass 8-24D), which contains parallel variable gain differential amplifiers and strip chart recorders. Calibration signal source 8, an A.C. generator, is also connected through switch 7 to polygraph 10. Stimulus A 2 (e.g., Grass Model PS1 strobe light) and stimulus B 3 (e.g., click generator) present stimuli to the subject under the control of pseudorandom stimulus controller 9, which also provides pre-stimulus and stimulus trial marker signals (5 volt spikes) of opposite polarity to one of the input channels to 24-channel FM analog tape recorder 11 (e.g., Honeywell 5600E). In other embodiments, recorder 11 is eliminated and polygraph 10 is connected directly to filter 12 for real-time loading of data. The 21 active outputs of recorder 11 are connected to the inputs of 21 parallel variable band pass filters 12 (e.g., Butterworth filters; EEG Associates Mark 4×24) having variable gain controls. The 21 outputs of filters 12 are connected to 21 of the input terminals of two 16-channel, 12-bit analog-to-digital converters 15, 16 (Digital Equipment Corporation AA-11K), which comprise part of digital computer 13 (Digital Equipment Corporation PDP 11/60). Analog-to-digital converters 15, 16 are attached to data bus 14 (Digital Equipment Corporation Unibus). Also attached to data bus 14 are 4-channel, 12-bit digital-to-analog converter 17 (Digital Equipment Corporation AD-11K) whose three outputs control black and white television monitor 18 (Digital Equipment Corporation VR 17) for waveform displays; color display control 19 (Digital Equipment Corporation VSV 01) whose three outputs control 12″ color television monitor 20 (CONRAC) for topographic displays; 8 serial line controller 24 (Digital Equipment Corporation DZ 11) two outputs of which control interactive keyboard and video character display terminal 22 (Digital Equipment Corporation VT 100) and printer 23 (Digital Equipment Corporation LA 120); 256K byte memory 24 containing operating system software 27 (Digital Equipment Corporation RSX 11/M), BEAM software 28 (Agrippa Data Systems), and analytic software 29 (TICAS; University of Arizona); floating point processor 25 (Digital Equipment Corporation FPP-11); central processing unit 26 (Digital Equipment Corporation PDP 11/60); and disk controller 27 controlling at least one disk drive 28.

Software Description

In general, the brain electrical activity mapping system creates color topographic displays reflecting brain electrical activity using, as input, continuous electrical waveforms recorded from a number of points on the skull. The color topographic displays consist of discrete matrices of a large number of display points (also called pixels), each of which has a color or intensity or other visible characteristic which indicates a certain value or values at the location of that point analogous to a point on the skull. In order to generate discrete topographic display matrices having many thousands of display points from continuous analog waveforms at a limited, e.g. 20, number of points on the skull, the brain electrical activity mapping system, as illustrated in FIG. 2,

7

converts the data to digital form and generates discrete sample frames 40, each sample or frame initially comprising 20 recorded values 41 from 20 channels of information. The system treats related groups of samples 40 as segments 42. In the case of EP data, for example, a segment would consist of a series of frames or samples, each 4 milliseconds in length, the series together representing one transient response sequence from the beginning of a pre-stimulus period to the end of the post-stimulus transient response. In the case of steady-state EEG data, a segment would consist of 2 seconds of data divided into 256 samples. A spectral analysis of the EEG data then produces 256 samples, each of which reflects the energy level in a small, e.g. $\frac{1}{2}$ Hz, energy band and a segment consists of the entire series of 256 spectral samples. For signal averaging purposes, the system considers a set of segments together, e.g., 500 segments each representing a transient response to a given stimulus. The 500 segments taken together are known as an ensemble 43. Frames of data can be raw data or data which has been processed or transformed by the system. In any case, as illustrated in FIG. 3, when a frame 40 is to be displayed it is expanded into a matrix 45 consisting of a large number of display points 46 which are determined by an interpolation process from the original frame data points 47. Each point of the matrix is then converted to a visual display point 47 which forms part of the final topographic display 48.

FIG. 4 illustrates the organization of the operations which comprise brain electrical activity mapping software 28 and TICAS analytic software 29. Raw and processed data is stored in disk files 51. Operations 52–65 and 67–69 use data stored in files 51 to perform data manipulation, data display and data storage functions. Operations 54 and 55 also process data from the outputs of converters 15, 16.

FIG. 5 illustrates the function of define protocols operation 53. Protocol files 73 are generated and edited by program 'SETPAR' 71 based on control information 70 provided by the operator through terminal 22, the results of the operation being displayed (block 72) on terminal 22 to the operator. Each protocol file 73 contains information which governs the manner in which other operations are performed on a particular type of data file (e.g., one protocol might apply to the processing of EP transient response data from strobe light stimuli). The protocol information may include the number and identity of input channels, the labeling of the output channels to correspond to specific points on the final display, the identity of the trial marker channel, the voltage level above which to search for the trial markers, the rate in samples per second of sampling of the data, the number of samples in a segment, the number of segments in an ensemble, the number of ensembles, the number of points in a baseline, the microvolt level of the calibration signal (e.g., 100 microvolts at 10 Hz), a multiplication factor, the number (up to 20) and size (width) of integration bands, the label of the protocol, the percent of taper of samples in a segment of data for fast fourier transform processing, the number of automatic smoothing passes, the high and low values for automatic rejection of data during accumulation, the stimulus interval and location in seconds, and channel labels related to electrode positions on the skull.

FIG. 6 illustrates the function of disk data sampling operation 54. Program 'DATCOL' 75 loads raw data from the output of converters 15, 16 into raw data file 79, which is divided into 19 buffers 80 which hold en-

8

sembles of data related to particular brain states or stimuli. The operator provides control information 76 designating the patient to whom the data relates and the name of the applicable protocol file 73. Other control information 76 governs the beginning, end, and pauses in data sampling, and the performance of a calibration of signal levels. Calibration data is initially stored in a buffer 80 of raw data file 79. When the operator requests (block 76) a calibration, and designates which buffer 80 contains the raw calibration data, program 'DATCOL' computes the root mean square value and the mean of at least 30,000 points in each channel of calibration data and divides the root mean square value by 0.707 to establish the assumed peak value of the calibration signal. The peak value, representing the level of the original calibration voltage, and the mean value, representing the D.C. offset of the calibration voltage value for each channel, are stored in calibration file 78.

The format of raw data as stored in raw data file 79 is illustrated in FIG. 7. Each buffer 80 contains header block 81, having protocol and other housekeeping information concerning the data stored in the buffer; calibration block 82 containing for each channel of data the calibration value in microvolts per bit and the number of microvolts by which the calibration signal was offset from zero both of which values were found in calibration file 78 at the time raw data was loaded; bad segment block 83 identifying segments of data which the operator will later decide to exclude from subsequent operations; an unused segment 84; and a series of data segments 85, which hold a series of data samples, each containing values for all 20 channels. The data segments 85 are interleaved with no gaps.

FIG. 8 illustrates the function of core averaging operation 55, usually usef for loading and signal averaging raw EP transient responses. Data from converters 15, 16 is read by program 'CORAVG' 86. User provided control information 88 designates the protocol, obtained from protcol file 73, under which the operation is performed, and determines start, end, and pauses of the operation. Program 'CORAVG' 86 samples data beginning at points labeled by the prerecorded trial markers and forms signal averaged EP transient responses from a series of transient responses resulting from repetition of a stimulus. The series of transient response data are accumulated and held in EP file 87, which is a reduced data file as described below. Calibration file 78 holds calibration information accumulated from the data channels in the manner previously described. Program 'CORAVG' 86 automatically rejects as "bad data" any segment which contains values outside of preset limits. Program 'CORAVG' also automatically adjusts the zero baseline with respect to each electrode's average EP transiet response, by subtracting the mean of the pre-stimulus period values for a channel from each point in that channel's transient response curve.

FIG. 9 illustrates a plot of an average EP transient response 90 of microvoltage against time as it could be displayed on monitor 18 following core averaging operation 55. The stimulus was presented at time 93, the transient response includes pre-stimulus period between time 92 and time 93, and the plot shows calculated zero baseline 91.

FIG. 10 illustrates the function of raw data quality control operation 56, which enables the operator interactively to review and eliminate bad segments of raw data before other operations are performed. By means

4,408,616

9

of control information **94** the operator can select for review the contents of any buffer **80** in raw data file **79**. The buffer data is displayed (block **105**) segment by segment by program 'GLITCH' **95** on television monitor **18** to the operator as an analog waveform. The operator can label any segment of bad data, which causes the bad data segment to be identified on bad segment block **83**. Control information **94** can also include the insertion of trial markers indicating a point on a waveform at which subsequent operations should begin, and display to the operator the microvolt value of individual points on a displayed curve.

FIG. **11** illustrates raw data topographic display operation **57**, which provides topographic time sequenced displays (cartoons) of raw data frames. Program 'RAW-MOV' **96** expands the 20 channels of each data frame into a matrix of 128×128 data points by three-point linear interpolation. The operator provides control information **102** designating the disk buffer **80** on raw data file **79** which contains the data to be displayed; the number of display matrices to be produced; the parameters for interframe interpolation; and the parameters and options (described below) for scaling the data points among the available grey color tones of the display. Program 'RAWMOV' **96** calculates each interpolated data point for the display matrix using three-point linear interpolation from the three closest original channels and scales the data to the available grey color tones of the display. The interpolation is performed using preset coefficients stored in interpolation file **97** by an operation described below.

The display matrices produced by program 'RAW-MOV' **96** are stored in sequence in disk movie file **98**. Program 'RAWDIS' will display (block **101**) the frames stored in disk movie file **98** on monitor **20**. Control information **100** permits the operator to designate the file to be displayed, the frame rate, and the starting, stopping and reversing of the display sequence. The displays include labels of information taken from the protocol block, e.g., patient identification.

FIG. **12** illustrates the functions of create interpolation file operation **52**. Program 'POINTS' **110** creates points file **115** reflecting the X and Y coordinates of each point in the original electrode layout with respect to the 128×128 grid and associating with each point in the 128×128 display matrix the identity of the three original electrode points with respect to which it should be interpolated. Control information **120** provided by the operator includes the X and Y coordinates of each channel and the identity of the three interpolation points for each display point. Program 'OUTLINE' **111** identifies and stores in outline file **116** the X and Y coordinates of the points which outline the plan view of the skull to be included in the display, based on control information **121**. Program 'MAKCOF' **112** generates and stores in coefficient file **117** the coefficients needed to perform the three-point linear interpolation for each matrix display point within the skull outline, using points file **115** and outline file **116** as input. Program 'MAKOVR' **113** stores in overlay file **118** the operator provided (block **123**) coordinates of the overlay of the skull, nose and ears outline for the display. Program 'SETOVR' **114** generates interpolation file **119** from overlay file **118** and coefficient file **117**. Interpolation file **119** then contains the information required to compute interpolated matrix data points and the skull overlay for display.

10

FIG. **13** illustrates the function of the raw data reduction operation **58**. Three alternative programs can operate on data in buffers **80** to produce reduced data files **125**. Program 'DSKFFT' **126** accepts segments of EEG data from raw data file **79**, performs a fast fourier transform analysis which produces a new segment of data reflecting the spectral energy in each of a sequence of frequency bands. Program 'DSKFFT' **126** also generates, for each group of segments, an ensemble consisting of the sums (used in a later step to form the average values) and sums squared (used in a later step to form the standard deviations) for each channel across all segments in the group, values reflecting each of the sums as a percentage of the total spectral energy in the segment, and values reflecting the coefficient of variation (the standard deviation divided by the mean) for each channel across an ensemble. FIG. **15** illustrates the format of the resulting ensemble of FFT data stored in reduced data file **125**. The sums data **130** is filed in sequence by channel for the first frequency band **131**, e.g., 0.5 Hz. Similar sums data follows for the other frequency bands. After all sums data is stored, the sums squared data **132**, the normalized power spectral density sums, and the coefficient of variation data are stored in similar fashion. In addition to storing the sums and sums squared data for all segments in the ensemble, program 'DSKFFT' can store spectral information for each segment analyzed. As illustrated in FIG. **16**, the data is stored as sine and cosine coefficients for each channel for each frequency band, and as normalized sine and cosine coefficients as a percentage of total spectral energy. As illustrated in FIG. **18**, the FFt data file **191** stored on reduced data file **125** also includes a header block **192** housekeeping information.

In FIG. **13**, program 'DSKAVG' **127** performs a function similar to core averaging operation **55** in signal averaging EP transient response waveforms, but uses as input raw data stored in raw data file **79** and permits the operator to review each waveform and select those to be used in the averaging process, rejecting others. Program 'MANAVG' **128** permits a similar operator-assisted signal averaging process when the raw data does no contain preset stimulus trial markers, requiring the operator to indicate the point at which averaging is to begin for each waveform. FIG. **14** illustrates the format of signal averaged data produced by programs 'CORAVG' **86**, 'DSKAVG' **127** and 'MANAVG' **128**. The sums of each channel for all trials for the first time frame **133**, e.g., 0–4 milliseconds, are loaded in order, followed by similar information with respect to all subsequent time frames for a given segment. As illustrated in FIG. **17**, such EP files **190** are preceded by header block **193**.

FIG. **19** illustrates the function of reduced data quality control operation **59**, which permits the operator interactively to review and modify data in reduced data file **125**. By providing control information **204**, the operator can select the file to be reviewed and indicate whether it contains FFT spectral information or EP time-sequenced information. For FFT information, program 'FFTLUK' **201** displays (block **202**) selected channels of spectral data as frequency-voltage curves on monitor **18** and permits the operator to low-pass filter the waveforms and display the value of particular data points. For EP data, program 'EPLUK' **203** displays (block **202**) selected channels as time-voltage curves and permits the operator to reset the zero baseline, to filter high frequency noise from a channel, and

4,408,616

11

to display the value of any point on a curve. FIG. 20 illustrates the function of manual baseline relocation. Because pre-stimulus period response 180 was not level, automatic baseline 176 set by program 'CORAVG' 86 inaccurately reflects the true zero level for transient response curve 175. The operator can relocate the baseline to a new level 177 by moving cursor 179 to the desired level, causing that voltage value to be subtracted from each point of data along curves 180 and 175.

FIG. 21 illustrates the functions of reduced data topographic display operation 60. For single frame display of FFt data, program 'FFTTVM' 206 reads data from reduced data file 125 as selected by operator control information 214. The data is scaled in accordance with instructions included in control information 214. The selected frame is provided to program 'TVM16' 213 which interpolates a matrix of 128 × 128 points using the coefficients and other information contained in interpolation file 97, and provides the resulting matrix to color display 212. For single frame EP display, program 'EPTVM' 205 performs an analogous process to that of program 'FFTTVM' 206. Programs 'EPTVM' 205 and 'FFTTVM' 206 also perform compilations of sequences of frames into one display matrix, in accordance with predefined groupings set forth in protocol blocks.

A sequence of FFT matrices or EP matrices can be displayed in rapid time sequence as a cartoon by the use of program 'FFTMOV' 208 and program 'EPMOV' 207, respectively, each of which processes sequences of selected matrices of data from reduced data file 125, using scaling control information 215; interpolates full 128 > 128 matrices for each frame; interpolates a selected number of additional matrices between the original frames; and stores the resulting matrices in movie file 211. Based on control information 216 specifying data to be displayed, the frame rate of display, start, stop, backward, forward and pause, program 'FFTDIS' 210 and program 'EPDIS' 209 provide cartooned matrices for viewing on color display 212.

FIG. 22 illustrates group file production operation 61. Program 'GRPBLD' 221 creates and updates a composite group file 223 working from selected individual reduced data files 125. Control information 222 provided by the operator indicates the identity of individual reduced data files to be included. The group files 223 consist of the sums and the sums squared for all homologous points in the reduced data files 125 of all individuals in the group. Normalized sums and coefficients of variation may also be produced and stored. Hard copy 224 listing the individuals in each group and the values of group file data are available based on control information 222.

FIG. 23 illustrates the function of group topographic data display operation 62 which is analogous to the operation of the single frame display of reduced data file information, illustrated in FIG. 21, except that the data displayed is from group file 223 instead of reduced data file 125.

FIG. 24 illustrates the function of individual versus group comparison operation 63. Programs 'EPTVM' 205 and 'FFTTVM' 206 are performed respectively on EP and FTT data. In each case, the program generates a frame of points, each of which is the number of standard deviations (z-statistics) by which an individual's point, taken from individual file 226 differs from the average of the group's corresponding points taken from group file 223. The resulting frame is displayed (block

12

216) by program 'TVM16' 213, which interpolates additional data points to form a 128 × 128 matrix in the manner previously described.

FIG. 25 illustrates the function of group difference detection and feature selection operation 64, which computes frames of t-statistics reflecting the level of statistical difference between two groups based on the means and standard deviations of homologous data points for the two groups. Program 'GRPCMP' 230 computes t-statistics and degrees of freedom from the sums and sums squared data contained in two different group files 223 designated in control information 231 provided by the operator. The resulting frames are stored in group comparison file 232. Based on file and frame designations set forth by the operator in control information 235, program 'GRPDIS' 234 transmits a selected statistic frame for display by program 'TVM16' 213 as previously deascribed. Program 'TVM16' 213 also returns a fully expanded 128 × 128 matrix back to program 'GRPDIS' 234. Through control information 235, the operator may store such a t-statistic matrix in saved frame file 233. FIG. 26 illustrates the format of saved frame file 233. Header block 240 contains the number of saved frames, and for each frame identifies the time frame length or frequency band and the protocol under which the data was collected. Frames 241 contain 128 × 128 matrices of floating point t-statistics generated by program 'GRPDIS' 234.

FIG. 27 illustrates the functions of the brain electrical activity mapping to TICAS file transfer operation 65, which converts features of brain electrical activity mapping data to a form usable with TICAS software 29. Program 'FEADEF' 245 generates feature list file 247 from feature definitions and names of saved frame files 234 provided by the operator in control information 246. Program 'FEAGET' 248 then generates TICAS formal file 249 from reduced data files 125, saved frame file 233, and feature list file 247, identified by the operator in control information 250. The feature definitions which may be selected and stored in TICAS format file 249 for subsequent TICAS analysis include nearly all combinations of data found in all individual files, all combinations of integrated bands of frames (e.g., alpha bands) in individual files grouped according to preset protocol specifications, or combinations of individual frame files weighted by the values in a saved t-statistic frame.

FIG. 28 illustrates the functions of TICAS feature selection and evaluation operation 67. In control information 266, 264 the operator designates two groups 262, 263 from TICAS format file 249 whose features are to be analyzed, the type of data to be analyzed, and the number of input features to be analyzed, and the number of output features to be produced. Program 'UTEST' 261 peforms a standard two-sample Wilcox-Mann-Whitney U-test and provides a list of U-test scores in rank order which are printed on printer 23 and stored. Program 'FMTST' 260 performs a final merit value (FMV) test and provides and stores a list of values for features in order of final merit values. Program 'FMTST' 260 first determines intermediate merit values as a combination of the standard receiver operating characteristic (ROC) curve or d' value and the results of an ambiguity function analysis. The final merit values for each feature are then determined by correlation of the intermediate merit value with all features ranked higher in intermediate value. Program 'MERGE' 267 selects from Group

4,408,616

<table>
<tr><td>13</td><td>14</td></tr>
</table>

A features 268 and group B features 269, based on the FMV values and U values, those features which are most useful, which are then stored in disk files 270 and 271.

FIG. 29 illustrates the functions of TICAS generate discision rules operation 68. Program 'SLPRT' 275 uses an operator controlled (block 278) subset of selected Group A features 276 and selected Group B features 277 to generate disk stored interim rules 279, by a method controlled (block 278) by the operator. The computation method may be a non-parametric d-selection technique, a parametric classification technique, or a combination of the two. Program 'CLSFY' 284 uses operator selected (block 285) interim rules 279 to classify operator selected subjects having operator selected features, from selected group features files 280 or refined group features files 281, 282, printing the results on printer 23, thereby permitting the operator to evaluate the efficacy of each selected interim rule 279. Progran 'DSC' 286 combines operator chosen (289) features from selected Group A features 287 and selected Group B features 288 into new features on the basis of the weighting functions of a standard linear discriminate analysis, subject to the operator's choice (group 289) of discriminant function parameters. Discriminant function weights for the best features are then loaded into a disk file 290. Program 'LINCOM B' 293 uses the original selected Group A features 291 and selected Group B features 292 and the discriminate function weights 29 to create refined Group A features 294 and refined Group B features 295, which are linear or other operator selected (block 296) combinations of the original features. Refined Group A features 294 and refined Group B features 295 can replace the original selected features 276 and 277 as input to program 'SLPRT' 275 to permit an iterative process of decision rule generation.

FIG. 30 illustrates test decision rules operation 69. Program 'CLSFY' 284 uses final sets of decision rules, e.g., rules A 304 and rules B 305, to classify individuals in original Group A 300, original Group B 301 and new unknown groups, e.g., Group C 302 and Group D 303, to determine the efficacy of the final decision rules, the results being provided on printer 23.

Operation

Data Gathering

Accumulation of raw EEG and EP data is accomplished by first attaching 20 electrodes 5 to the scalp of an individual subject in a conventional international 10–20 format. In other embodiments, information from between 10 and 200 electrodes can be gathered and analyzed. Before recording, and if desired during recording, the operator observes the signal levels on the 20 channels of chart recording of polygraph 10 and adjusts the gain on weak signals to produce usable waveforms. A calibration signal of 100 microvolts (10 Hz) from source 8 is recorded on all twenty channels on tape recorder 11 at the beginning of each session and whenever any of the gain levels on polygraph 10 is adjusted.

Data gathering typically begins with a careful administration of a sequence of tests, each of which is intended to establish a particular steady-state electrical condition in the subject's brain. The sequence of tests usually includes instructions to relax and remain still with eyes open, to relax and remain still with eyes closed, to become drowsy, to breathe deeply for hyper-

ventilation, to listen to music and to listen to speech. Other tests rewquire the subject to (1) listen carefully to a story and answer simple questions about its content when completed, (2) remember a set of six abstract figures (often resembling an unknown language alphabet) in black ink on index cards presented by the examiner, (Kimura Figures-Instruction) (3) select the six previously presented figures from a set of 38 figures, verbally indicating yes or no (Kimura Figures-Test), (4) associate each of four abstract figures on index cards with a particular artificial name spoken by the examiner (Paired Associates-Instruction), (5) name each of the four abstract figures when tested by the examiner (Paired Associates-Test), (6) read silently three previously unread paragraphs (e.g., example text from the Gray Oral Reading Test) so as to answer questions subsequently (Reading Test-Instruction), (7) identify whether 34 typed sentences presented by the examiner were previously included in the three paragraphs (Reading Test-Test), and (8) read text upside down: The tests are designed to permit recording of brain electrical signals during simple resting brain activity and during different levels of activation of the left hemisphere, the right hemisphere and both hemispheres of the brain together. This permits the demonstration of pathologies present at rest and those present upon brain activation. The development of specific tests and the choice of tests is determined by the user based in part on the subject being tested and the information eing sought as described in greater detail below. Between twenty seconds and three minutes of steady state brain electrical activity is recorded on all 20 channels during each of the tests. Appropriate records of the tape location of each test are kept. These tests have been used with the brain electrical activity mapping system to demonstrate group differences between normal subjects and those with dyslexia or specific reading disability at the 10–12 year age level and at the six-year age level; to differentiatedemented patients from normals and aged patients from younger patients in clinical settings; to identify patients with an organic basis for sociopathic behavior and other forms of mental illness; to demonstrate epilepsy when the resting background EEG failed to show any abnormalities; to demonstrate abnormalities in EEg and EP data for schizophrenic subjects; and to determine when a brain tumor, previously treated, is about to recur.

With young infants, the brain states tested include sleep, alert and attending to visual and auditory stimuli, alert but not attending to visual and auditory information, and drowsiness. Using these states, it is possible to discriminate among children with poor behavioral scores on a psychological test and those with high psychological scores.

A series of sensory evoked potential (EP) transient responses are then recorded from all electrodes while the subject is repeatedly exposed to a selected stimulus, e.g., a strobe light or a click generator or to a predetermined sequence of two alternate stimuli. Because the EP transient response is weak compared to the background steady-state brain electrical activity, the stimulus must be presented many times (e.g., 500) to the subject for later signal averaging. The total response period of interest is typically 1024 milliseconds, comprising 512 milliseconds before stimulus and 512 milliseconds after stimulus. The process is repeated for different stimuli.

4,408,616

15

Stimuli presented to the subject can range from simple flash, simple click, simple pattern reversal and simple somatosensory stimulation to those requiring complex decisions. Requiring a subject to discriminate between subtly different auditory stimuli (e.g., the words "tight" and "tyke") is useful in diagnosing dyslexia. This procedure is known as the Tight-Tyke evoked potential phenomic discrimination test. Picking an infrequently different stimulus from among other more frequent stimuli is useful in evaluating subjects who have functional brain disorder.

Auditory stimuli generate a set of fast and a set of slow transient responses. The fast responses eminate from the brainstem and have a typical duration of 20 milliseconds. Brainstem responses are normally sampled for a total response period of 40 milliseconds comprising 20 milliseconds before stimulus and 20 milliseconds after stimulus. Filters 12 are adjusted to exclude frequencies below 300 Hz and to include frequencies up to 8000 Hz.

When EP transient responses from such stimuli are averaged to eliminate noise, two types of interference can occur. The first type, known as contingent negative variation (CNV), relates to the connection made by the brain between consecutive equally spaced stimuli when the subject is told to count the stimuli. The D.C. component of the resulting transient response shows a gentle dip and a sharp rise immediately before each stimulus, attributable to the subject's anticipation of the next stimulus. The sharp rise contaminates the evoked potential transient response and makes it difficult to establish a zero baseline. By including as part of the interval between stimuli a first pseudorandom time element which varies from 0 to a period longer than the post-stimulus response and is also a multiple of the wavelength of the interfering frequency described below, the CNV effect is greatly reduced.

The second type of interference results from the existence of background noise at certain characteristic frequencies, e.g., 10 Hz, which reflect prominent bands of steady-state brain wave activity. The major interfering frequency of a given subject may be determined by a spectral analysis of his background EEG signal. The interference problem is especially significant in adults with prominent alpha waves and children with prominent slow brain wave activity. By including in the time interval between stimuli a second pseudorandom time element whose period varies from zero to the wavelength of the major interfering frequency, the background noise can be substantially reduced in the averaging process.

The inclusion of a prestimulus period of recoding for each transient response permits an accurate baseline determination at a later stage of signal processing in order to establish a true zero level for the post-stimulus response and permits a determination of the quality of the signal averaging process.

Pseudorandom stimulus controller 9 measures the interval between stimuli as a combination of the post-stimulus response period, the first pseudorandom period described above, the second pseudorandom period described above, and the pre-stimulus response period.

As illustrated in FIG. 31, pseudorandom stimulus controller 9 comprises a four-stage timer, each stage of which in turn measures one of the four periods included in the interval between stimuli. The first stage comparator 406 measures the pre-stimulus period p_1/f_{c1} where P_1 is a number preset by the operator in register 408 and

16

f_{c1} is the frequency set on variable frequency clock 404. When the first stage timing is completed, the second stage times the post-stimulus period as P_2/f_{c2} where P_2 is a number preset in register 414 and f_{c2} is the preset frequency on clock 410. At the end of the first stage timing period, a stimulus trial marker (5 volt spike) is recorded on the trial marker channel of tape recorder 11 and stimulus 409 is triggered. The selected post-stimulus period is long enough to permit a full decay of the transient response being observed. At the end of the second stage timing period, the third stage measures the first pseudorandom time period P_3/f_{c3}, where P_3 is the next pseudorandom number in programmable read only memory (PROM) 419 and f_{c3} is the preset frequency of variable clock 415. PROM 419 has been preloaded with a pseudorandom sequence of numbers. At the end of the third stage timing, the fourth stage measures a second pseudorandom period in an analogous manner based on a pseudorandom sequence in PROM 424 and a preset frequency on clock 420. When the fourth stage timing period is over, a pseudorandom trial marker (5 volt spike) is recorded on the trial marker channel of recorder 11. A new timing cycle is then completed and the process is reiterated until the total number of transient responses recorded equals a preset number in register 426 or the process is stopped by the operator. The entire process is begun by pushing button 401, which causes the recording of a pre-stimulus trial marker. Temporary delay button 431 can be used to temporarily delay the continued operation of the timer at the operator's discretion, as for example when the subject is distracted in a manner which would render the transient response useless. A low order bit in PROM 424 or PROM 419 can be set to 0 or 1 by the operator for each number loaded into PROM 24 or PROM 19 so that two different stimuli (e.g., auditory and visual) can be triggered in a preselected order or pattern, with one stimuli being presented more frequently than the other.

The result of the recording session is an analog tape of raw EEG and EP voltage data and calibration voltages on 20 channels with trial markers on a twenty-first channel. The next step is to load the data into computer 13.

As previously described, brain electrical activity mapping software 28 performs data collection, data manipulation, and data display functions in accordance with central information provided by the operator. The various operations can be performed in any sequence and the operator can perform a series of functions iteratively. The operator provides control information through the keyboard of terminal 22 and receives information concerning the various operations on printer 23, waveform monitor 18 and topographic color monitor 20. The flexibility of operation heightens the system's utility as a diagnostic and analytical tool.

Data Loading

Under operator control, EEg data for each brain state and related calibration signals are loaded directly onto disk storage from recorder 11 after passing through filters 12 set to pass frequency components between 0.5 and 50 Hz or between 0.5 and 1000 Hz and epileptic spike data. Gain controls on the filters are adjusted to fully utilize the signal capacity of converters 15, 16. EEG data can be sampled at rates as high as 20,000 samples per second.

Under operator control, EP data is passed through filters 12 set to eliminate frequencies above a selected

4,408,616

17

frequency of between 40 and 100 Hz, or below 300 Hz for brainstem data, and is signal averaged in core memory using core averaging operation 55, which automatically rejects bad data and sets the zero baseline.

Typically EP data is sampled every 4 milliseconds, or every microseconds for brainstem analysis, and 256 sampled are taken, 128 pre-stimulus and 128 post-stimulus. If the operator determines that the EP transient response data is very noisy, he may alternatively record the data as raw data and use raw data reduction operation 58 to average only selected transient response trials. In cases where the transient response data may not contain the necessary stimulus trial markers, such as in recordings of rapid eye movement (REM) sleep, the data can similarly be recorded as raw data and trial markers can be added manually by the operator, using raw data operation 58, before signal averaging is done.

Raw Data Quality Control and Display

To assure the maximum accuracy and utility of raw data, the operator can, using raw data quality control operations 56, display recorded waveforms, accept or reject each waveform for later processing, have mathematical smoothing operations performed, reset baselines or eliminate certain points of data.

The operator views the EP transient responses for the 20 channels for the purpose of evaluating the utility of each curve and specifying modifications which will improve their utility when displayed. The operator may direct a further adjustment of the baseline, which has already been set automatically, by having a constant number added to or subtracted from the value in each frame, or can determine to have the automatic baseline determination redone using a smaller number of the later pre-stimulus frames as the baseline. This procedure is particularly useful when the early pre-stimulus frames are found to contain the tail end of the transient response of the prior stimulus. By reviewing the relative levels of V_{RMS} (pre-stimulus) and V_{RMS} (post-stimulus) for a given channel, the operator can determine whether the background noise level is unacceptably large with respect to the transient response, necessitating another recording session with the subject. The operator may also filter any high frequency noise in the post-stimulus period by three-point interpolation.

As part of the raw data quality control process, if a channel contains spurious values (e.g., voltage spikes) in particular frames, the operator can eliminate those values and substitute values interpolated from the next prior and next later frames. If the voltage levels on one channel are substantially higher than for the other channels, the operator can flag that channel to indicate that the channel should be excluded from the subsequent display scaling procedure (described below). Based on the operator's instructions, the automatic baseline determination may be redone and the results are viewed again until the operator is satisfied that the set of transient responses contain satisfactorily low noise levels and are properly zeroed.

Raw data topographic display operation 57 enables the operator to display a cartoon series of topographic maps of raw data, which has been expanded by interpolation into a matrix of 128×128 points. The cartoon can be started or stopped and run forward or reversed at will. When raw EEG data is to be cartooned, the operator can sample the data at a high rate, e.g., 400 frames per second, and then display the information at slower speed or in a series of matrices, each of which is an

18

average of a sequence of frames. The averaging can be done on a running basis, so that the first N frames are averaged and displayed, then the N frames beginning with the second frame are averaged and displayed, and so on.

EEG Data Reduction

Raw EEG data is converted to spectral data using the fast Fourier transform process of raw data operation 58, as previously described. The segments of raw EEG curves whose spectral data is averaged are generally about 2 seconds in length each, which is shorter than the average period between spurious artifact signals. Typically from 15 to 90 segments are spectrally analyzed and the spectra averaged. The spectra usually consist of 128 frequency bands of $\frac{1}{2}$ Hz in width covering the spectrum from 0 to 64 Hz. The ends of each segment can be tapered in accordance with the operator's discretion in connection with the Fourier transform process.

Reduced Data Quality Control and Topographic Display

Working with reduced EP and EEG data, that is sequences of time frames of transient response data and groups of spectral band data, the operator can use reduced data quality control operation 59 to view the waveforms, discard bad data reflecting movement artifact, eye blink, or muscle activity and eliminate high frequency noise. The reduced data can then be topographically displayed on a frame by frame or cartooned basis using the reduced data topographic display operation 60. In either case, the operator can form frames which represent combinations of underlying frames. For example, groups of $\frac{1}{2}$ Hz bandwidth frames can be combined into larger bandwidth frames corresponding with typical spectra of clinical interest, e.g., alpha, beta, delta and theta. Bands of any desired width can be formed. In addition to displaying raw spectral energy information from EEG data, it is possible to display normalized spectral energy in which the points on each display are normalized to the overall spectral energy of each electrode or to the average overall spectral energy at all electrodes. In the case of EP data, it is similarly possible to display each point as a normalized value to the value at one specific electrode, e.g., the vertex electrode designated "C_z", or to a standardized value, or to a selected value, or to the V_{RMS} of the background activity at each electrode, or to the V_{RMS} of all electrodes. Similarly, the 128 frames of an EP transient response can be grouped into frames of greater time duration for display.

Group Data Analysis

By accumulating a number of stored data frames, it is possible for the operator to assemble and display group data files using group file production operation 61 and group topographic data display operation 62.

Significance Probability Mapping (SPM)

Using stored data for various groups and individuals, the operator can perform and display topographically t-statistic comparisons between groups of frames and z-statistic comparisons between an individual frame and a group of frames. Any other statistical group comparison can also be used to form a display matrix to illustrate group differences. This type of analysis, significance probability mapping (SPM), enables the operator

19   4,408,616   **20**

to identify significant brain activity features related to various neurophysiological illnesses and conditions.

Grid Sector Analysis

Frames produced by the SPM procedure may be further analyzed by a Grid Sector Analysis (GSA). While the frames produced by the SPM procedure reflect regional abnormalities, the GSA procedure produces numerical measures of the degree of global or focal deviations from normal, which can assist in automatic determination of the existence of regional abnormalities in unknown subjects.

The first step of the GSA process conceptually requires the division of a frame into a number of different grids, each divided into sectors of a uniform size. Within each grid sector, the mean of all values of the data points lying within the sector is determined as the value of that sector. The process is repeated for grids of different fineness. Preferably three grids, of 4000 sectors, 64 sectors, and 16 sectors respectively, are used. Histograms of sector values are then prepared for each grid reflecting sector t-statistic or z-statistic values on the horizontal axis and numbers of sectors having that value on the vertical axis for each grid. Various analyses of the histrograms, which differ for focal and global abnormalities, will indicate whether an abnormality is focal, i.e., localized in one area, or global, i.e., diffused over a large part of the brain. One such analysis would simply be the observation that the peak number of sectors for the coarser grids will be at lower z or t values in the case of a global abnormality than in the case of a focal abnormality.

In the case of focal abnormalities, there is a marked difference in the histograms for the three grids, while in the case of global abnormalities, there is little or no difference for the three grids. A variety of features can be developed from the histograms to serve as possible diagnostic rules. The maximum z-value for each grid, the maximum amount of asymmetry between homologous grid regions, the mean asymmetry between homologous grid regions, and the difference between the absolute values of the sum of all left hemisphere and all right hemisphere values. Also, one can calculate the number of regions above certain criterion levels for each histogram.

A group of spectral maps or a series of EP responses can be analyzed as an ensemble by forming at each matrix point the mean of the values of each map in the ensemble. The grid region on each individual map showing the largest value is given a score of 4, the next largest a score of 2, the third largest a score of 1, and the rest a score of 0. The scores are then summed by region across all maps in the ensemble, and the regions having the three largest scores and their sum are stored as indications of focal features. The same process is repeated for the three regions having the greatest asymmetries in each image between corresponding grid sectors. The resulting information can serve as features which can be processed using TICAS to develop diagnostic rules to classify unknown subjects between a group of normals and a group having a particular dysfunction. The numerical descriptors generated by GSA, when used for statistical analysis are approximately as successful in the identification of patients with brain tumors as visual inspection of EEG data by expert clinicians.

Coefficient of Variation Analysis

Given an ensemble of segments of data, the operator can determine the mean and the standard deviation of each point across the segments. By displaying the standard deviations as percentages of mean at each point, the coefficient of variation (C/V) across the skull can be observed topographically. The normal expect range of C/V values is 40–60% and deviations from that range are immediately evident from the displays. The C/V display is useful in demonstrating head regions where there are wide variations in activity, e.g., epileptogenic regions.

Difference Maps

A display matrix can be formed to represent at each point, the difference in value of corresponding points on two underlying frames. This permits, for example, displays which suggest the regions of the brain activated by patterned light, by comparing the frames corresponding to plain light stimulation and to patterned light stimulation.

Automatic Diagnostic Rules

Working from significant brain activity features and using TICAS-related operations 65, 67, 68 and 69, the operator can develop and test diagnostic rules for accurately classifying unknown subjects between normal and abnormal groups.

Scaling

Several of the available BEAM system operations produce color topographic displays. Video monitor displays typically involve assigning to each point on the display a grey tone of color which represents the value of the point. Sixteen tones of color represent 16 different graduated values. For example, red can be used for positive values and blue can be used for negative values with the grey tone of blue or red indicating the level of positive or negative value. An absence of color represents zero. In order to maximize the visual effectiveness of the display, it is desirable to scale the values of the data points to the available color tone levels in such a way that the useful variations in value are spread among the maximum range of color tones. The scaling can be done according to a variety of options. The data points can be scaled so that the maximum absolute value of the data points over a set of matrices will be equivalent to the maximum positive and negative color tones and all other points will be scaled linearly to the intermediate color tones. Scaling can be done from zero to the maximum absolute value. The same scaling technique can be accomplished with one or more channels excluded by the operator from the scaling process so that unusually high value data points will not skew the scaling process. Scaling can be done on a matrix by matrix basis rather than across a group of matrices. Scaling can be done to a maximum value chosen by the operator. In the scaling process, any data value which is larger than the brightest available grey color will be truncated and displayed as that brightest color.

Three-Point Linear Interpolation

Since the data frames to be presented for display originally contain a relatively small number of points, e.g., 20 points, and the display is preferably of a continuous matrix of 128×128 points, expansion of the data by some form of interpolation is required. The expansion is

4,408,616

21 22

accomplished by three-point linear interpolation, in which each display point is determined as a sum of the values of the three nearest data points on the original data frame, each multiplied by a predetermined coefficient which reflects the precise location of the display point. As an alternative to the software previously described, the calculation of the display point can be done on hardware having an extremely short processing time, making possible "real-time" displays, that is, each display matrix is calculated in a time shorter than the display time for each display matrix. A detailed description of the three-point interpolation technique is contained in U.S. patent application Ser. No. 221,830 (hereby incorporated by reference).

Display Features; Multidimensional Display

As illustrated in FIG. 32, the each topographic display comprises an outline of the skull with an indication of its orientation with respect to the ears and nose. All display points outside the outline are suppressed. Within the skull outline are displayed the grid of data points, each of which reflects a value or values for that point on the skull. The number of dimensions of information which may be represented by a given point varies with the display method. Frequently only one dimension of information is presented at any point in the form of a grey-tone of color on a predetermined grey-tone scale. Alternatively additional dimensions may be reflected at a point as a unique combination of three colors. Three dimensions can be represented by the quantity of each of the original colors which is mixed into the combination and a fourth dimension could be the lightness or darkness of the three. In this manner, for example, spectral EEG data for four frequency bands of brain activity could be displayed simultaneously. A detailed description of this four-dimensional display is contained in U.S. patent application Ser. No. 221,830.

Whenever displays are cartooned, the operator may select the frame rate of display from stationary to ten frames per second minimum. The cartoon can also be displayed legarithmically with time, so that the later matrices are displayed in faster sequence then the earlier ones, which visually compensates for the fact that more EP response information is available just after the stimulus than toward the end of the response period.

Examples of System Use

The brain electrical activity mapping system offers a powerful brain diagnostic and research tool by permitting immediate video display of information about steady-state brain waves, EP transient responses, spectral analyses of EEG signals, and statistical information based on these types of data, and the ability to develop diagnostic rules from selected features of data. The following examples illustrate the versatility and utility of the system.

Suspected Epilepsy

Although the "spike and wave" as seen on routine EEG graphs is virtually diagnostic of epilepsy, over 10% of all true epileptics fail to demonstrate this abnormality. Use of special electrodes, sleep studies, and activating drugs often fails to produce spikes in true epileptics. This means that although an epileptic may have brain cortex that is capable of demonstrating sufficient irritability at times to produce a seizure, that at other times it fails to be sufficiently irritative to produce a spike on the EEG and thus eludes diagnosis. Topographic display is of great assistance in such situations. Such suspected epileptic patients should have eyes open (EO) and eyes closed (EC) topographic studies performed. Irritative cortex presents itself as focal increases of activity over all frequency bands, especially the high frequency beta bands. The visual evoked EP response (VER) topographic study should also be performed. Irritative cortex leads to focal increases of both positive and negative waves. If the epilepsy is associated with an atrophic lesion, a region of reduced EEG and EP activity may be found in close association with the focal irritability.

When spikes are found, displays of their topographic extent are extremely useful in determining their point of origin. In this case, raw EEG data is displayed in cartoon form thus delineating the epileptic dipole.

Suspected Supratentorial Brain Lesion

Patients are often referred for EEG tests in order to rule in or out a lesion of one or both cerebral hemispheres. This includes tumor, stroke, abscess, atrophy, arterio-venous malformation, congenital malformation, hemorrhage, regional encephalitis. These subjects should be subjected to topographic studies in the eyes open and eyes closed brain states, and for the VER and bilateral somotosensory evoked response (BSER) EP situations. In general these lesions may be recognized by the pattern of hypo- or hyperactive cortex that become visible on the brain electrical activity mapping images. For example, tumors show decrease in activity early, excessive activities later, and reduced activity at the vertex. Brain electrical activity mapping greatly adds to the information obtained by radiographic scanning as it is sensitive to the functional disturbances produced by these lesions which usually extend beyond the anatomical limits of the lesion.

To pinpoint abnormalities the technique of significance probability mapping (SPM) should be used. Furthermore, quantification of a lesion by grid sector analysis (GSA) is often useful.

Brain electrical activity mapping is most useful when tests must be applied to a large population for screening purposes or repeatedly to a single person. Such uses would include screening for tumor and stroke, determining whether a lesion is increasing or decreasing, and assessing the effects of treatment on a lesion. Brain electrical activity mapping is completely non-invasive, and not dangerous as radiographic techniques would be in such circumstances. There is also evidence that many lesions produce electrical (functional) disturbances before they can be detected by radiographic means.

Suspected Learning Disabilities

Brain electrical activity mapping studies are most useful in the elucidation of regional abnormalities of brain activity found in dyslexia, hyperactivity, dyscalculia, and combinations of the above. For example, dyslexia reveals abnormalities not just in the classic left temporal lobe speech areas but in the medial frontal lobe bilaterally. To demonstrate these abnormalities, one needs to perform the full test battery which includes: right hemispheric activating tests (the Kimura Figures task and listening to music as described elsewhere); left hemispheric activating (listening to speech and reading Grey Oral passages as described elsewhere); and bi-hemispheral tests (Paired Associates test and the Tight-Tyke evoked potential phenomic discrimination test as described elsewhere).

Automated classification tests to discriminate among these clinical entities can be developed.

Emotional Dysfunction

Many forms of emotional disorder can be caused by the lesions mentioned above. Brain electrical activity mapping can be more useful in the recognition of covert pathology in this patient population than radiographic techniques. In addition, certain forms of psychopathology have recognizable brain electrical activity mapping signatures. For example sociopathic behavior is associated with lack of synchrony between the frontal lobes; e.g., the VER may show different electrical polarity between the right and left frontal lobes. Schizophrenia shows markedly increased EEG slow activity overlying the frontal regions. In this group of subjects, the eyes open and eyes closed EEG and VER studies are most useful.

Infant Competence

Discrimination between babies at risk for future learning and emotional problems is a frequent clinical request. Brain electrical activity mapping has proven useful in accomplishing such discrimination. In addition to studying the EEG and VER in stages 1 and 2 sleep, the EEG should be studied while the babies are brought into the alert state and maintained there as discussed elsewhere. Less competent babies, for example, show paradoxical increases in frontal delta slowing as they are alerted.

Suspected Dementia

Senile and pre-senile dementia represent a major problem for gerontologists and neurologists. Radiograpic evidence of brain abnormality may not be found until the clinical symptom complex is well established. On the other hand, brain electrical activity mapping studies demonstrate early abnormalities in a non-invasive manner. The best battery of tests is similar to those described above for suspected learning disabilities, but generally the tight-tyke EP is replaced by another EP where the subject must discriminate between frequently and infrequently heard tone pips of differing frequency. A difference EP between the response to the two different tone pips is produced. The topographic display of the difference EP shows a marked reduction in dementia and may be used to follow the course of dementia and the response of dementia to pharmacotherapies.

Headache

Headache may be caused by many factors. Brain electrical activity mapping is very useful to screen out serious lesions of the types described as supratentorial lesions above. The specific syndrome of migraine headache has a frequently seen pattern on brain electrical activity mapping of excessive 8–11 Hz occipital oscillations and excessive occipital activity. It is best to use the EO and EC EEG and VER for headache. Occasionally the BSEP is useful.

Comparison of Individual to Group

As described above, the brain electrical activity mapping system is generally able to compare an individual statistically to a group and display the result topographically. In a clinical setting, the individual in question, who may have displayed a normal CT scan, is compared to an age matched/sex matched group of normals, and abnormalities are then displayed in color-

mapped form, wherein bright colors show high abnormality and dull colors show insignificant abnormality. This technique provides an effective diagnostic tool.

Comparisons of Groups; Automatic Diagnosis Rules

The result of a group comparision under the system is a topographic display of statistical difference expressed as t-statistics, which when coupled with the number of degrees of freedom available in the calculation, produce a probability level of significant difference between two groups at a particular brain state. For instance, a group of normals could be compared to a group of schizophrenics by the creation of t-statistic displays with respect to a variety of brain states and stimuli. The user looks for displays which exhibit high degrees of coherence and statistical difference. This is normally shown on a screen in color. The larger statistical differences appear as brighter colors. The degree to which the differences are focused at particular points or diffused over the skull is also apparent. Smoothness in the lines dividing areas of different brightness suggests focused differences, while diffuse differences are suggested by ragged edges between dim and bright areas. It is possible for the researcher, upon selection of a particular map that shows something interesting, to save the matrix for later analysis. Such a saved matrix of t-statistics can be used to non-linearly weight the underlying data frames to create features which can be analyzed using TICAS. Once a set of saved frames representing group difference information is accumulated, he then converts all of the saved information, representing features which tend to distinguish the two groups into a file format which is suitable for analysis by TICAS, which is a multi-variate classification system, publicly available from the University of Arizona, courtesy of Dr. Peter H. Bartell.

TICAS is designed to sift through all of the features saved in the course of the inter-group analysis and pick those which prove to be the most discerning mathematically to produce a set of features which succinctly allows automatic diagnosis of a patient.

This procedure has been used to successfully discriminate between normal subjects and those with dyslexia, to discriminate between normal subjects and those with supertentorial brain tumor, and to discriminate between subjects with exposure to organophosphate compounds and nonexposed controls.

Dyslexia Analysis

An article, *Dyslexia Regional Differences in Brain Electrical Activity by Topographic Mapping*, Duffy et al. (Annals of Neurology, Vol. 7, No. 5, May, 1980), hereby incorporated by reference, describes the use of the brain electrical activity mapping system to identify the parts of the brain whose electrical activity differs for individuals suffering from reading disability (dyslexia) as compared with normal individuals, and to establish objective standards for diagnosing dyslexia. The previously described battery of brain state tests were administered to a dyslexic group and a control group. Visual and auditory stimuli were repeatedly presented to both groups and recorded with the appropriate trial markers. The stimuli were offered in pseudorandom fashion. Using the brain electrical activity mapping system, topographic displays of the alpha (8 to 11.75 Hz) and theta (4 to 7.75 Hz) activity at each electrode for each tested brain state for each subject were produced. Similar cartoons of 128 frames (4 milliseconds each) were prepared for each type of EP response for each subject. The resulting brain state frames and EP response frames for the dyslexic group and the control group were then averaged to form mean frames of each group for each state and stimulus. The two groups of mean images were then compared using the t-statistic function. A further transformation produced a matrix of percentile index values (PI) whose value is related inversely to t-values. The PI values permit a graphic localization of regions of maximum difference between the dyslexic group and the control group. By topographically displaying the PI matrices for alpha and theta for each brain state and for each EP stimulus, it was possible to identify the brain regions which differed between the dyslexics and the controls. As a final step, a new display matrix was formed which summarized the differences reflected in all of the PI matrices as indicated by the occurrence of a certain PI level on at least one of the underlying PI matrices. The map of PI differences having a value of at least 2 identified four brain areas related to dyslexia: (1) bilateral medical frontal, (2) left anteriolateral frontal, (3) left mid-temporal and (4) left posterolateral quadrant. Classic concepts of dyslexia had not suggested the involvement of all of these brain areas in dyslexics. The study also indicated that alpha brain activity was involved in dyslexia as well as the theta activity which has previously been viewed as of primary importance.

In *Dyslexia: Automated Diagnosis by Computerized Classification of Brain Electrical Activity,* Duffy et al. (Annals of Neurology, Vol. 7, No. 5, May, 1980) hereby incorporated by reference, specific highly effective diagnostic rules for identifying dyslexics were developed by a rule selection process applying TICAS software to the brain wave data derived in the study described immediately above. Working from displays of brain electrical activity, 183 features were identified for particular regions and brain states in which the strongest differences between the dyslexic group and the normal group occurred. Two of the 183 features were identified as capable of classifying unknown subjects as dyslexic or normal with a success of 80–90%.

Localization of Tumor

In *Brain Electrical Activity Mapping (B.E.A.M.); A Method for Extending the Clinical Utility of EEG and Evoked Potential Data,* Duffy, et al (Annals of Neurology, Vol. 5, No. 4, April, 1979), hereby incorporated by reference, the use of brain electrical activity mapping system topographic displays to identify the location of a brain tumor was discussed. Spectral EEG data in the four classic bands (delta, theta, alpha, and beta) was recorded for various tested brain states. Average EP response data for strobe light stimuli comprising 128 time frames of 4 milliseconds each was also recorded. After three-point linear interpolation to expand the matrix, displays of spectral EEG data, and cartooned EP data were obtained. FIG. 5 of the article illustrates the spectral EEG displays in the four classic bands of brain activity for a patient with a known tumor, which had been located by CT scanning. The assymmetries in the spectral displays also identify the area of the tumor, although the suggested lesion size was larger than indicated by CT scanning. Analysis of 7 tumor patients, whose classic EEG's were normal or non-localizing, showed that brain electrical activity mapping studies were able to define the lesions almost as effectively as CT scan.

Use of Significance Probability Mapping with B.E.A.M. to Compare Groups and Compare Individuals to Groups

In *Significant Probability Mapping: An Aid in the Topographic Analysis of Brain Electrical Activity,* Duffy et al., accepted for publication the authors describe the use of topographical displays of statistical transformations of data. In one application, EP response data was obtained from a group of subjects with brain tumors and a second control group of subjects. The data was broken into sequential frames of 4 milliseconds each. For the control group, new matrices of mean and variance of each electrode over all members of the group were prepared. A z-statistic matrix was formed for each tumor subject to illustrate his deviation from the normal population. Using the z-statistic display a clinical neurophysiologist was able to identify 11 of 12 tumor subjects.

In a second application, discussed in the same article, EEG steady-state signals were recorded for three different brain states (resting but alert with no external stimulation, listening to a tape recording of speech, and listening to a tape recording of music) for individuals in a group of dyslexics and individuals in a group of normal readers. Matrices of alpha band activity were produced for each individual, and mean and variance matrices were prepared for each of the two groups. For each group t-statistic matrices were formed to compare the resting and listening to speech states and the resting and listening to music states. By examining the t-statistic displays for the two groups it was possible to infer the differences in speech-induced and music-induced brain activity between the dyslexics and the normal readers. Those determinations could not have been made from an analysis of the underlying EEG alpha matrices.

Use of Grid Sector Analysis of B.E.A.M. SPM Data to Determine Degree of Focal or Global Deviation From Normal

In an unpublished article, "Quantification of Focal Abnormalities in BEAM Data by Grid Sector Analysis: Automated discrimination Between Normal Subjects and Patients with Supratentorial Brain Tumor", Duffy, et al., describes uses of grid sector analysis as part of the brain electrical activity mapping system for the purpose of automated neurophysiological diagnosis of brain tumor. In this application, EEG and visual EP data were recorded from a group of patients with confirmed supratentorial brain tumor and from a control group. SPM matrices were prepared comparing the tumor subjects to a normal group and comparing the control group to the tumor group. Four 96 millisecond time periods of EP data were analyzed. Grid sector analyses on the data resulted in a set of 1096 combined global and focal features from the combined EEG and EP data. By a process of features selection and rule development and testing, two features were identified as most useful in distinguishing the tumor subjects from the control subjects. When classification rules developed on the initial group of 30 subjects were applied to a new group of 10 subjects, containing 5 normals and 5 subjects with brain tumor, all ten were correctly classified.

Other Embodiments

Other embodiments of the invention are within the following claims. For example, the input data may be

4,408,616

27   28

obtained from any type of transducer capable of measuring brain electrical activity, and

topographic displays can be prepared from the signals taken from the skull, without interpolation of additional points to form a display matrix.   5

Related Applications

This application is related to the following applications, each of which is hereby incorporated by reference: 10

(1) Frank H. Duffy, Brain Electrical Activity Mapping (BEAM)
(2) Norman David Culver, Brain Electrical Activity Mapping (BEAM)   15
(3) Norman David Culver, Analysis of Brain Electrical Activity
(4) Norman David Culver, Apparatus and Method for Topographic Display of Multichannel EEG Data, U.S. Ser. No. 221,830.   20

What is claimed is:
1. Apparatus for generating a topographic display of information on the electrical activity of the brain, said apparatus comprising   25
a plurality of electrical-activity transducers adapted to be placed at spaced apart locations on the skull of a patient,
stimulus means for repeatedly providing a sensory stimulus for activating the brain to produce EP   30
responses to said transducers,
response averaging means connected to be responsive to said transducers, to produce average responses for each transducer,
processing means connected to be responsive to said 35
averaging means for processing said average responses to generate a time sequence of matrices,
display means connected to be responsive to said processing means, for displaying said matrices as a time sequence of topographic maps of the skull, 40
said matrice having elements defining discrete points of said maps,
said display means including means for displaying said topographic maps at a variable frame rate, said maps corresponding to different portions of said 45
average responses being displayed respectively at different selected frame rates.
2. The apparatus of claim 1 wherein said display means includes means for displaying maps corresponding to initial portions of said average responses at a 50
slower rate than maps corresponding to later portions of said average responses.
3. The apparatus of claim 1 wherein said display means includes means to display said topographic maps at a frame rate that varies logarithmically.   55
4. Apparatus for generating a topographic display of information on the electrical activity of the brain, said apparatus including
a plurality of electrical-activity transducers adapted to be placed at spaced apart locations on the skull, 60
processing means connected to be responsive to said transducers, for processing responses of said transducers to generate a time sequence of matrices, each of said matrices having elements representing the instantaneous amplitudes of said responses at 65
various locations on the skull and there being a sufficient number of said matrices for a selected time period of actual brain activity for capturing

onset of a transient event that occurs with a rapidity on the order of that of an epileptic spike,
said processing means including means to generate from said time sequence of matrices a running-average matrix which at any given time represents the current matrix averaged with a selected number of the matrices preceding it in time,
display means connected to be responsive to said processing means, for displaying said matrices as a time sequence of topographic maps of the skull, said elements defining discrete points of said matrice having maps,
said display means including means for displaying said topographic maps at a variable frame rate and for selectably slowing said frame rate to permit observation of said transient event.
5. The apparatus of claim 4 wherein said processing means includes means for generating 200 or more matrices for each second of real time.
6. Apparatus for generating a topographic display of information on the electrical activity of the brain, said apparatus comprising
a plurality of electrical-activity transducers adapted to be placed at spaced apart locations on the skull of a patient,
storage means connected to be responsive to said transducers for storing responses of said transducers during first and second time periods,
processing means connected to be responsive to said transducers, for processing said responses to generate first and second matrices each having elements representing brain activity at different skull locations, said first matrix representing information on brain activity during said first period, and said second matrix representing information on brain activity during said second period,
different means connected to be responsive to said processing means, for forming a difference matrix having elements each corresponding to the difference between corresponding elements of said first and second matrices,
display means connected to be responsive to said different means, for displaying said different matrix as a topographic map of the skull, said matrix elements each forming a discrete point of said topographic map.
7. The apparatus of claim 6 further comprising stimulus means for providing a sensory stimulus to generate an EP response and wherein at least one of said first and second periods of time are during said EP response.
8. Apparatus for generating a topographic display of information on the electrical activity of the brain, said apparatus comprising
a plurality of electrical-activity transducers adapted to be placed at spaced apart locations on the skull of a patient,
stimulus means for repeatedly generating a sensory stimulus for the brain, to produce at said transducers repeated segments of data, each said segment having a pre-stimulus response and a post-stimulus response,
response averaging means connected to be responsive to said transducers, for averaging said segments to produce average pre-stimulus and average post-stimulus responses for each transducer,
baseline means connected to be responsive to said responsive averaging means, for determining a zero baseline for said average segments from the mean

4,408,616

29

level of at least a portion of the respective average pre-stimulus response, and

subtraction means connected to be responsive to said baseline means, for generating zeroed average segments by subtracting from each average segment the zero baseline determined by said baseline means,

processing means connected to be responsive to said subtraction means, for processing said zeroed average segments to generate one or more matrices, each said matrix having element representing information on the electrical activity of the brain at one location on the skull,

display means connected to be responsive to said processing means, for displaying said one or more matrices as topographic maps of the skull, said matrix elements forming discrete points of said maps.

9. The apparatus of claim 8 further comprising

means connected to be responsive to said stimulus means, for storing the time of occurrence of each said stimulus and

means connected to be responsive to said means for storing, for dividing each said segment into a predetermined pre-stimulus subinterval during which the pre-stimulus response occurs and a predetermined post-stimulus subinterval during which the post-stimulus response occurs, by using said stored times of stimuli occurrence as an indication of the boundary between said subintervals.

10. The apparatus of claim 8 wherein said processing means includes means to generate from said zeroed average segments a time sequence of said matrices, the display elements of each matrix representing the instantaneous amplitude of an EP response at various locations on said skull, and

said display means includes means for displaying said matrices in sequence, to thereby display said EP response as a time-varying topographic map.

11. The apparatus of claim 10 wherein said processing means includes means to generate said sequence of matrices in an endless loop, to thereby produce a cyclical display of said EP response.

12. The apparatus of claim 8 further comprising sampling means connected to be responsive to said transducers, for sampling and storing as a sequence of digital words said segments, and wherein said response averaging, baseline, and subtraction means all include means for performing the respective functions digitally.

13. The apparatus of claim 12 wherein said response averaging means includes

a summing buffer connected to be responsive to said sampling means, and having locations for storing each said sampled digital word for each transducer and

means connected to be responsive to said sampling means, for adding to said buffer locations new digital words corresponding to each new segment, to thereby generate said average pre- and post-stimulus responses.

14. The apparatus of claim 13 wherein said sampling means includes means for taking from 20 to 2000 equally-spaced-in-time samples of said pre-stimulus response and for taking 20 to 2000 equally-spaced-in time samples of said post-stimulus response.

15. The apparatus of claim 13 further comprising means connected to be responsive to said sampling means, for comparing said new digital words to prede-

30

termined limits and rejecting digital words falling outside said limits, thereby not adding said words to said buffer locations.

16. The apparatus of claim 12 further comprising means connected to be responsive to said transducers, for filtering high-frequency components from the post-stimulus response for any selected transducer by multipoint interpolation of the digital words for the selected response.

17. The apparatus of claim 8 wherein said baseline means includes means for selectively eliminating from the mean level computation portions of an average pre-stimulus response for a selected transducer, to thereby provide a more accurate baseline for the response of the selected transducer.

18. The apparatus of claim 8 further comprising means connected to be responsive to said baseline means, for displaying said pre-stimulus and post-stimulus responses and said baseline for a selected transducer, to permit an operator to evaluate the appropriateness of said baseline.

19. The apparatus of claim 8 wherein

said baseline means includes means for calculating the root mean square average value of the average pre-stimulus response and of the average post-stimulus response and

said display means includes means for displaying said root mean square average values along with said responses,

whereby such root mean square value can be used in connection with said displayed responses to evaluate whether the noise level in the responses for any particular transducer is unacceptably large and for thereby determining whether new data should be taken.

20. The apparatus of claim 8 or 19 further comprising means connected to be responsive to said baseline means, for an operator to adjust the baseline value up or down for any selected transducer average response.

21. The apparatus of claim 8, 18, or 20 further comprising means connected to be responsive to said baseline means, for repeating the steps of calculating said baseline and viewing said responses for selected transducers, whereby adjustments can be made to said baseline until said responses are satisfactory.

22. Apparatus for generating a topographic display of information on the electrical activity of the brain, said apparatus comprising

a plurality of electrical-activity transducers adapted to be placed at spaced apart locations on the skull of a patient or measure the EEG response at said locations,

sampling means connected to be responsive to said transducers, for sampling said EEG responses during time intervals shorter than the anticipated interval between interruptions in the state of brain activity,

spectral processing means connected to be responsive to said sampling means, for computing, for each of said transducers, the Fourier transforms of the sampled EEG responses and for computing from said Fourier transforms, for each of said transducers, the spectral energy contained in selected frequency bands,

processing means connected to be responsive to said spectral processing means, for processing the output of said spectral processing means to generate a plurality of matrices, one said matrix for each se-

31

lected frequency band, each said matrix having elements each of which represents the spectral energy within the respective frequency band at one location on the skull,

display means connected to be responsive to said processing means, for displaying said matrices as topographic maps of the skull, said matrix elements forming discrete points of said maps.

23. The apparatus of claim 22 wherein said sampling means is arranged for sampling and storing as a sequence of digital words selected portions of said EEG responses, and wherein said spectral processing means includes means for digitally performing said Fourier transform determination.

24. The apparatus of claim 23 wherein said sampling means includes means to sample said EEG responses at at least 3 times the highest frequency in said selected frequency bands.

25. The apparatus of claim 24 wherein said sampling means includes means to sample said EEG responses at from 4 to 5 times said highest frequency.

26. The apparatus of claim 22 wherein said sampling means includes marking means for storing the start and stop times of a particular brain activity.

27. The apparatus of claim 22 wherein a time maximum interval for sampling said EEG responses is on the order of two seconds.

28. The apparatus of claim 22 wherein said sampling time interval of said EEG responses is from 0.1 to 4.0 seconds long.

29. The apparatus of claim 22 further comprising averaging means connected to be responsive to said spectral processing means, for averaging said Fourier transforms to generate, for each transducer, the average spectral energy contained within said frequency bands.

30. The apparatus of claim 22 wherein said frequency bands comprise the alpha, beta, delta, and theta bands.

31. The apparatus of claim 22 further comprising filtering means connected to be responsive to said transducers, for removing from said EEG responses frequency components outside the prominent frequency bands of brain electrical activity.

32. The apparatus of claim 31 wherein said filtering means includes means for removing from said EEG responses at least frequency components below 0.5 Hz and above 50 Hz.

33. The apparatus of claim 31 wherein said filtering means includes means for removing from said EEG responses at least frequency components below 0.5 Hz and above 1000 Hz.

34. The apparatus of claim 31 wherein said filtering means includes means for removing from said EEG responses at least frequency components below 300 Hz and above 5000 Hz.

35. The apparatus of claim 22 wherein said spectral processing means includes means for tapering the beginning and end portions of said responses prior to determination of the Fourier transform to reduce high frequency artifacts.

36. Apparatus for generating a topographic display of information of the electrical activity of the brain, said apparatus comprising

a plurality of electrical-activity transducers adapted to be placed at spaced apart locations on the skull of a patient,

processing means connected to be responsive to said transducers, for processing electrical responses measured at said transducers, said processing

32

means including means for generating one or more matrices, each matrix containing a plurality of elements, said elements representing information on the electrical activity of the brain at particular skull locations,

statistical processing means connected to be responsive to said processing means, for processing at least two said matrices to generate a statistical comparison matrix having elements, each element being representative of a statistical difference between the corresponding elements in said two matrices,

display means connected to be responsive to said statistical processing means, for displaying said statistical comparison matrix as a topographic map of the skull, said matrix element forming discrete points of said map.

37. The apparatus of claim 36 further comprising interpolation means connected to be responsive to said statistical processing means, for expanding said statistical comparison matrix to a larger matrix prior to display, and larger matrix having additional statistical comparison elements for skull locations intermediate said transducer locations, said additional elements being generated by interpolation from the elements of said statistical comparison matrix.

38. The apparatus of claim 36 further comprising interpolation means connected to be responsive to said processing means, for expanding said matrices to larger matrices prior to said statistical processing, said larger matrices having additional elements for skull locations intermediate said transducer locations, said additional elements being generated by interpolation from the elements of said matrices.

39. The apparatus of claim 36 wherein said statistical processing means includes means to generate as said statistical comparison matrix a matrix of t values representing the statistical difference between a first and a second group of matrices, each group having matrices having a plurality of elements.

40. The apparatus of claim 39 wherein said statistical processing means includes

means connected to be responsive to said means to generate a matrix of t values, for generating a first mean-value matrix having elements which are representative of the mean values of the respective elements the matrices said first group,

means connected to be responsive to said means to generate a matrix of t values, for generating a first standard-deviation matrix having elements which are representative of the standard deviations of the respective elements of the matrices of said first group,

means connected to be responsive to said means to generate a matrix of t values, for generating a second mean-value matrix having elements which are representative of the mean values of the respective elements of the matrices of said second group,

means connected to be responsive to said means to generate a matrix of t values, for generating a second standard-deviation matrix having elements which are representative of the standard deviations of the respective elements of the matrices of said second group,

means connected to be responsive to said means to generate a matrix of t values, for generating said matrix of t values from said first and second mean-

4,408,616

33

value matrices and said first and second standard-deviation matrices.

41. The apparatus of claim 36 wherein said statistical processing means includes means to generate as said statistical comparison matrix a matrix of z values representing the statistical difference between one matrix and a group of matrices.

42. The apparatus of claim 41 wherein said statistical processing means includes

means connected said means to generate a matrix of z values, for generating a first matrix representative of the mean of said group of matrices,

means connected said means to generate a matrix of z values, for generating a second matrix representative of the standard deviation of said group of matrices,

said matrix of z values being generating from said one matrix and said first and second matrices, each of said matrices having a plurality of elements.

43. The apparatus of claim 42 wherein said first matrix is representative of the mean of a normalized reference population, said second matrix is representative of the standard deviation of said population, and the elements of said matrix of z values are thereby representative of the number of standard deviations by which the elements of said one matrix differ from the mean of said population.

44. The apparatus of claim 36 further comprising

means connected to be responsive to said statistical processing means, for producing from said statistical comparison matrix one or more quantitative features which are each determined by processing the elements within selected regions of said statistical matrix,

means connected to be responsive to said means for producing features, for determining a statistical merit value for selected features,

means for determining how to combine said features to form decision rules, and

means connected to be responsive to said means for determining, for classifying individuals using said decision rules.

45. Apparatus for generating a topographic display of information on the electrical activity of the brain, said apparatus comprising

a plurality of electrical-activity transducers adapted to be placed at spaced apart locations on the skull of a patient,

statistical processing means connected to be responsive to said transducers, for processing responses at said electrical-activity transducers to generate a coefficient-of-variance matrix, said matri having element each of which represents the normalized standard deviation of the responses at one skull location, the normalized standard deviation being the standard deviation divided by the mean,

display means connected to be responsive to said statistical processing means, for displaying said coefficient-of-variance matrix as a topographic map of the skull, thereby providing a map of the level of variation in brain activity.

46. Apparatus for generating a topographic display of information on the electrical activity of the brain, said apparatus comprising

a plurality of electrical-activity transducers adapted to be placed at spaced apart locations on the skull of a patient,

34

processing means connected to be responsive to said transducers, for generating from responses measured at said transducers a time sequence of first matrices, each said first matrices having display elements representing the instantaneous response at various locations on said skull,

temporal interpolation means connected to be responsive to said processing means, for generating by interpolation second matrices interspersed in said sequence of first matrices, said second matrices having elements representing the approximate response at instants of time intermediate the instants of time associated with said first matrices,

display means connected to be responsive to said processing means, for displaying said first matrices and said interspersed second matrices as a time sequence of topographic maps of the skull, said matrix elements forming discrete points of said maps, said second matrices enhancing the visual smoothness of the transitions over time between said first matrices.

47. Apparatus for generating a topographic display of information on the electrical activity of the brain, said apparatus comprising

a plurality of electrical-activity transducers adapted to be placed at spaced apart locations on the skull of a patient,

processing means connected to be responsive to said transducers, for generating one or more matrices from the responses measured at said transducers, each matrix having elements representing information on electrical activity of the brain at one location on the skull,

display means connected to be responsive to said processing means, for displaying said matrices as topographic maps of the skull, said matrix elements forming discrete points of said maps,

waveform quality control means for previewing said transducer responses or processed versions thereof, said quality control means including at least two of the following means

means for tagging a response with information on its waveform quality, including an indication of whether the response should be used in later processing,

means at the discretion of the operator for eliminating a response from further processing,

means for automatically eliminating a response from further processing if a portion thereof exceeds a predetermined threshold,

means for smoothing a response to eliminate undesired high frequency components,

means for adjusting a zero baseline of a response, said zero baseline having been previously set automatically,

means for eliminating selected portions of a response from further processing, and

means for displaying in numerical form the value of a response at a point in time selected by the operator.

48. Apparatus for generating a topographic display of information on the electrical activity of the brain, said apparatus comprising

a plurality of electrical-activity transducers adapted to be placed at spaced apart locations on the skull of a patient,

means connected to be responsive to said transducers, for sampling responses measured at said transduc-

4,408,616

35

ers and storing the sampled responses as a series of data matrices, one matrix for each sampling time,

means connected to be responsive to said means for sampling, for selectively viewing the sampled responses corresponding to a single transducer as a plot of transducer output versus time,

quality control means for adjusting portions of said selectively viewed responses or eliminating said responses from further processing,

processing means connected to be responsive to said means for sampling, for processing said data matrices to generate one or more processed matrices, said processed matrices having elements each corresponding to one transducer location,

interpolation means connected to be responsive to said processing means, for generating expanded matrices by expanding the number of elements in said processed matrices to provide elements corresponding to skull locations intermediate said transducer locations,

display means connected to be responsive to said interpolation means, including a video monitor capable of generating a matrix of grey tones for displaying said expanded matrices as topographic maps of the skull, said expanded matrices having elements defining the grey tones of discrete points on said maps.

49. The apparatus of claim 48 further comprising matrix storage means connected to be responsive to said means for sampling, processing means, and interpolation means, for tagging selected data, processed, or expanded matrices and storing them for later recall and processing.

50. The apparatus of claim 48 further comprising means connected to be responsive to said transducers, for storing calibration responses from said transducers and means for calibrating said responses matrices by determining from said stored calibration responses a DC offset and gain for each said transducer.

51. Apparatus for generating a topographic display of information on the electrical activity of the brain, said apparatus comprising

a plurality of electrical-activity transducers adapted to be placed at spaced apart locations on the skull of a patient,

processing means connected to be responsive to said transducers, for processing responses measured at said transducers to generate one or more matrices, each matrix having elements representing information on brain activity at different skull locations,

display means connected to be responsive to said processing means, for displaying said one or more matrices as topographic maps of the skull, said matrix elements forming discrete points of said maps, said display means including a video monitor which generates a visible grey tone at each said discrete point, said tone being variable from a maximum tone to a minimum tone, and

scaling means connected to be responsive to said processing means, for scaling said matrix elements to the available tones.

52. The apparatus of claim 51 wherein said video monitor generates a zero tone intermediate said maximum and minimum tone and said scaling means comprises at least two of the following means

means connected to be responsive to said processing means, for scaling the maximum matrix element to

36

the maximum tone and the minimum matrix element to the minimum tone and linearly interpolating inbetween,

means connected to be responsive to said processing means, for scaling the maximum matrix element to the maximum tone and the minimum matrix element to the zero tone and linearly interpolating inbetween,

means connected to be responsive to said processing means, for scaling the maximum matrix element to an operator supplied tone,

means connected to be responsive to said processing means, for scaling the minimum matrix element to an operator supplied tone,

means connected to be responsive to said processing means, for excluding from the scaling operation selected unusually high or low valued matrix elements and for assigning to matrix elements that fall outside the available tone range the closer of the maximum or minimum tone.

53. The apparatus of claim 51 wherein said video monitor generates colored grey tones of a first and a second color, with grey tones of said first color forming said grey tones between said maximum tone and said zero tone, with grey tones of said second color forming said grey tones between said minimum tone and said zero tone, and with the absence of a color tone forming said zero tone.

54. The apparatus of claim 53 wherein said two colors are complementary colors.

55. The apparatus of claim 53 wherein there are at least 6 grey tones of each of said two colors.

56. The apparatus of claim 51 wherein there are a plurality of said matrices to be displayed and said scaling means includes means for independently performing said tone scaling for each matrix displayed.

57. The apparatus of claim 51 wherein there are a plurality of said matrices to be displayed and said scaling means includes means for scaling with respect to the display elements in all said matrices so that the scaling remains the same for each matrix displayed.

58. The apparatus of claim 51 further comprising preview means connected to be responsive to said transducers, for viewing selected segments of the transducer responses and for tagging selected segments for exclusion from the scaling operation and wherein said scaling means includes means for identifying the presence of said tagging and for excluding data so tagged from said scaling operation.

59. Apparatus for generating a topographic display of information on the electrical activity of the brain, said apparatus comprising

a plurality of electrical-activity transducers adapted to be placed at spaced apart locations on the skull of a patient,

processing means connected to be responsive to said transducers, for processing responses measured at said transducers to generate one or more matrices, each matrix having elements representing information on brain activity at different skull locations,

display means connected to be responsive to said processing means, for displaying said one or more matrices as a topographic map of the skull, said matrix elements forming discrete points of said map, said display means including a video monitor which generates a tone at each said discrete point, said tone varying from a maximum tone to a minimum tone,

4,408,616

37

normalizing means connected to be responsive to said processing means, for normalizing said matrix elements to a selected value, and

scaling means connected to be responsive to said processing means, for scaling said matrix elements to the available tones, said scaling means including means for assigning a selected tone to said selected normalization value.

60. The apparatus of claim 59 wherein said normalizing means includes means for normalizing said matrix elements to the matrix element representing brain electrical activity at the vertex.

61. The apparatus of claim 59 wherein said normalizing means includes means for normalizing each individual matrix element to the root mean square value of the background electrical activity at the skull location represented by the individual matrix element.

62. The apparatus of claim 59 wherein said normalizing means includes means for normalizing said matrix elements to the average root mean square value of the background electrical activity over all skull locations.

63. The apparatus of claim 59, 60, 61 or 62 further comprising

stimulus means for repeatedly providing a sensory stimulus for the brain, to produce repeated EP responses at said transducers,

response averaging means connected to be responsive to said transducers, for averaging said repeated responses for each transducer to produce an average response for each transducer, and

wherein said processing means includes means for generating from said average responses a time sequence of said matrices, and

said display means includes means for displaying said matrices in sequence.

64. The apparatus of claim 59 wherein

there is further provided spectral processing means connected to be responsive to said transducers, for computing the Fourier transforms of the responses measured by said electrical-activity transducers and for computing from said Fourier transforms the spectral energy contained in selected frequency bands,

said processing means includes means for processing the output of said spectral processing means to generate a plurality of matrices, one said matrix for each selected frequency band, each matrix having elements representing the spectral energy within the selected frequency band at various locations on the skull, and

said normalizing means includes means to normalize said matrix elements either to the total spectral energy for all said frequency bands at the skull location corresponding to said matrix element or to the average total spectral energy for all said frequency bands for all matrix elements.

65. The apparatus of claim 1, 4, 6, 8, 22, 45, 46, 47, 48, 51, or 59 wherein said processing means includes interpolation means for generating by interpolation additional matrix elements for skull locations intermediate the locations of said transducers.

66. The apparatus of claim 65 wherein said interpolation means includes means for computing the values of said additional matrix elements by three point interpolation from the values associated with the three closest transducer locations.

67. The apparatus of claim 66 wherein said three point interpolation is linear.

38

68. The apparatus of claim 1, 4, 6, 8, 22, 36, 45, 46, 47, 48, 51, or 59 wherein the number of said electrical-activity transducers is in the range of 10 to 200 and the number of elements in said topographic maps is at least 5 times the number of transducers.

69. A method for generating a topographic display of information on the electrical activity of the brain, said method comprising the steps of

placing a plurality of electrical-activity transducers at spaced apart locations on the skull of a patient,

storing responses of said transducers during first and second time periods,

processing said responses to generate first and second matrices each having elements representing brain activity at different skull locations, said first matrix representing information on brain activity during said first period, and said second matrix representing information on brain activity during said second period,

forming a difference matrix having elements each corresponding to the difference between corresponding elements of said first and second matrices, and

displaying said difference matrix as a topographic map of the skull, said matrix elements each forming a discrete point of said topographic map.

70. The method of claim 69 further comprising the step of providing as a stimulus for the brain during said first period a source of patterned light and providing as a stimulus for the brain during said second period a source of nonpatterned light.

71. A method of generating a topographic display of information on the EP response of the brain, said method comprising the steps of:

placing a plurality of electrical-activity transducers at spaced apart locations on the skull of a patient,

repeatedly providing a sensory stimulus for the brain so as to produce at said transducers repeated segments of data, each segment including a pre-stimulus response and a post-stimulus response,

averaging the repeated segments to produce an average segment for each transducer,

determining a zero baseline for each average segment from the mean level of at least a portion of the average pre-stimulus response,

subtracting the zero baselines from the respective average segments to produce zeroed average segments,

processing the zeroed average segments to generate one or more matrices of elements, with each matrix element representing information on the EP response at one location on the skull, and

displaying said one or more matrices as topographic maps of the skull, with each display point forming a discrete point on said maps.

72. A method for generating a topographic display of information on the electrical activity of the brain, said method comprising the steps of

placing a plurality of electrical-activity transducers at spaced apart locations on the skull of a patient,

repeatedly providing a sensory stimulus for activating the brain to produce EP responses at said transducers,

averaging said responses to produce average responses for each transducer,

processing said average responses to generate a time sequence of matrices,

4,408,616

39

displaying said matrices as a time sequence of topographic maps of the skull, said matrices having elements defining discrete points of said maps, and displaying said topographic maps at a variable frame rate,

maps corresponding to different portions of said average responses being displayed respectively at different selected frame rates.

73. A method for generating a topographic display of information on the electrical activity of the brain, said method including the steps of

placing a plurality of electrical-activity transducers at spaced apart locations on the skull,

processing responses of said transducers to generate a time sequence of matrices, each said matrix having elements representing the instantaneous amplitudes of said responses at various locations on the skull and there being a sufficient number of said matrices for a selected time period of actual brain activity for capturing onset of a transient event that occurs with a rapidity on the order of that of an epileptic spike,

generating from said time sequence of matrices a running-average matrix which at any given time represents the current matrix averaged with a selected number of the matrices preceding it in time,

displaying said matrices as a time sequence of topographic maps of the skull at a variable frame rate, each running-average matrix having elements defiring discrete points of said maps, and

selectably slowing the frame rate at which said topographic maps are displayed so as to permit observation of said transient event.

74. A method for generating a topographic display of information on the electrical activity of the brain, said method comprising the steps of

placing a plurality of electrical-activity transducers at spaced apart locations on the skull of a patient to measure the EEG response at said locations,

sampling the EEG responses during time intervals shorter than the anticipated interval between interruptions in the state of brain activity,

computing, for each of said transducers, the Fourier transforms of the sampled EEG responses and computing from said Fourier transforms, for each of said transducers, the spectral energy contained in selected frequency bands,

processing said computed spectral energy of said selected frequency bands to generate a plurality of matrices, one said matrix for each selected frequency band, said matrices having elements representing the spectral energy within the respective frequency band at one location on the skull, and

displaying said matrices as topographic maps of the skull, said matrix elements forming discrete points of said maps.

75. A method for generating a topographic display of information on the electrical activity of the brain, said method comprising the steps of

placing a plurality of electrical-activity transducers at spaced apart locations on the skull of a patient,

processing electrical responses measured at said transducers, said processing means including means for generating one or more matrices, each matrix containing a plurality of elements, said elements representing information on the electrical activity of the brain at particular skull locations,

40

processing at least two said matrices to generate a statistical comparison matrix said statistical comparison matrix having elements each of which representative of a statistical difference between the corresponding elements in said two matrices, and

displaying said statistical comparison matrix as a topographic map of the skull, said matrix elements forming discrete points of said map.

76. A method for generating a topographic display of information on the electrical activity of the brain, said method comprising the steps of

placing a plurality of electrical-activity transducers at spaced apart locations on the skull of a patient,

statistically processing responses at said electrical-activity transducers to generate a coefficient-of-variance matrix, said matrix having elements each of which represents the normalized standard deviation of the responses at one skull location, the normalized standard deviation being the standard deviation divided by the mean,

displaying said coefficient-of-variance matrix as a topographic map of the skull, thereby providing a map of the level of variation in brain activity.

77. A method for generating a topographic display of information on the electrical activity of the brain, said method comprising the steps of

placing a plurality of electrical-activity transducers for placement at spaced apart locations on the skull of a patient,

generating from responses measured at said transducers a time sequence of first matrices, each said first matrix having display elements representing the instantaneous response at various locations on said skull,

generating by interpolation second matrices interspersed in said sequence of first matrices, said second matrices having elements representing the approximate response at instants of time intermediate the instants of time associated with said first matrices,

displaying said first matrices and said interspersed second matrices as a time sequence of topographic maps of the skull, said matrix elements forming discrete points of said maps, said second matrices enhancing the visual smoothness of the transitions over time between said first matrices.

78. A method for generating a topographic display of information on the electrical activity of the brain, said method comprising the steps of

placing a plurality of electrical-activity transducers at spaced apart locations on the skull of a patient,

generating one or more matrices from responses measured at said transducers, each matrix having elements representing information on the electrical activity of the brain at one location on the skull,

displaying said one or more matrices as topographic maps of the skull, said matrix elements forming discrete points of said maps,

previewing said transducer responses or processed versions thereof, said previewing including at least two of the following steps

tagging a response with information on its waveform quality, including an indication of whether the response should be used in later processing,

eliminating a response from further processing at the discretion of the operator,

4,408,616

41

automatically eliminating a response from further processing if a portion thereof exceeds a predetermined threshold,

smoothing a response to eliminate undesired high frequency components,

adjusting a zero baseline of a response, said zero baseline having been previously set automatically

eliminating selected portions of a response from further processing, and

displaying in numerical form the value of a response at a point in time selected by the operator.

79. A method for generating a topographic display of information on the electrical activity of the brain, said method comprising the steps of

placing a plurality of electrical-activity transducers at spaced apart locations on the skull of a patient,

sampling responses measured at said transducers and storing the sampled data as a series of data matrices, one matrix for each sampling time,

selectively viewing the sampled data corresponding to a single transducer as a plot of transducer output versus time,

adjusting portions of said selectively viewed data or eliminating said data from further processing,

processing said data matrices to generate one or more processed matrices said one or more processed matrices having elements each corresponding to one transducer location,

expanding the number of elements in said one or more processed matrices to provide elements corresponding to skull locations intermediate said transducer locations,

providing a video monitor capable of generating a matrix of grey tones for displaying said expanded matrices as topographic maps of the skull, said expanded matrix elements defining the grey tones of discrete points on said maps.

80. A method for generating a topographic display of information on the electrical activity of the brain, said method comprising the steps of

placing a plurality of electrical-activity transducers at spaced apart locations on the skull of a patient,

processing responses measured at said transducers to generate one or more matrices, each matrix having elements representing information on brain activity at different skull locations,

42

displaying one or more said matrices as topographic maps of the skull, said matrix elements forming discrete points of said maps,

providing a video monitor which generates a visible grey tone at each said discrete point, said tone being variable from a maximum tone to a minimum tone, and

scaling said matrix elements to the available tones.

81. The method of claim **80** wherein

said providing step comprises providing a said video monitor which generates a zero tone intermediate said maximum and minimum tone, and

said scaling step comprises at least two of the following steps

scaling the maximum matrix element to the maximum tone and the minimum matrix element to the minimum tone and linearly interpolating inbetween,

scaling the maximum matrix element to the maximum tone and the minimum matrix element to the zero tone and linearly interpolating in between,

scaling the maximum matrix element to an operator supplied tone,

scaling the minimum matrix element to an operator supplied tone,

excluding from the scaling operation selected unusually high or low valued matrix elements and assigning to matrix elements that fall outside the available tone range the closer of the maximum or minimum tone.

82. A method for generating a topographic display of information on the electrical activity of the brain, said method comprising the steps of

placing a plurality of electrical-activity transducers at spaced apart locations on the skull of a patient,

processing responses measured at said transducers to generate one or more matrices, each matrix having elements representing information on brain activity at different skull locations,

displaying said one or more matrices as a topographic map of the skull, said matrix elements forming discrete points of said map,

providing a video monitor which generates a tone at each said discrete point, said tone varying from a maximum tone to a minimum tone,

normalizing said matrix elements to a selected value, and

scaling said matrix elements to the available tones, said scaling means including means for assigning a selected tone to said selected normalization value.

* * * * *

United States Patent [19]

Monroe

[11] **Patent Number:** 5,213,562

[45] **Date of Patent:** May 25, 1993

US005213562A

[54] **METHOD OF INDUCING MENTAL, EMOTIONAL AND PHYSICAL STATES OF CONSCIOUSNESS, INCLUDING SPECIFIC MENTAL ACTIVITY, IN HUMAN BEINGS**

[75] Inventor: **Robert A. Monroe**, Nelson County, Va.

[73] Assignee: **Interstate Industries Inc.**, Faber, Va.

[21] Appl. No.: **514,460**

[22] Filed: **Apr. 25, 1990**

[51] Int. Cl.⁵ A61M 21/00
[52] U.S. Cl. 600/28; 128/732
[58] Field of Search 600/26–28;
128/731–732, 905

[56] **References Cited**

U.S. PATENT DOCUMENTS

2,466,054	4/1949	Siebel .
3,160,159	12/1964	Hoody et al. .
3,576,185	4/1971	Schulz et al. .
3,712,292	1/1973	Zentmeyer, Jr. .
3,753,433	8/1973	Bakerich et al. .
3,826,243	7/1974	Anderson .
3,837,331	9/1974	Ross .
3,884,218	5/1975	Monroe 600/28
4,034,741	7/1977	Adams et al. .
4,141,344	2/1979	Barbara .
4,227,516	10/1980	Meland et al. .
4,335,710	6/1982	Williamson .
4,573,449	3/1986	Warnke .
4,834,701	5/1989	Masaki 600/28
5,036,858	8/1991	Carter et al. 128/732

Primary Examiner—Lee S. Cohen
Assistant Examiner—John P. Lacyk
Attorney, Agent, or Firm—Sughrue, Mion, Zinn, Macpeak & Seas

[57] **ABSTRACT**

A method having applicability in replication of desired consciousness states; in the training of an individual to replicate such a state of consciousness without further audio stimulation; and in the transferring of such states from one human being to another through the imposition of one individual's EEG, superimposed on desired stereo signals, on another individual, by inducement of a binaural beat phenomenon.

6 Claims, 5 Drawing Sheets

FIG.1A

FIG.1B

FIG.1C

FIG.2A

FIG.2B

FIG.2C

FIG.2D

FIG.3A

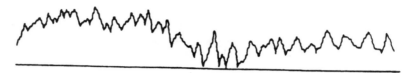

FIG.3B

AMPLITUDE

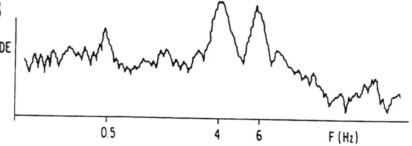

0.5   4   6   F (Hz)

FIG.3C

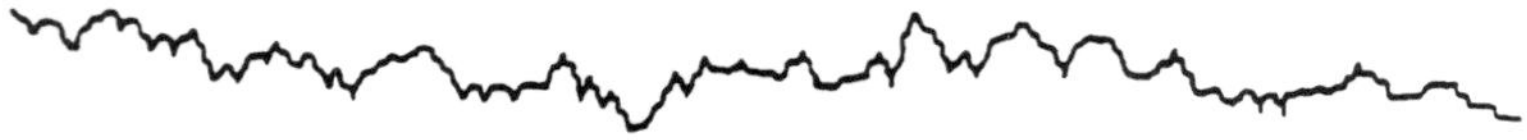

FIG.3D

AMPLITUDE

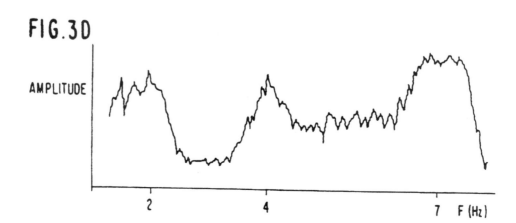

2   4   7   F (Hz)

FIG.3E

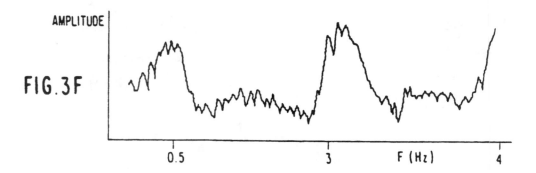

FIG.3F

FIG.3G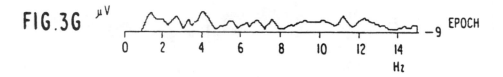

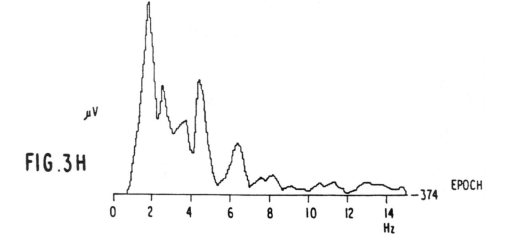

FIG.3H

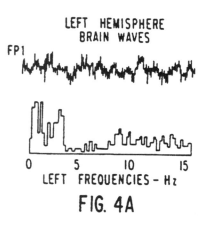

LEFT HEMISPHERE
BRAIN WAVES

FP1

LEFT FREQUENCIES – Hz

FIG. 4A

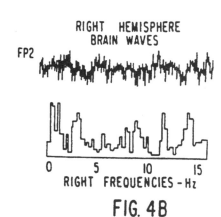

RIGHT HEMISPHERE
BRAIN WAVES

FP2

RIGHT FREQUENCIES – Hz

FIG. 4B

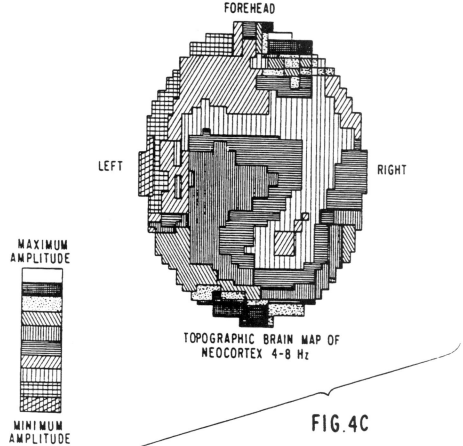

FOREHEAD

LEFT

RIGHT

MAXIMUM
AMPLITUDE

MINIMUM
AMPLITUDE

TOPOGRAPHIC BRAIN MAP OF
NEOCORTEX 4-8 Hz

FIG.4C

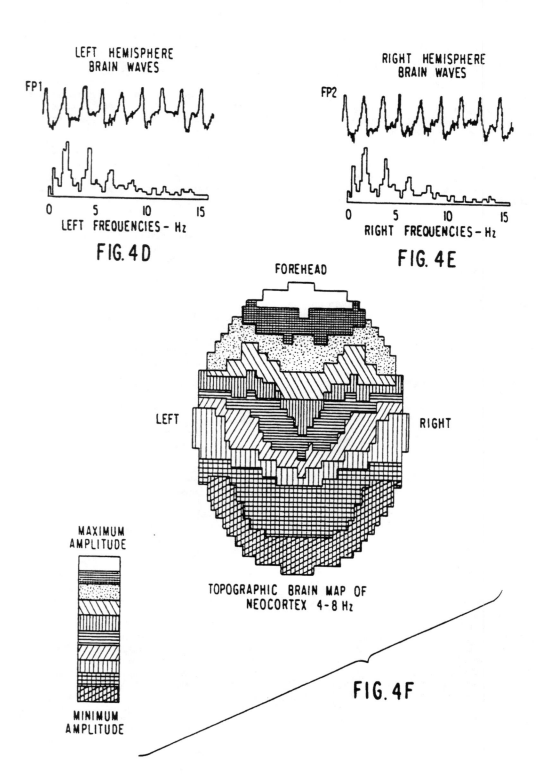

LEFT HEMISPHERE
BRAIN WAVES

FP1

0   5   10   15
LEFT FREQUENCIES — Hz

FIG. 4D

RIGHT HEMISPHERE
BRAIN WAVES

FP2

0   5   10   15
RIGHT FREQUENCIES — Hz

FIG. 4E

FOREHEAD

LEFT   RIGHT

MAXIMUM
AMPLITUDE

MINIMUM
AMPLITUDE

TOPOGRAPHIC BRAIN MAP OF
NEOCORTEX 4-8 Hz

FIG. 4F

5,213,562

1

METHOD OF INDUCING MENTAL, EMOTIONAL AND PHYSICAL STATES OF CONSCIOUSNESS, INCLUDING SPECIFIC MENTAL ACTIVITY, IN HUMAN BEINGS

BACKGROUND OF THE INVENTION

The present invention relates to a method of inducing various states of consciousness in human beings. More particularly, the invention relates to a method of inducing such states of consciousness through generation of stereo audio signals having specific wave shapes which act as a carrier of a binaural beat. The resultant binaural beat acts to entrain brain waves into unique waveforms characteristic of identified states of consciousness. The invention is applicable in areas of learning and behavior replication as well as in the area of sleep inducement, and thus represents a significant departure from and improvement over known audio-based sleep inducement techniques, some of which will be discussed below.

The binaural beat phenomenon was discovered in 1839 by H. W. Dove, a German experimenter. Generally, this phenomenon works as follows. When an individual receives signals of two different frequencies, one signal to each ear, the individual's brain detects a phase difference or differences between these signals. When these signals are naturally occurring, the detected phased difference provides directional information to the higher centers of the brain. However, if these signals are provided through speakers or stereo earphones, the phase difference is detected as an anomaly. The resulting imposition of a consistent phase difference between the incoming signals causes the binaural beat in an amplitude modulated standing wave, within each superior olivary nucleus (sound processing center) of the brain. It is not possible to generate a binaural beat through an electronically mixed signal; rather, the action of both ears is required for detection of this beat.

FIGS. 1A and 1B show two superposed waves of different frequencies. FIG. 1C shows the resulting wave, which has a clear beat phenomenon. Assuming the two waves have equal amplitude but different respective frequencies f_1, f_2, the combination of the two waves may be represented mathematically as follows:

$$
\begin{aligned}
X &= X_1 + X_2 \\
&= a\,{}^*\cos(2\pi f_1 t) + a\,{}^*\cos(2\pi f_2 t) \\
&= a\,{}^*[\cos(2\pi f_1 t) + a\,{}^*\cos(2\pi f_2 t)] \\
&= 2a\,{}^*\cos\left(2\pi\,\frac{[f_1 - f_2]}{2}\,t\right){}^*\cos\left(2\pi\,\frac{[f_1 + f_2]}{2}\,t\right)
\end{aligned}
$$

The beat phenomenon arises from the variation in amplitude of a resulting carrier frequency. Pulses appear every $\frac{1}{2}(f_1-f_2)$, with two maxima occurring each cycle, when $\cos(2\pi)\frac{1}{2}[f_1-f_2] = \pm 1$. That is, the beat frequency is simply f_1-f_2, a result which agrees with experience.

Known consciousness state inducing techniques have not used this binaural beat phenomenon, but have relied on other techniques, as follows. For example the use of audio generators to induce a state of consciousness known as sleep is well known in the prior art, as exemplified by U.S. Pat. No. 2,711,165 and 3,384,074. In one type of technique exemplified in these patents, generated audio signals include pleasing and harmonious

2

study sounds or vibrations, fixed frequency signals which are buried cyclically with respect to amplitude, and repetitive sounds such as the falling of rain on the roof and the sighing wind through the trees.

U.S. Pat. No. 2,304,095 relates to a method of inducing sleep by generation of an audible or tactual signal which is related to the physiological process of heartbeat and respiration. In the disclosed method, the pitch and amplitude of a pleasing audio signal are varied at a rate somewhat slower than either the rate of heartbeat or the rate of respiration. As a result, heartbeat and respiration tend to synchronize with the audio signal, thus lowering heartbeat and respiration rates and inducing sleep.

Of course, there are other naturally-occurring sounds which have been recorded, and which are not varied, but which instead induce a state of relaxation which leads to sleep for a similar reason. For example, the pounding of waves on a shore line occurs at a frequency generally lower than that of heartbeat or respiration, and induces a state of relaxation.

The use of an electroencephalogram (EEG) as a research and diagnostic tool has led to findings that particular brain wave patterns are indicative of different states of consciousness. In 1934, researchers discovered that brain waves, and their associated states of consciousness, could be altered with repetitive visual stimulation at a known frequency, an effect known as entrainment. Scientific interest in entrainment continued throughout the 1960's. In the 1970's, numerous independent studies repeatedly confirmed that rhythmic flashing lights rapidly entrained brain waves.

A sonic equivalent of photic entrainment also is known, as disclosed for example in commonly-assigned U.S. Pat. No. 3,884,218, the inventor of which is the inventor of the present application. This patent discloses a method of inducing sleep in a human being by generating an audio signal which is made up of a familiar pleasing repetitive sound modulated by frequencies usually associated with an EEG sleep pattern. There are different EEG patterns related to various levels or depths of sleep, and it has been found that by modulating the repetitive sound with these different sleep patterns, it is possible to induce various levels of sleep. The inventor has coined the term frequency following response, or FFR, to describe this phenomenon.

Other known techniques for inducing various states of consciousness, or for performing brainwave analysis and related functions, are shown, for example, in the following U.S. patents:

2,466,054	4,034,741	3,160,159	4,141,344
3,576,185	4,227,516	3,712,292	4,335,710
3,753,433	4,573,449	3,826,243	4,834,701
3,837,331.			

The binaural beat phenomenon described above also can create a frequency entrainment effect. If a binaural beat is within the range of brain wave frequencies, generally less than 30 cycles per second, the binaural beat will become an entrainment environment. This effect has been used to study states of consciousness, to improve therapeutic intervention techniques, and to enhance educational environments. However, the modulation of the binaural beat signals with brain waves associated with particular activities has not been attempted previously.

5,213,562

3

SUMMARY OF THE INVENTION

In view of the foregoing, it is one object of the invention to provide a method of inducing states of consciousness by generating stereo audio signals having specific wave shapes. These signals act as a carrier of a binaural beat. The resulting beat acts to entrain brain waves into unique waveforms characteristic of identified states of consciousness.

The method of the invention extends beyond the confines of the frequency entraining concept, and incorporates waveform entrainment by altering the wave shape of the binaural beat. Conventional binaural beat frequency entrainment previously has been limited to conventional wave shapes, i.e., square triangular sinusoidal, or in some cases, the various musical instruments. For example, it is known that radiant energy, such as sound in this case, may be defined by its frequency, amplitude, and wave shape. A musical note is a particularly suitable example of this. Generally, the musical note A above middle C in the twelve tone diatonic scale is assigned a frequency of 440 cycles per second. The amplitude of that note is expressed as the loudness of the signal. However, the wave shape of that note is related strongly to the instrument used. An A played on a trumpet is quite different from an A played on a violin.

The similarity results from the distinct shapes of the waveforms of each instrument. Similarly, human brain waves also have unique wave shapes, wave contours which are neither sinusoidal, nor square, nor triangular, nor like those of any musical instrument.

In accordance with the invention, human brain waves, in the form of EEGs, are superimposed upon specific stereo audio signals, known as carrier frequencies which are within the range of human hearing. Thus the invention relates not only to techniques of generating the binaural beat, but also to specific waveforms of the binaural beat in frequency, waveshape, and amplitude, and most particularly to the source of the data used to produce such waveforms.

BRIEF DESCRIPTION OF THE DRAWINGS

FIGS. 1A–1C show two waves at different frequencies, and the resulting binaural beat, respectively;

FIGS. 2A–2D show an input wave, two stereo carrier waves as determined by Fourier analysis, and the resultant binaural beat wave, which matches the contour of the input wave;

FIGS. 3A–3B, 3C–3D, 3E–3F, and 3G–3H are pairs of graphs showing a normal waking EEG and FFR responses in different signal ranges, respectively; and

FIGS. 4A–4F show topographic brain maps of the neocortex of a subject in a normal waking state, and after listening to a binaural beat sound pattern.

DETAILED DESCRIPTION OF THE PREFERRED EMBODIMENT

As will be discussed below, different regions of the brain produce distinct electrical waveforms during various physical, mental, and emotional states of consciousness. In the method of the invention, binaural beat audio wave shapes are made to match such particular brain waves as they occur during any mental physical, and emotional human condition of consciousness. Thus, it is possible to convert waveforms from specific brain regions, as well as complete brain surface electrical topography.

4

In the audio application of the invention, using sampled EEG waveforms from a subject in specific states of consciousness and activity, mental and/or physical, these waveforms are impressed upon multiple sets of sound carrier waves within the human spectrum of hearing. Thus, the waveforms translate into wave amplitude modulations of the carrier to effect what is called a frequency following response, or FFR, as mentioned above.

Some description of the empirical procedure used in the course of developing the invention will be useful, as background. In the 1970s, testing was done on various subjects for effective EEG frequencies using audio signals as a human stimulus. Such frequencies were replicated as amplitude modulation of single-channel audio signals within human hearing ranges, for use in sleep-inducing, attention-focusing, etc.

Where particular subjects responded especially well, those signals were converted to binaural beat patterns. The binaural beat signals were derived by first selecting frequencies of the single-channel audio signals based on the well-known "Oersted Curve", named after the famous 19th century physicist. Using this curve permitted selection of specific audio frequencies to provide the greatest binaural beat frequencies at a much lower range. The effectiveness of the tests were doubled as a result of using binaural beat signals.

In the mid 1980s, EEG waveforms themselves were examined as produced by the binaural signals employed. FFR and entrainment factors thought to be responsible for success were verified. One of the results identified as the probable cause of such effectiveness was the synchronization of the brain hemispheres in such signal frequency ranges (i.e. the induced signals were present simultaneously in major portions of both brain hemispheres).

Experimentation expanded to different subjects in similar states of consciousness. Isolation of EEG patterns in these states of consciousness, and conversion of these patterns to binaural sound, with subsequent reapplication of the binaural sounds produced significantly enhanced results. The effect was especially apparent among naive subjects.

Recently, EEG neuromapping began of subjects with particular talents, where those subjects could utilize those talents (e.g. playing a piano sonata, or solving a mathematical equation) at a mental or visualization level. It was possible to isolate the EEG waveforms related to utilization of those talents, and to convert those waveforms to binaural sound. Subsequent exposure of the subject to such patterns enhanced the individual's ability to replicate the process. Exposing other subjects to the signals produced a learned response through repetition.

Thus, the inventor believes that the inventive process, while not necessarily creating a musician or a mathematician, will set up an EEG ambiance in which learning will be facilitated.

Looking more closely now at the implementation and effects of the invention, FIGS. 2A–2D show a phenomenon wherein an input brain wave signal from a particular brain region is superimposed on stereo carrier waves. FIG. 2D shows the resultant binaural beat wave which matches the contour of the input wave.

The generation and propagation of the binaural beat may be understood from the following series of equations, based on the following.

Taking the components from FIGS. 1A–1C, and scaling each component to an appropriate factor (say, α and β).

These components could be recombined to form a beat in accordance with the original components. Linearity and orthogonality principles make these manipulations possible. First, assign the measured wave to be the beat frequency, x.

$$x = \alpha - \beta$$

From the beating waves discussed with respect to FIGS. 1A–1C:

$$\sin(\alpha) + \sin(\beta) = 2\cos\left(\frac{\alpha - \beta}{2}\right)\sin\left(\frac{\alpha + \beta}{2}\right) =$$

$$2\cos\left(\frac{x}{2}\right)\sin\left(\frac{2\alpha - x}{2}\right)$$

$$\cos(\alpha) + \cos(\beta) = 2\cos\left(\frac{\alpha - \beta}{2}\right)\cos\left(\frac{\alpha + \beta}{2}\right) =$$

$$2\cos\left(\frac{x}{2}\right)\cos\left(\frac{2\alpha - x}{2}\right)$$

Now, let us alter the Fourier series $f(x)$ to produce the beat in the shape of the original wave, $f'(x)$:

$$f'(x) = \tfrac{1}{2}a_0 + \tfrac{1}{2}\sum_{n=1}^{\infty}\cos\left(\frac{nx}{2}\right)\left[a_n\cos\left(n\frac{2\alpha - x}{2}\right) + b_n\sin\left(n\frac{2\alpha - x}{2}\right)\right])$$

$$= \tfrac{1}{2}a_0 + \tfrac{1}{2}\sum_{n=1}^{\infty}\cos\left(n\frac{\alpha - \beta}{2}\right)\left[a_n\cos\left(n\frac{\alpha + \beta}{2}\right) + b_n\sin\left(n\frac{\alpha + \beta}{2}\right)\right])$$

$$= \tfrac{1}{2}a_0 + \tfrac{1}{2}\sum_{n=1}^{\infty}\cos\left(n\frac{\alpha - \beta}{2}\right)a_n\cos\left(n\frac{\alpha + \beta}{2}\right) + \cos\left(n\frac{\alpha - \beta}{2}\right)b_n\sin\left(n\frac{\alpha + \beta}{2}\right)\right])$$

$$= \tfrac{1}{2}a_0 + \tfrac{1}{2}\sum_{n=1}^{\infty}a_n[\cos(\alpha) + \cos(\beta)] + b_n[\sin(\alpha) + \sin(\beta)])$$

$$= \tfrac{1}{4}a_0 + \tfrac{1}{2}\sum_{n=1}^{\infty}[a_n\cos(\alpha) + b_n\sin(\alpha)] + \tfrac{1}{4}a_0 + \tfrac{1}{2}\sum_{n=1}^{\infty}[a_n\cos(\beta) + b_n\sin(\beta)]$$

$$= \tfrac{1}{2}\left\{\tfrac{1}{2}a_0 + \sum_{n=1}^{\infty}[a_n\cos(\alpha) + b_n\sin(\alpha)]\right\} + \tfrac{1}{2}\left\{\tfrac{1}{2}a_0 + \sum_{n=1}^{\infty}[a_n\cos(\beta) + b_n\sin(\beta)]\right\}$$

$$= \tfrac{1}{2}g(\alpha) + \tfrac{1}{2}h(\beta)$$

From the foregoing, it can be seen readily that $g(\alpha)$ and $h(\beta)$ have become two waves, each having half the amplitude of the original wave, the combination of these waves producing a beat which is the input shape $f(x)$.

Thus, using two-channel stereo sound, it is possible to modulate two separate sets of carrier waves so that the replicated EEG waveforms are created as differential beat frequencies between the separate sets. Thus, the method permits the direct application on a frequency base without having to consider the limitation of the spectrum of human hearing. The brain itself synthesizes the signals which cause the effect.

One example may be as follows. If a carrier frequency of 100 Hz were employed in one channel of the audio signal, and a carrier frequency of 104 Hz were employed in the other channel, a binaural beat of 4 Hz would result. In EEG waveform synthesis, as many as 100 separate carrier pairs may be used or a single broadbanded carrier pair may be used to generate a similar number of specific binaural beats that replicate the EEG waveforms in both frequency and amplitude.

A 4 Hz, or a 5 Hz binaural beat would be too low in frequency to hear. Using the Oersted curve mentioned above, the most effective harmonic carrier would be 275 Hz, which is within hearing range. For the multiple waveform situation just discussed, the differential between carrier waves on a single channel also is utilized to produce an FFR.

One type of audio pattern found to be particularly useful in implementing the inventive method is what is known to the inventor as Phased Pink Sound. The full spectrum of audible sound is known commonly as "white" noise. "Pink" sound is known to result from an adjustment in amplitude of white sound to compensate for decline in perception by the human ear at both ends of the audible spectrum.

Phased Pink Sound results from the relative rotational shifting of pink sound from one stereo audio channel to another with cyclic changes in amplitude, frequency, and rate of panning. Such changes generally are synchronous with selected waveforms within the multiple patterns of the binaural beat generating system. Studies have shown that using Phased Pink Sound at a level at least 10 dB lower than the binaural beat signals produces as much as a 30% enhancement in FFR within the EEG waveforms of the listening individual. There is some basis for concluding that Phased Pink Sound provides an audio base that assists the brain in "synthesizing" the binaural beat frequencies normally inaudible in the human hearing process.

Basically, Phased Pink Sound is generated by a digital processor, which converts mathematical sequences, derived from appropriate algorithms, into audible sound. Such digital processors and their operation are well-known in the art, and so are not discussed here. Inherent in such a system is a frequency sensor that synchronizes the phasing with dominant EEG waveforms as those waveforms are introduced from another source.

Examples of suitable algorithms for implementing Phased Pink Sound are as follows:

```
/*************************************************************************
 * Algorithm to generate 8-bit PCM samples in array pink[] of the        *
 * single channel sound that serves as the source for the stereo         *
 * "phased pink" sound                                                    *
 *************************************************************************/

#include <math.h>
#include <stdio.h>


#define M2PI    -6.283185307179586
#define SAMPLES_PER_SECOND 10466.5
#define CUTOFF 200.0        /* cutoff frequency for low-pass filter */
#define S 83732             /* number of samples to generate */
#define MINDELAY 60         /* minimum flanging delay (samples) */
#define MAXDELAY 80         /* maximum flanging delay (samples) */

extern short w[];           /* 8192 entry table of 16-bit sine values
                               scaled from 0x8001 to 0x7FFF */
extern double st_entries;   /* count of entries in sine table */

long phase;                 /* random number generator phase */
long fa;                    /* filter accumulator */
long fc;                    /* filter constant */
long sweep;                 /* flanging filter phase */
long sweep0;                /* flanging filter initial phase */
long ds;                    /* flanging filter phase step */
long count;                 /* samples remaining in flanging filter cycle */
long count0;                /* samples in flanging filter cycle */
long delay;                 /* current flanging filter delay (XXXX.XXXX) */
long delay0;                /* flanging filter delay constant */
long range;                 /* flanging filter delay range */
short gainNS;               /* noise sound gain (gain = gainNS/1024) */
short gainFS;               /* flanging sound gain (gain = gainFS/1024) */
short noise[S+MAXDELAY];    /* array to receive noise samples */
short offset;               /* final sample offset to balance values */
short scaleF;               /* final scale factor to range samples */
char pink[S];               /* array to receive "phased pink" samples */


/*************************************************************************
 * Main program                                                          *
 *************************************************************************/

main()
{
    long control_base;      /* initial flanging delay */
    long control_range;     /* range of flanging control */
    int i;                  /* loop index */
    short *np;              /* pointer to filtered noise sample array */
    short *fsnp;            /* pointer to initial/final noise sequence */
    short NoiseGen();       /* next filtered noise sample */
    short Flange();         /* flanging sample */
    short xx;               /* output before final scaling */
    /* Initialize the white noise generator */
    phase = 0x8000;
```

```
/* Initialize low-pass filter */
fa = 0;
fc = (1.0 - exp(M2PI * CUTOFF / SAMPLES_PER_SECOND)) * 65536.0;

/* Initialize flanging filter for 8 second cycle.  Delay sweeps
   sinusodially around 5*PI/2.  Flanginging tone gain is 75%
   of the noise tone */
sweep = sweep0 = ((long)((.75 * st_entries) * 65536.0 + 0.5))
   & 0x1FFFFFFF;
control_base = w[sweep0 >> 16];
control_range = 0x0007FFFFL - control_base;
range = (((double)(MAXDELAY - MINDELAY) * 32767.0) / control_range)
   * 16.0 + 0.5;
delay0 = (MINDELAY << 16) - control_base * (range >> 3);
ds = (st_entries / (8.0 * SAMPLES_PER_SECOND)) * 65536.0 + 0.5;
count = 8.0 * SAMPLES_PER_SECOND + 0.5;
gainNS = 585;
gainFS = 439;

/* Initialize the final offset and scale factor for these filter
   parameters (empirically determined) */
offset = 153;
scaleF = 0x245;

/* Generate an initial sequence of noise samples to provide for
   delayed samples */
np = fsnp = noise;
for (i = 0; i < MAXDELAY; i++) *np++ = NoiseGen();

/* Generate the next S samples of "phased pink" sound */
for (i = 0; i < S; i++) {

   /* Generate the next colored noise sample.  For looping,
      finish off with the initial noise sequence */
   if (i < S-MAXDELAY) *np = NoiseGen();
   else *np = *fsnp++;

   /* Apply a sweeping cosine comb filter to flange the sound */
   xx = (*np*gainNS + Flange(np)*gainFS) >> 10;
   pink[i] = ((xx + offset) * scaleF) >> 16;
   np++;

   }
}

/******************************************************************
 * NoiseGen — function to generate a filtered noise sample       *
 ******************************************************************/

short NoiseGen(nsp)
{
   long x;               /* current noise sample */
   long y;               /* current filtered noise sample */

   /* Generate sinusodial density noise from white */
   phase = phase << 1;
```

5,213,562

11

12

```
if (phase & 0x10000) phase = phase ^ 0x1087;
phase = phase & 0xFFFF;
x = w[phase >> 3];

/* Apply 1st order low-pass digital filter */
y = (fc*fa) >> 16;
fa += (x >> 4) - y;
return((short)(y << 4));
}



/****************************************************************
 * Flange — function to generate a flanging noise sample        *
 ****************************************************************/

short Flange(nsp)
   short *nsp;              /* pointer to current noise sample */
{
   short f;                 /* flanging noise sample */
   short *dnp;              /* pointer to delayed noise sample */

   /* Apply a sinusodially sweeping comb filter to flange the sound */
   if (count--) sweep = (sweep + ds) & 0x1FFFFFFF;
   else {
      sweep = sweep0;
      count = count0;
   }

   /* Compute the filter delay and linearly interpolate between
      noise samples to simulate a continuously variable delay */
   delay = delay0 + ((w[sweep >> 16] * range) >> 3);
   dnp = nsp - (delay >> 16);
   f = *dnp +
      ((((*(dnp-1) - *dnp) >> 1) * ((delay & 0xFFFF) >> 1)) >> 14);
   return(f);
}
```

Looking at some results of the inventive method, FIG. 3A shows the EEG of a subject in a normal waking state. FIG. 3B shows an EEG of the individual after listening to binaural beat sounds produced in accordance with the invention. The Figure shows an FFR response in the 1.5, 4, and 6 Hz signal range.

Likewise, FIG. 3C shows the EEG of a subject in a normal waking state, and FIG. 3D shows an EEG of the individual after listening to other binaural beat sounds produced in accordance with the invention. The Figure shows an FFR response in the 2, 4, and 7 Hz signal range.

FIG. 3E shows the EEG of a subject in a normal waking state, and FIG. 3F shows an EEG of the individual after listening to still other binaural beat sounds produced in accordance with the invention. The Figure shows an FFR response in the 0.5, 3, and 4 Hz signal range.

Finally, FIG. 3G shows the EEG of a subject in a normal waking state, and FIG. 3h shows an EEG of the individual after listening to still other binaural beat sounds produced in accordance with the invention. The Figure shows FFR response to 1.5, 2, and 4 Hz signals in amplitude, by frequency.

FIGS. 4A–4C shows a typical contour map of a subject in a normal waking state. It should be noted that the map shows a lack of continuity. Note also the lack of significant amplitude patterns ranging between temporal lobes, and the relative lack of intensity within the frontal area.

In contrast, FIGS. 4D–4F shows a contour map of the same individual after listening to binaural beat sound in accordance with the invention. Note the synchronization between hemispheres, and the high amplitude of activity at the frontal portion of the brain. Note also how the left and right hemisphere brain waves exhibit significantly higher amplitudes in the frequencies found in the original sound stimulus.

The application of the binaural beat signals by headphones or other second producing devices causes the following results:

1. When such audio signals are provided simultaneously with the state of being itself, those specific states can be enhanced. The additional pattern superposed upon the original provides a powerful setting to maintain and/or expand the condition.
2. By recording the audio signals and playing them back, an individual may return to an original or

5,213,562

13

previously-experienced state of consciousness whenever desired.

3. By listing to recordings of these audio signals, an original pattern or condition induced in one individual may be replicated in other individuals.

4. An individual can be trained, based on sufficient repetition of application of these waveforms, to the point that the individual can recall and replicate these waveforms themselves, without further outside stimulation.

The method of the invention has applications in a number of different areas, not the least of which is the inducement of a state of sleep. Other areas of application include inducement of wakefulness of varying degrees; focusing of attention; inducement of mental and physical relaxation; enhancing intellectual performance in various mental disciplines such as mathematics; enhancement of creativity; the reexperience of previous activity; the acquisition of new abilities which others already have; reinforcement and restoration of weak areas in the mind and body; enhancement and strengthening of mental and/or muscular coordination; and development of integration of entire brain function. Human beings have EEG patterns which are unique to the various states of consciousness and mental and/or physical activity just mentioned, so that the imposition of the appropriate stereo audio signals on the desired EEG wave produces the binaural beat which is necessary to induce the state.

While the invention has been described above in detail with reference to a particular specific embodiment, various modifications within the spirit and scope of the invention will be apparent to those of working skill in this technological field. Thus, the invention should be considered as limited only by the scope of the appended claims.

14

What is claimed is:

1. A method of inducing states of consciousness in human beings, comprising:

providing a replicated electroencephalogram (EEG) waveform indicative of a desired state of consciousness;

superimposing said EEG waveform on two separate sets of carrier waves using stereo sound;

creating differential beat frequencies between said sets of carrier waves in accordance with said superimposing step; and

providing the resulting signals in audio form to respective ears of a human being, to induce said state of consciousness.

2. A method as claimed in claim 1, wherein said creating step includes the step of combining pink with said sets of carrier waves by shifting of said pink sound with respect to said EEG waveform from one stereo audio channel to another, with cyclic changes in amplitude, frequency, and rate of panning.

3. A method as claimed in claim 1, wherein all of said steps are performed repeatedly on a particular individual over a period of time so that the individual is able eventually to reproduce said desired state of consciousness without further audio stimulation.

4. A method as claimed in claim 1, wherein all of said steps are performed using the EEG of one individual, but said applying step is carried out with another individual, so as to transfer the desired state of consciousness of one individual to another.

5. A method as claimed in claim 1, wherein said first providing step comprises the step of providing a plurality of EEG waveforms, indicative of different respective states of consciousness, and each of said superimposing, creating, and second providing steps are performed with each of said plurality of EEG waveforms.

6. A method as claimed in claim 1, wherein said second providing step results in substantial synchronization of major portions of both brain hemispheres of said human being.

* * * * *

US005356368A

United States Patent [19]

Monroe

[11] **Patent Number:** **5,356,368**

[45] **Date of Patent:** * **Oct. 18, 1994**

[54] **METHOD OF AND APPARATUS FOR INDUCING DESIRED STATES OF CONSCIOUSNESS**

[75] Inventor: **Robert A. Monroe**, Nelson County, Va.

[73] Assignee: **Interstate Industries Inc.**, Faber, Va.

[*] Notice: The portion of the term of this patent subsequent to May 25, 2010 has been disclaimed.

[21] Appl. No.: **664,176**

[22] Filed: **Mar. 1, 1991**

[51] Int. Cl.⁵ **A61M 21/00**
[52] U.S. Cl. **600/28; 128/732**
[58] Field of Search 600/26–28; 128/731–732

[56] **References Cited**

U.S. PATENT DOCUMENTS

2,466,054	4/1949	Siebel .
3,160,159	12/1964	Hoody et al. .
3,576,185	4/1971	Schulz et al. .
3,712,292	1/1973	Zentmeyer, Jr. .
3,753,433	8/1973	Bakerich et al. .
3,826,243	7/1974	Anderson .
3,837,331	9/1974	Ross .
3,884,218	5/1975	Monroe .
4,034,741	7/1977	Adams et al. .
4,141,344	2/1979	Barbara .

4,227,516	10/1980	Meland et al. .	
4,335,710	6/1982	Williamson .	
4,573,449	3/1986	Warnke .	
4,834,701	5/1989	Masaki .	
4,883,067	11/1989	Knispel et al.	600/28
5,036,858	8/1991	Carter et al. .	
5,101,831	4/1992	Koyama et al.	600/26

Primary Examiner—Lee S. Cohen
Assistant Examiner—J. P. Lacyk
Attorney, Agent, or Firm—Sughrue, Mion, Zinn, Macpeak & Seas

[57] **ABSTRACT**

Improved methods and apparatus for entraining human brain patterns, employing frequency following response (FFR) techniques, facilitate attainment of desired states of consciousness. In one embodiment, a plurality of electroencephalogram (EEG) waveforms, characteristic of a given state of consciousness, are combined to yield an EEG waveform to which subjects may be susceptible more readily. In another embodiment, sleep patterns are reproduced based on observed brain patterns during portions of a sleep cycle; entrainment principles are applied to induce sleep. In yet another embodiment, entrainment principles are applied in the work environment, to induce and maintain a desired level of consciousness. A portable device also is described.

28 Claims, 21 Drawing Sheets

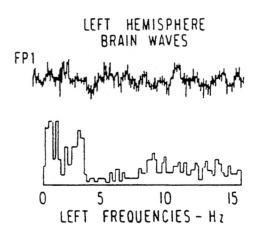

LEFT HEMISPHERE
BRAIN WAVES

FP1

0   5   10   15
LEFT FREQUENCIES - Hz

U.S. Patent   Oct. 18, 1994   Sheet 1 of 21   **5,356,368**

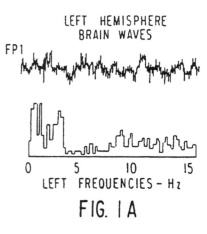

LEFT HEMISPHERE
BRAIN WAVES

FP1

0   5   10   15
LEFT FREQUENCIES – Hz

FIG. 1A

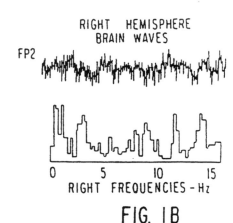

RIGHT HEMISPHERE
BRAIN WAVES

FP2

0   5   10   15
RIGHT FREQUENCIES – Hz

FIG. 1B

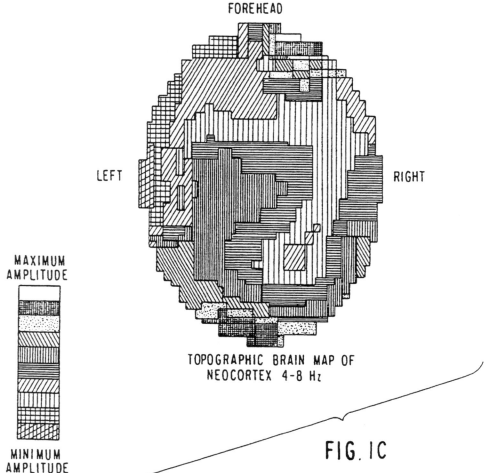

FOREHEAD

LEFT   RIGHT

MAXIMUM
AMPLITUDE

MINIMUM
AMPLITUDE

TOPOGRAPHIC BRAIN MAP OF
NEOCORTEX 4-8 Hz

FIG. 1C

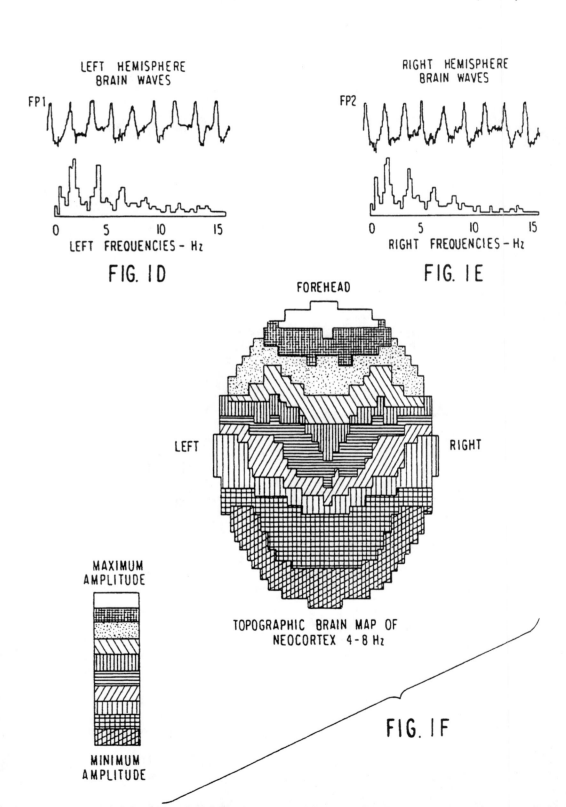

LEFT HEMISPHERE
BRAIN WAVES

FP1

LEFT FREQUENCIES - Hz

FIG. 1D

RIGHT HEMISPHERE
BRAIN WAVES

FP2

RIGHT FREQUENCIES - Hz

FIG. 1E

FOREHEAD

LEFT

RIGHT

MAXIMUM
AMPLITUDE

MINIMUM
AMPLITUDE

TOPOGRAPHIC BRAIN MAP OF
NEOCORTEX 4-8 Hz

FIG. 1F

FIG. 2

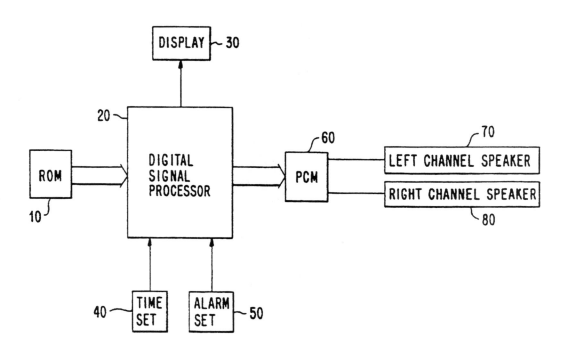

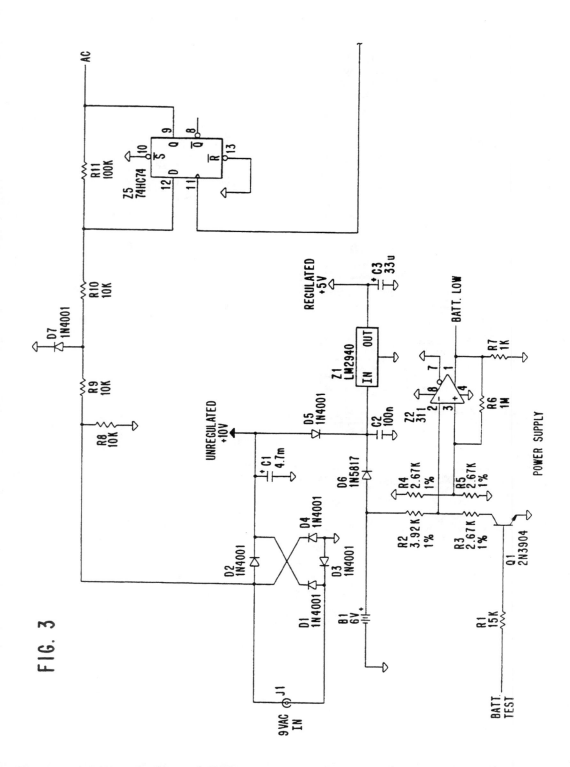

FIG. 3

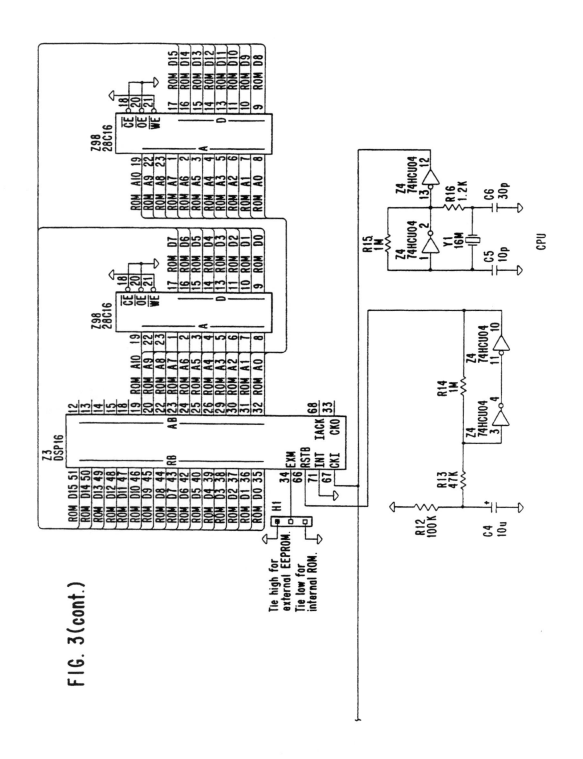

FIG. 3 (cont.)

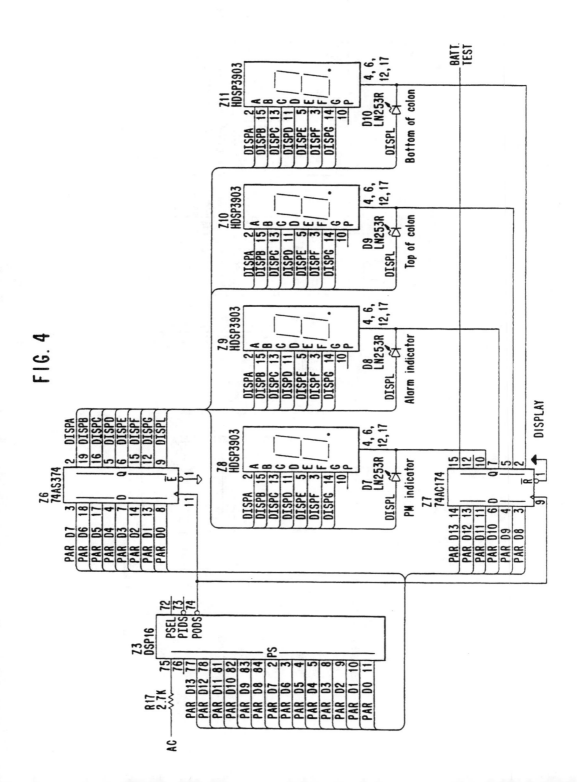

FIG. 4

U.S. Patent　　　Oct. 18, 1994　　　Sheet 7 of 21　　　5,356,368

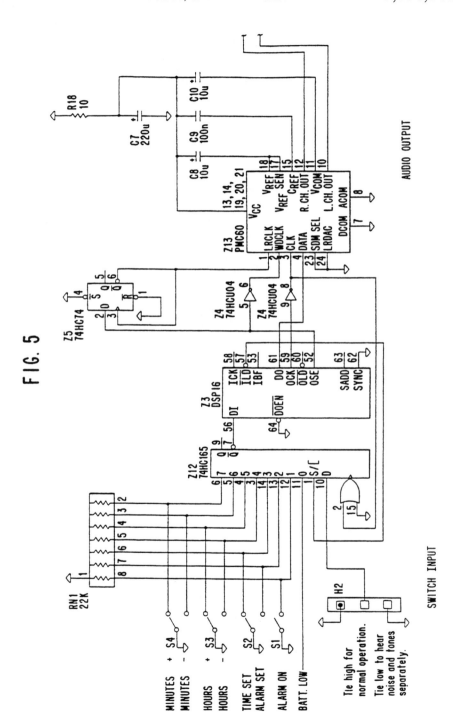

FIG. 5

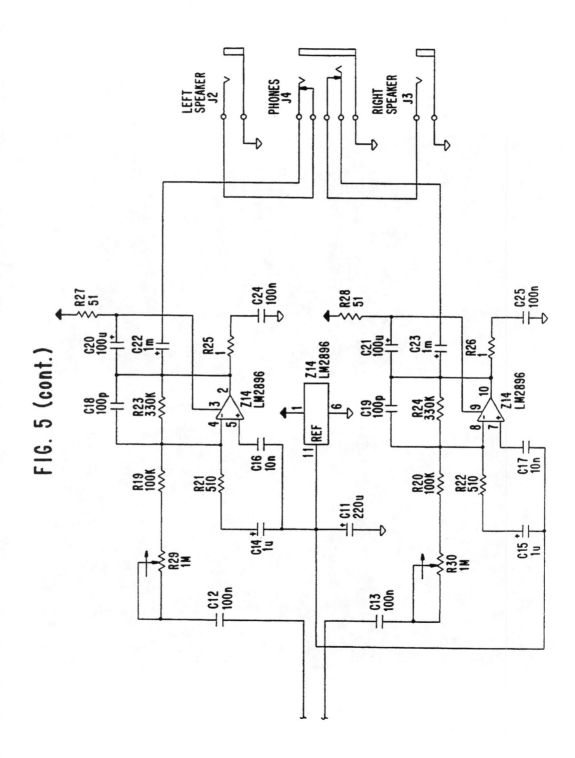

FIG. 5 (cont.)

FIG. 6A

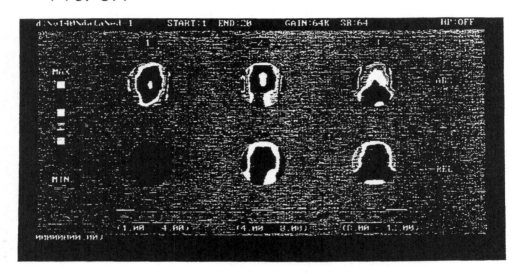

FIG. 6B

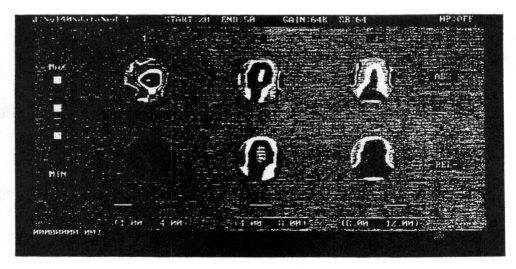

FIG. 6C

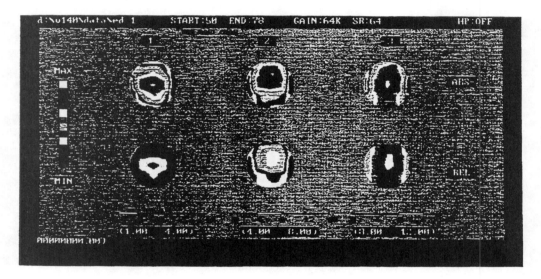

FIG. 6D

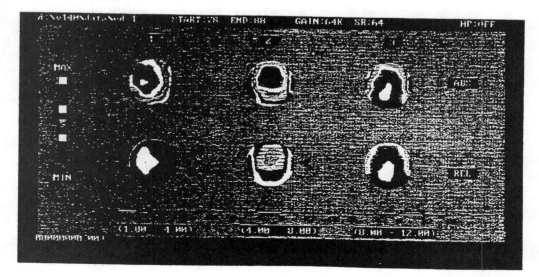

FIG. 6E

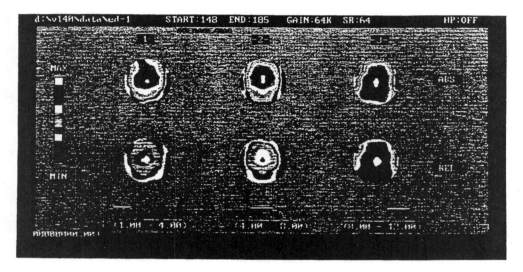

FIG. 6F

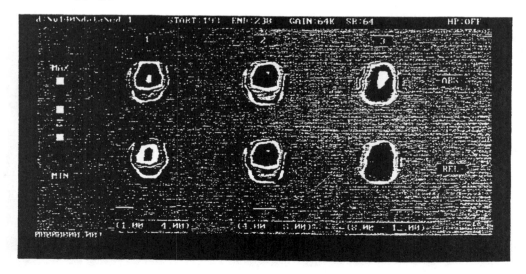

FIG. 6G

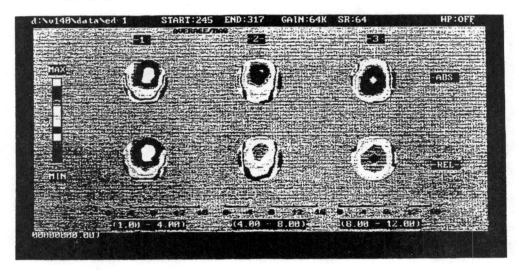

FIG. 6H

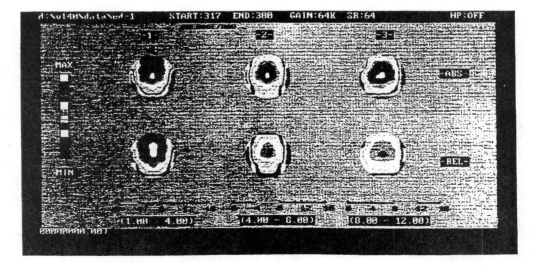

FIG. 6I

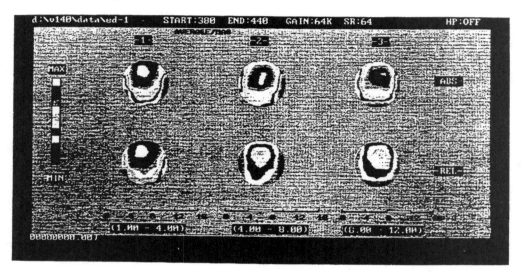

FIG. 6J

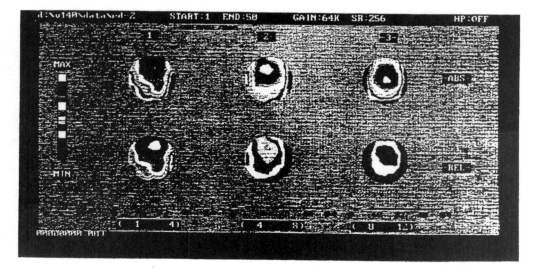

FIG. 7

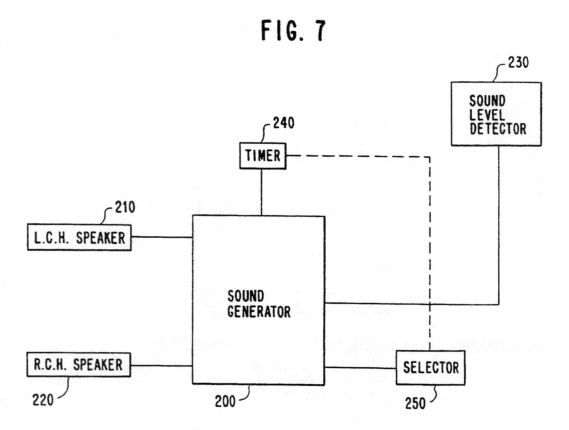

U.S. Patent

Oct. 18, 1994

Sheet 15 of 21

5,356,368

FIG. 8A

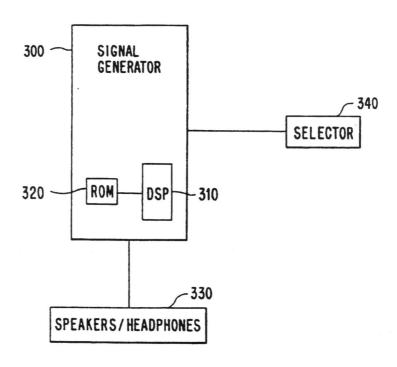

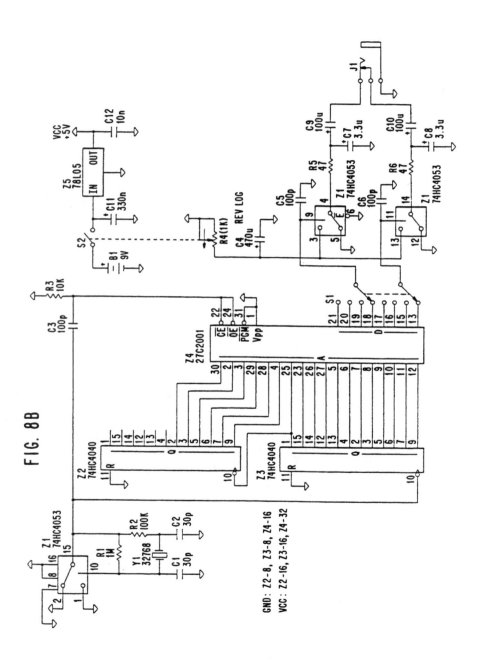

FIG. 8B

FIG. 9A

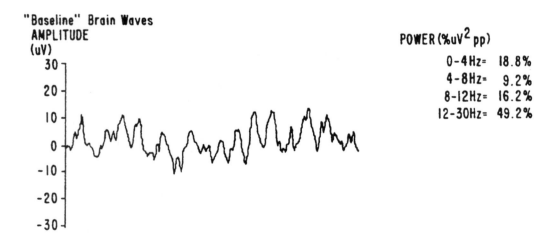

"Baseline" Brain Waves
AMPLITUDE
(uV)

POWER (%uV^{2}pp)

0-4Hz= 18.8%
4-8Hz= 9.2%
8-12Hz= 16.2%
12-30Hz= 49.2%

FIG. 9B

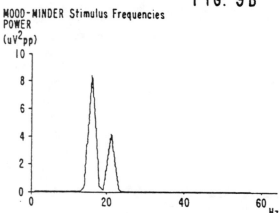

MOOD-MINDER Stimulus Frequencies
POWER
(uV^{2}pp)

POWER(%uV^{2}pp)

16Hz= 47.6%
21Hz= 23.2%

Awake and Alert

FIG. 9C

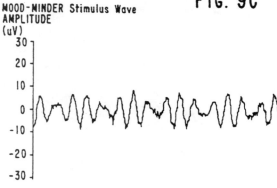

MOOD-MINDER Stimulus Wave
AMPLITUDE
(uV)

POWER(%uV^{2}pp)

16Hz= 47.6%
21Hz= 23.2%

Awake and Alert

FIG. 9D

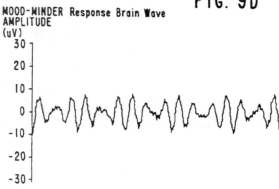

MOOD-MINDER Response Brain Wave
AMPLITUDE
(uV)

POWER(%uV^{2}pp)

16Hz= 46.5%
21Hz= 23.7%

Awake and Alert

U.S. Patent   Oct. 18, 1994   Sheet 19 of 21   5,356,368

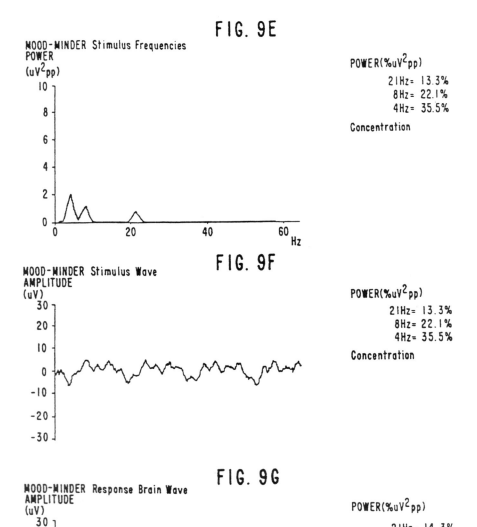

FIG. 9E

MOOD-MINDER Stimulus Frequencies
POWER
(uV^{2}pp)

POWER(%uV^{2}pp)

21Hz= 13.3%
8Hz= 22.1%
4Hz= 35.5%

Concentration

FIG. 9F

MOOD-MINDER Stimulus Wave
AMPLITUDE
(uV)

POWER(%uV^{2}pp)

21Hz= 13.3%
8Hz= 22.1%
4Hz= 35.5%

Concentration

FIG. 9G

MOOD-MINDER Response Brain Wave
AMPLITUDE
(uV)

POWER(%uV^{2}pp)

21Hz= 14.3%
8Hz= 21.5%
4Hz= 31.5%

Concentration

FIG. 9H

MOOD-MINDER Stimulus Frequencies

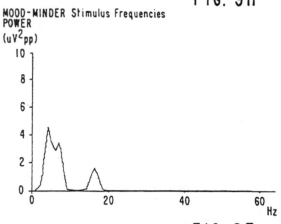

POWER($\%uV^2pp$)

16Hz= 11.5%
7Hz= 28.4%
4Hz= 30.2%

Attention

FIG. 9I

MOOD-MINDER Stimulus Wave

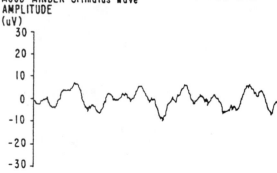

POWER($\%uV^2pp$)

16Hz= 11.5%
7Hz= 28.4%
4Hz= 30.2%

Attention

FIG. 9J

MOOD-MINDER Response Brain Wave

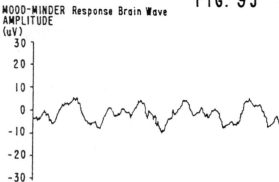

POWER($\%uV^2pp$)

16Hz= 8.2%
7Hz= 28.7%
4Hz= 32.6%

Attention

U.S. Patent Oct. 18, 1994 Sheet 21 of 21 **5,356,368**

FIG. 9K

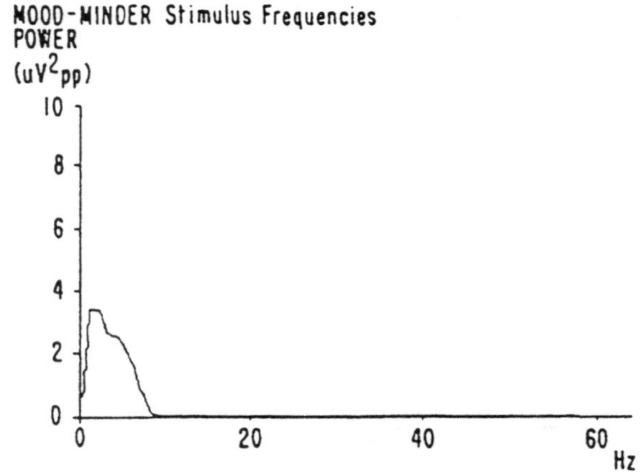
MOOD-MINDER Stimulus Frequencies
POWER
(uV²pp)
10
8
6
4
2
0
0
20
40
60
Hz

POWER(%uV²pp)

6Hz= 9.5%
4Hz= 15.4%
1.5Hz= 19.6%

Relaxation

FIG. 9L

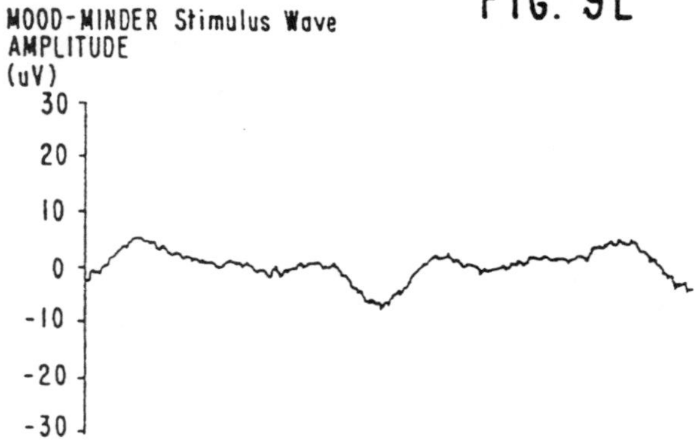
MOOD-MINDER Stimulus Wave
AMPLITUDE
(uV)
30
20
10
0
-10
-20
-30

POWER(%uV²pp)

6Hz= 9.5%
4Hz= 15.4%
1.5Hz= 19.6%

Relaxation

FIG. 9M

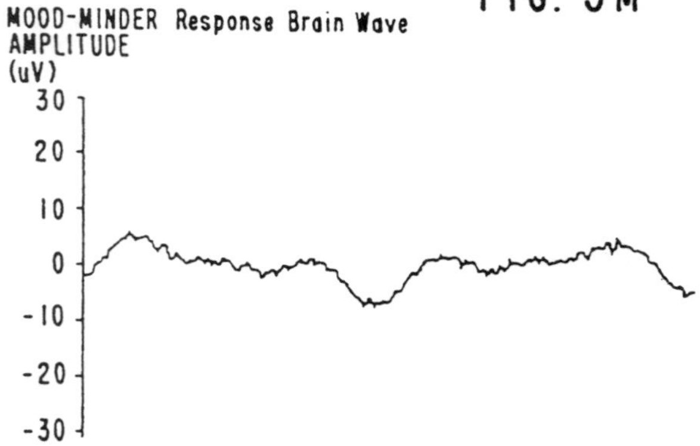
MOOD-MINDER Response Brain Wave
AMPLITUDE
(uV)
30
20
10
0
-10
-20
-30

POWER(%uV²pp)

6Hz= 7.9%
4Hz= 16.8%
1.5Hz= 20.0%

Relaxation

1

5,356,368

2

METHOD OF AND APPARATUS FOR INDUCING DESIRED STATES OF CONSCIOUSNESS

CROSS-REFERENCE TO RELATED APPLICATION

The present application is related to copending application No. 07/514,460, filed Apr. 16, 1990 now U.S. Pat. No. 5,213,562.

BACKGROUND OF THE INVENTION

1. Field of the Invention

The present invention relates to an improved method of inducing desired states of consciousness, including different levels of sleep, in human beings, using a technique known as frequency following response (FFR), developed by the present inventor. The invention also relates to apparatus for performing the method. A number of areas of applicability of the invention are described, in accordance with different preferred embodiments.

2. Description of the Background Art

In a prior patent, U.S. Pat. No. 3,884,218, the present inventor described a method of inducing different levels of sleep, using the FFR technique, in which brain waves could be made to follow superimposed frequency patterns. These frequency patterns were provided as sine waves, at frequencies known to correspond to different levels of sleep, such as alpha (exhibiting brain wave activity in the range of 8–12 Hz), theta (6–8 Hz), and delta (1–4 Hz). EEGs exhibiting frequencies between 12 and 30 Hz (known as a beta range) are characteristic of awake individuals, though beta activity at even higher frequencies has been observed in different types of mental activities. Gamma activity has been characterized as all activity above 30 Hz; until recently, it has not been possible to monitor brain activity in the gamma range. (It should be noted that the boundaries between gamma and beta, beta and alpha, alpha and theta, and theta and delta are somewhat arbitrary; the foregoing delineations are intended to be exemplary and not limiting.)

The present inventor discovered that the human brain could be entrained to output brain wave patterns these different frequencies. While frequencies corresponding to these different levels of sleep are not audible, by superimposing those frequencies on some type of sound, such as music, it was determined to be possible to induce desired levels of sleep. The individual listening to the music would "hear" the low frequencies, with the desired effect on brain activity.

An improvement on the inventor's patented technique, to induce varied states of alertness, is the subject of copending Application No. 07/514,460, the contents of which are hereby incorporated herein by reference. This copending application describes a general FFR technique using what is known as a binaural beat phenomenon, details of which are provided in that application. Briefly, a binaural beat is produced by sending signals at different frequencies (some Hz apart, depending on the desired effect) to an individual's left and right ears. The difference between the frequencies defines the frequency of the binaural beat. Using this technique, the desired frequency can be introduced into the individual's brain activity, inducing the desired state of consciousness.

The induction of FFR in the human brain in this manner results in the synchronization of activity in the hemispheres of the brain. FIG. 1A shows brain activity without FFR, and FIG. 1B shows brain activity with FFR. The inventor has coined the term HEMI-SYNC (for Hemisphere Synchronization) to describe this phenomenon.

The copending application describes a technique wherein, in one form, sine waves having a frequency corresponding to a consciousness state are superimposed on two different carrier frequencies to form two different signals to set up the binaural beat. In another form, an actual brain pattern, based on an electroencephalogram (EEG) waveform indicative of that consciousness state is superimposed on the different carrier frequencies to form two different signals. In use, each signal is provided to one ear of a subject. The difference in carrier frequencies sets up the binaural beat.

Another, more limited application of the binaural beat phenomenon is found in U.S. Pat. No. 4,834,701. In contrast to the narrow range of frequencies discussed in that patent, in the above-mentioned copending application, the applicability of the binaural beat phenomenon is investigated over a much wider range of frequencies, spanning the spectrum of brain activity.

Through additional investigation involving mapping of brain activities of different individuals, the present inventor has discovered some significance to the fact that, while brain waves at certain frequencies are characteristic of different levels of sleep, brain patterns of different individuals still vary. The inventor has investigated possible enhancements to the FFR effect by making it more generic among individuals, yet still more specific to brain activity than a simple sine wave, or an EEG of a particular individual.

Another area of investigation being performed by the present inventor relates to human sleep patterns. Based on current knowledge of human sleep patterns, it appears that sleep is composed of a series of 90-minute cycles. As stated earlier, the beta stage is one of alertness. The first sleep state is alpha, or mental and physical relaxation. The second is theta, or light sleep. Next is delta, or deep sleep. The inventor has investigated the possibility of providing FFR waveforms in cyclic patterns, replicating these human sleep patterns, to facilitate sleep. Another possibility is to take advantage of the cyclic nature of sleep patterns to provide a more gentle wake-up for a sleeper.

In considering the need for alertness during activities such as work, the inventor also considered how it might be possible to introduce FFR waveforms into ambient noise in one's surroundings to facilitate maintenance of desired states of consciousness. Particularly in environments such as factories, or in offices where office equipment puts out consistent types of noise, it would be desirable to be able to introduce a binaural beat into that noise at different frequencies, to enhance the degree of alertness of factory or office workers as desired.

SUMMARY OF THE INVENTION

In view of the foregoing, according to one aspect of the invention, EEGs for a number of individuals in different states of consciousness are sampled, and EEG waveforms for the group of individuals, corresponding to each identifiable state of consciousness, are combined. A binaural beat then is generated using the combined EEGs.

According to this aspect of the invention, it has been determined that using groups of EEG waveforms from different individuals and combining them to obtain a

5,356,368

3

representative waveform yields a waveform that a person's brain is more likely to replicate than an individual EEG waveform, or a sine wave representation of the EEG waveform. The combination may be simple averaging, though other combination techniques, such as weighted averaging, for combining different numbers of EEG waveforms as desired, are contemplated. Now that the inventor has discovered that combinations of EEG waveforms provide a particularly effective entrainment environment, it will be seen that various ways of combining these waveforms may yield greater or lesser effects.

In accordance with another aspect of the invention, a method for replicating cyclic sleep patterns for a desired sleep period is provided. In a preferred embodiment according to this aspect of the invention, a subject is led from beta, to alpha, to theta, to delta, then back to theta, then alpha, then a rapid-eye movement (REM) or light dreaming sleep, in a sequence of 90-minute cycles, during a sleep period of desired duration. After the expiration of the period, the subject may wake up voluntarily. Alternatively, the invention can provide a gentle external stimulus to lead the subject to a beta state.

With respect to this aspect of the invention, an apparatus is provided which automatically leads an individual through these cyclic sleep patterns, and enables the individual to set a desired sleep period. This device preferably takes advantage of the techniques to be described relative to the first-mentioned aspect of the invention, but is not so limited. The inventive contributions of this second aspect of the invention are considered to lie in the combination of hardware itself which generates the desired sequence of binaural beats, as opposed to the particular software which determines the nature of those binaural beats. In one form, the invention is constituted by an alarm clock which provides a fade-in theta-alpha signal followed by a strong beta-gamma signal shortly before a desired wake-up time.

According to yet another embodiment of the invention, selectable mind-affecting sound patterns are provided to supplement constant ambient noise in any environment. When the noise is not present, the patterns are not provided. The patterns vary in amplitude in accordance with changes in the environmental noise.

In accordance with still another embodiment of the invention, a portable system is provided to enable the wearer to introduce binaural beat signals of frequencies that are selectable in accordance with a desired level of awareness. Depending on the level of sophistication of the device, the binaural beat may be generated using the combined EEG waveforms of the first aspect of the invention, but this last aspect of the invention is not so limited.

BRIEF DESCRIPTION OF THE DRAWINGS

The foregoing and other aspects of the invention will be understood by those of working skill in this technological field by reference to the following detailed description of the preferred embodiments of the invention, read in conjunction with the accompanying drawings, wherein:

FIGS. 1A–1C and 1D–1F taken from the above-mentioned copending application, show one example of the results which can be achieved using the inventive techniques;

4

FIG. 2 is a block diagram of the hardware according to a second embodiment of the invention, and FIGS. 3–5 are more detailed schematics therefor;

FIGS. 6A–6J are drawings, similar to FIGS. 1A and 1B, but showing brain activity during various stages of a sleep cycle, using a technique in accordance with the second embodiment of the invention;

FIG. 7 is a block diagram of hardware in accordance with a third embodiment of the invention;

FIG. 8A is a block diagram of hardware in accordance with a fourth embodiment of the invention, and FIG. 8B a schematic of that hardware; and

FIGS. 9A–9M are graphs of different possible effects of the embodiment of FIGS. 8A and 8B, showing a baseline brain pattern, selected stimulus frequencies and corresponding stimulus waves, and associated response waves.

DETAILED DESCRIPTION OF THE PREFERRED EMBODIMENTS

The method according to a first preferred embodiment of the invention, which has been developed through extensive experimentation, derives from the empirically-observed phenomenon that brain patterns of human subjects are entrained more readily to brain patterns which more closely match their own. In prior implementations of the FFR technique, such as in the inventor's prior patent, in which sine waves having frequencies corresponding to desired levels of sleep were superimposed upon a given frequency, entrainment did occur. Use of the binaural beat phenomenon yielded better results, through synchronization of the hemispheres of the brain.

However, simple repetitive frequencies, or even combinations of such frequencies within different ranges, do not represent brain patterns per se, but rather provide entrainment environments for the brain to follow. It has been determined that, the more closely the entrainment environment parallels normal brain function at different levels of consciousness, the more effective the entrainment effect. This phenomenon is what led to the improvement disclosed in the above-mentioned copending application.

As a further improvement on that technique, as mentioned above, the present inventor investigated the possibility of creating more generic models of brain function at different levels of consciousness. As a result of that investigation, it was determined that combinations of EEG waveforms from different individuals functioning at the same identifiable level of consciousness (e.g. alpha sleep, theta sleep, or delta sleep) provided a superior entrainment environment. In the inventive method according to this aspect of the invention, the brain patterns of 40 to 50 individuals were combined to yield the entrainment environment.

One area of applicability of the techniques of the present invention is in the area of sleep therapy. Many individuals suffer from sleep disorders to varying degrees. It is possible to provide a suitable entrainment environment, based on known sleep cycles prevalent in humans, to help individuals to regulate their sleep patterns, and thus help to solve their sleep disorders. One embodiment of the invention, shown in FIG. 2 and also in FIGS. 3–5, implements the inventive techniques in what the inventor calls a Sleep Processor to aid in the regulation of human sleep cycles.

In FIG. 2, a read-only memory (ROM) 10 stores frequency sequences corresponding to different parts of

5,356,368

5   6

a human sleep cycle. The stored frequency sequences may be in accordance with a predetermined algorithm, or alternatively may provide a less complex entrainment environment, such as simple averaging. A digital signal processor (DSP) 20 selects different ones of these sequences based on the current time and the time to which an alarm is set. The time is displayed on display 30, and is set using time set 40. The alarm is set to a desired wake-up time using alarm set 50.

During operation, the DSP 20 accesses the ROM 10 and provides an output to a pulse code modulator unit (PCM) 60 accordingly. The PCM 60 provides an output to each of left and right channel speakers 70, 80 which are provided in close proximity to the ears of a human subject. Using headphones enhances the effect.

Some additional detail of operation of the DSP 20 in one aspect of this embodiment now will be provided. A serial port in the DSP 20 generates an interrupt at a 50 KHz rate. An interrupt handler in the DSP 20 computes the various sounds, in one form, by generating sine waves using a pair of integrators:

$$\text{cosine} = \text{cosine} + \text{frequency} \times \text{sine}$$
$$\text{sine} = \text{sine} - \text{frequency} \times \text{cosine}$$

The Sleep Processors needs ten frequencies, five for each channel, and all of these frequencies are generated at the same time. The results are multiplied by ten envelopes, most of which are zero at any moment.

Noise is generated by a well-known 16-bit shift-register algorithm. This algorithm generates a noise signal that repeats every 65535 samples, or about every five seconds. The noise is filtered to sound more like pink or red noise, and less like white noise, and is written into a delay line in RAM. For each channel, the filtered noise is averaged with an earlier sample from the delay line, thus imparting a comb filter response to it.

An additional low-frequency sine/cosine pair is generated, to sweep the comb filter delay. 32-bit arithmetic is used here. The approximate sweep rate is about 1/8 Hz. The low-frequency sine wave is used directly to sweep the delay on one channel. The delay on the other channel is controlled by some mix of the sine and cosine waves. By choosing these and other coefficients properly, any phase and amplitude relationship between the left and right sweep can be obtained. The comb filtered noise for each channel is multiplied by a noise envelope value.

The device is operated as follows. A desired wake-up time is set, much like an alarm clock, and the desired volume is selected. A start/stop button then is pressed to start the cycles for the selected sleep period. Throughout the sleep period, the device repeats a 90 minute cycle of sound that leads the subject through alpha, theta, delta, and back to dreaming sleep. Five minutes before the scheduled wake-up time, a beta signal is introduced to bring the subject back to complete physical wakefulness. When the subject wakes up, he/-she hits the start/stop button again to stop the sound sequence.

The sounds produced by the DSP 20 include binaural beat carrier sound patterns utilizing both amplitude and frequency modulation, masking pink sound (a known type of sound described in the copending application), and, optionally, occasional single-word voiced affirmations. The binaural beat audio signals may be in the form of appropriate sine waves, or alternatively may be replicas of actual EEG brain waveforms. In the latter case, either the just-described combined EEG waveforms or a single EEG waveform (as described in the copending

application) may be used. The entire pattern of sound and control is generated algorithmically.

One aspect of the effectiveness of the device of FIGS. 2–5 is the spacing of sound carriers at related frequencies so as to engender binaural beat signals not only from channel to channel, but also monaurally, in each audio channel. In this preferred embodiment, three binaural beat frequency signals are created between audio carrier channels, and two amplitude beats per channel also are created, yielding a total of seven beat signals. The inventor has coined the term Septon for this set of beat signals. One example of a septon is as follows:

Left Channel		Right Channel
200 Hz carrier (4 Hz monaural beat)	(4 Hz binaural beat)	204 Hz carrier (4 Hz monaural beat)
204 Hz carrier (4 Hz monaural beat)	(4 Hz binaural beat)	208 Hz carrier (4 Hz monaural beat)
208 Hz carrier	(4 Hz binaural beat)	212 Hz carrier

A standard program according to this preferred embodiment would employ the following sound sequence:
0–5 minutes:
Signal Group A (comprised of replicated EEG waveforms having dominant values in the alpha range)
Signal Group B (15 dB below Group A, generated simultaneously with the sounds of Group A, and comprised of replicated EEG waveforms having dominant values in the theta range)
Phased Pink Sound (six seconds, peak-to-peak, on both left and right channels, 20 dB below Group A)
Voice Inserts (repeated at 40 second intervals, 10 dB below Group A, simultaneously with the other sounds, and comprising short sequences of phrases like "relax" "let go", and "sleep")
5–20 minutes:
Signal Group B
Signal Group C (20 dB below Group B, generated simultaneously with Group B, and comprised of replicated EEG waveforms having dominant values in the delta range)
Phased Pink Sound (15 dB below Group B, having a duration as in the first interval)
Voice Inserts (10 dB below Group B, comprised as above)
20–40 minutes:
Signal Group C
Signal Group D (10 dB below Group C, generated simultaneously with Group C, and comprised of replicated EEG waveforms having dominant values in the lower delta range)
Phased Pink Sound (10 dB below Group C, having a duration as in the first interval)
Voice Inserts (20 dB below Group C, comprised as above) 40–65 minutes:
Signal Group D
Phased Pink Sound (10 dB below Group D, having a duration as in the first interval)
Voice Inserts (20 dB below Group D, comprised as above) 65–80 minutes:
Signal Group C
Signal Group D (10 dB below Group C, generated simultaneously with Group C)
Phased Pink Sound (15 dB below Group C, having a duration as in the first interval)

NO voice inserts
80–90 minutes:
Signal Group B
Signal Group C (10 dB below B, generated simultaneously with Group B)
Phased Pink Sound (15 dB below Group B, having a duration as in the first interval)
NO voice inserts

The foregoing sequence is repeated through the sleep period until the wakeup sequence, approximately five minutes before the set wake-up time:
Signal Group AA (a wakeup sequence, comprising replicated EEG waveforms having dominant values in the beta range, or alternatively a 400 Hz/416 Hz envelope yielding frequencies in the beta range)
Voice inserts (10 dB below Group AA, comprised of short phrases such as "waking up", "refreshed", "bright", and repeated at intervals)

One variation of the foregoing embodiment is an alarm clock which, instead of sounding a loud alarm or other jarring noise at wake-up time, starts a gentle sequence of signals some minutes before, to bring an individual up gently through the various levels of sleep to full wakefulness. A fade-in theta-alpha signal may be provided, followed by a stronger beta-gamma signal.

FIGS. 6A to 6J show the effects of the just-described "sleep processor" embodiment. Column 1 shows distribution of delta frequencies; column 2 shows distribution of theta frequencies; and column 3 shows distribution of alpha frequencies. The top row of graphs is the actual pattern observed in the individual, and the bottom row is the baseline pattern.

FIG. 6A corresponds to a normal waking state. Dominant alpha activity is shown in the occipital area of the brain. In FIG. 6B, pink noise has been applied, without any beat frequencies. A narrower focus of waking state is shown.

In FIG. 6C, a signal sequence corresponding to Signal Group A has been applied. Some gain in theta frequencies are seen, with rapid diffusion of alpha frequencies and movement toward the vertex of the head. In FIG. 6D, a signal sequence corresponding to Signal Group B has been applied. There is further diffusion of alpha frequencies, with some movement of delta and theta activity toward the pre-frontal cortex of the brain.

In FIG. 6E, a signal sequence corresponding to Signal Group C has been applied. There is rapid diffusion of alpha frequencies, and increased power of theta and delta frequencies. In FIG. 6F, a signal sequence corresponding to Signal Group D has been applied. Alpha frequencies are diffused further toward the pre-frontal cortex, and there is a marked increase in theta and delta frequencies.

FIG. 6G, continuing application of Signal Group D frequencies, shows a marked increase in delta activity in the pre-frontal cortex, with a steady decrease in alpha activity at the vertex. In FIG. 6H, another binaural beat stimulation has been applied, and characteristics of stage 3 and 4 sleep may be observed. In FIG. 6I, further evidence of the further binaural beat stimulation is observed. Delta is the dominant frequency here. Alpha and theta activity has moved to the prefrontal cortex. Finally, FIG. 6J shows early awakening activity, with a diffusion of delta activity.

FIG. 7 is a block diagram of hardware in accordance with another embodiment of the invention, having application to the work environment, or anywhere a constant source of noise is present, to allow workers, for example, to maintain a desired state of awareness. The device may contain suitable digital signal processor circuitry, as in the preceding embodiment. One difference is that the operation of the device is keyed to the presence of ambient noise, not to a given time duration or selected sleep period.

The device of FIG. 7 includes a sound generator 200 which, as just mentioned, may comprise a digital signal processor. The generator 200 outputs sound patterns via one or more speakers (left and right channel speakers 210, 220 are shown). A sound level detector 230 detects the level of ambient noise in the room, and provides a signal to the sound generator 200, or activates a cut-off switch (not shown), to discontinue output of the sound generator 200 when the ambient noise level drops below a predetermined level.

The sound level detector also preferably provides a signal to the sound generator 200 to boost the sound pattern output when the ambient noise level increases, so that the effect of the provision of the sound pattern is commensurate with the noise level in the room. Alternatively, the user may simply adjust the volume manually, using one or more knobs (not shown) on the sound generator 200.

A timer 240 may be provided to control the duration of provision of the selected sound pattern, or even to change the sound pattern at different times of day by controlling a selector 250 which the user accesses to select a particular sound pattern to be output. The user may select a given sound pattern in the morning, and the timer 240 may change that pattern automatically, based on a need at different times of day for sound patterns providing different states of alertness.

The sound pattern produced by the device of FIG. 7 varies automatically in amplitude in accordance with changes in the ambient noise, and is discontinued when the noise stops. As a result, the sound remains unobtrusive. Depending on the setting, the produced sound pattern can enhance wakefulness, promote relaxation (as, for example, in rest areas in the workplace), reduce anxiety and stress, or focus attention, among other characteristics.

The basic system of FIG. 7 produces and inserts four different sound patterns which are selected manually so as to merge the output into the constant ambient noise. More sound patterns are possible, depending on the desired overall capabilities of the system. Various modifications are possible. For example, a programmable version may be provided, which changes the form of the sound patterns throughout a work day or night, in accordance with the responses desired.

Selectability of patterns may be accomplished differently in a model intended for use in conjunction with a computer system. The computer operator can input a selection, and may vary that selection as desired throughout the work day.

FIG. 8A is a diagram of a portable embodiment of the invention, for use in providing a desired level of consciousness on an individualized basis. A signal generator 300 preferably includes a digital signal processor 310 and a ROM 320 for storing predetermined signals or sequences of signals which correspond to various desired states of awareness. The signal generator 300 may be a simple tone generator or pair of tone generators which provide outputs to speakers or headphones 330 (such as button-sized headphones) to set up a binaural beat. Output of pink sound or phased pink sound by the generator 300 is desirable to facilitate defocusing of the

9

5,356,368

10

listener and consequent ability to concentrate on the sounds being produced. A selector 340 enables a user to instruct the signal generator 300 to output signals corresponding to the level of consciousness (e.g. focused concentration, relaxation, alertness) that a user desires.

FIG. 8B shows a schematic of this embodiment, which the inventor calls a "Mood Minder". This embodiment includes a selector for selecting one of four possible types of signals, corresponding to four respective levels of awareness: awake and alert; concentration; attention; and relaxation. However, the invention is not so limited, as the generator 300 may be capable of producing other possible types of signals. Alternatively, pre-set patterns in the generator 300 may vary when specialized use is required. The key to this embodiment is its portability, enabling the user to carry the device everywhere. The device is battery-operated, and is small enough to fit in an upper coat pocket, for example.

FIGS. 9A–9M show examples of prestored patterns produced by the generator 300, and of results achieved in use. FIG. 9A shows baseline brain waves, with relative power output shown at the right for different frequencies. FIGS. 9B, 9E, 9H, and 9K show the stimulus frequencies produced for four different respective states of consciousness. FIGS. 9C, 9F, 9I, and 9L show the stimulus waves corresponding to the superposition of the stimulus frequencies on the baseline wave. FIGS. 9D, 9G, 9J, and 9M show the results achieved in use. As can be seen, the peak-to-peak amplitudes for the response brain waves correspond closely to those of the stimulus waves.

While the present invention has been described in detail with reference to preferred embodiments, various modifications within the scope and spirit of the invention will be apparent to those of working skill in this technological field. Consequently, the invention should be considered as limited only by the scope of the appended claims.

What is claimed is:

1. A method of inducing desired states of consciousness in human beings, comprising the following steps:

    combining a plurality of replicated electroencephalogram (EEG) waveforms, each indicative of a particular desired state of consciousness, to produce a combined EEG waveform;

    superimposing said combined EEG waveform on two separate sets of carrier waves using stereo sound;

    creating differential beat frequencies between said sets of carrier waves based on said superimposing step; and

    providing the resulting signals in audio form to respective ears of a human being, to induce said state of consciousness.

2. A method as claimed in claim 1, wherein said combining step comprises mathematically averaging said EEG waveforms to produce said combined EEG waveform.

3. A method as claimed in claim 1, further comprising the step of repeating said combining, superimposing, and creating steps for each of a set of desired states of consciousness, and producing a cycle of sets of resulting audio signals, said providing step comprising providing said cycle of sets of resulting audio signals to respective ears of a human being, to induce each of said desired states of consciousness in cyclic fashion.

4. A method as claimed in claim 3, wherein said cycle corresponds to human sleep patterns, said desired states of consciousness comprising wakefulness, alpha sleep, delta sleep, and theta sleep.

5. A method as claimed in claim 3, wherein said cycle corresponds to human sleep patterns, said desired states of consciousness comprising alpha sleep, delta sleep, and theta sleep, said cycle being approximately 90 minutes long.

6. A method as claimed in claim 5, said method further comprising the steps of providing a plurality of repetitions of said cycle, followed by providing a set of audio signals containing a binaural beat at a frequency indicative of beta consciousness.

7. A method as claimed in claim 1, wherein said creating step includes the step of combining pink sound with said sets of carder waves by shifting of said pink sound with respect to said combined EEG waveform from one stereo audio channel to another, with cyclic changes in amplitude, frequency, and rate of panning.

8. Apparatus for facilitating sleep in a human subject, comprising:

    means for setting a wake-up time to select a desired sleep duration;

    means for generating a first sequence of signals in a cycle corresponding to a human sleep pattern, frequencies of said signals in said first sequence being substantially equal to frequencies of human brain patterns at different levels of sleep;

    means for repeating said cycle a plurality of times based on the selected wake-up time; and

    means for waking up said human subject at the selected wake-up time.

9. Apparatus as claimed in claim 8, wherein said means for waking up said human subject comprises means for generating a second sequence of signals a predetermined time before the selected wake-up time, frequencies of said signals in said second sequence being substantially equal to frequencies of human brain patterns at or near an awakened state.

10. Apparatus as claimed in claim 9, wherein said predetermined time is approximately five minutes.

11. Apparatus as claimed in claim 8, wherein said first sequence of frequencies comprises, in order, alpha frequencies, theta frequencies, delta frequencies, and theta frequencies.

12. Apparatus as claimed in claim 8, further comprising means for generating phased pink sound in conjunction with said first sequence of frequencies.

13. Apparatus as claimed in claim 8, wherein said first sequence of signals comprises a plurality of sets of combined brainwaves, each of said sets corresponding to a different level of sleep, said combined brainwaves within a given set being constituted by combined electroencephalogram (EEG) waveforms of a plurality of individuals, taken when said individuals had attained a different respective level of sleep.

14. Apparatus as claimed in claim 13, wherein said EEG waveforms are mathematically averaged.

15. Apparatus for awakening an individual using brain pattern entrainment, said apparatus comprising:

    means for selecting a wake-up time;

    means for keeping time; and

    means, operative a predetermined period before said wake-up time as determined by said means for keeping time, for producing a first sequence of signals having frequencies in the theta-alpha range, followed by a second sequence of signals having frequencies in the beta-gamma range.

5,356,368

11

16. Apparatus as claimed in claim **15**, wherein said means for producing said first and second sequences of signals comprises means for producing said second sequence of signals at a higher amplitude than said first sequence of signals.

17. Apparatus as claimed in claim **15**, wherein said first sequence of signals comprises a plurality of sets of combined brainwaves, each of said sets corresponding to a different level of consciousness, said combined brainwaves within a given set being constituted by combined electroencephalogram (EEG) waveforms of a plurality of individuals, taken when said individuals had attained a different respective level of consciousness.

18. Apparatus as claimed in claim **16**, wherein said EEG waveforms are mathematically averaged.

19. Apparatus for inducing a desired state of consciousness, said apparatus comprising:

   means for detecting presence of a predetermined level of ambient noise;

   means, responsive to said detecting means, for generating signals having frequencies substantially equal to frequencies of human brain patterns when said ambient noise is present; and

   means for selecting said signals in accordance with desired human activity in said areas.

20. Apparatus as claimed in claim **19**, further comprising timer means, connected to said generating means, for generating said signals for a predetermined time set by said timer means.

21. Apparatus as claimed in claim **19**, wherein said timer means is connected to said selecting means to enable selection of different ones of said signals in accordance with desired human activity at different times of day.

22. Apparatus as claimed in claim **19**, wherein said generating means comprises means, responsive to said detecting means, for increasing an amplitude of said signals in response to an increase in amplitude of said ambient noise, and for decreasing an amplitude of said

12

signals in response to a decrease in amplitude of said ambient noise.

23. Apparatus as claimed in claim **22**, wherein said generating means further comprises means for discontinuing said signals when said ambient noise falls below said predetermined level.

24. Apparatus as claimed in claim **19**, wherein said generating means comprises a digital signal processor and a read-only memory (ROM) connected to said digital signal processor, said ROM storing a plurality of sets of signals, each of said sets of signals having frequencies substantially equal to human brain patterns at a desired state of consciousness.

25. Apparatus as claimed in claim **24**, wherein each of said sets of signals comprises a plurality of sets of combined brainwaves, each of said sets corresponding to a different level of consciousness, said combined brainwaves within a given set being constituted by combined electroencephalogram (EEG) waveforms of a plurality of individuals, taken when said individuals had attained a different respective state of consciousness.

26. Apparatus as claimed in claim **25**, wherein said EEG waveforms are mathematically averaged.

27. Apparatus for awakening an individual using brain pattern entrainment, said apparatus comprising:

   means for selecting a wake-up time; and

   means, operative a predetermined period before said wake-up time, for producing a first sequence of signals having frequencies in a first predetermined range corresponding to a first state of consciousness, followed by a second sequence of signals having frequencies in a second predetermined range corresponding to a second state of consciousness.

28. Apparatus as claimed in claim **27**, wherein said first predetermined range is the theta-alpha range, and said second predetermined range is the beta-gamma range.

*   *   *   *   *

ANTI-GRAVITY

THE ANTI-GRAVITY HANDBOOK
edited by David Hatcher Childress, with Arthur C. Clarke, Nikola Tesla, T.B. Paulicki, Bruce Cathie, Leonard G. Cramp and Albert Einstein

The new expanded compilation of material on Anti-Gravity, Free Energy, Flying Saucer Propulsion, UFOs, Suppressed Technology, NASA Cover-ups and more. Highly illustrated with patents, technical illustrationsand photos. This revised and expanded edition has more material, including photos of Area 51, Nevada, the government's secret testing facility. This classic on weird science is back in a 90s format!
* How to build a flying saucer.
* Arthur C. Clarke on Anti-Gravity.
* Crystals and their role in levitation.
* Secret government research and development.
* Nikola Tesla on how anti-gravity airships could draw power from the atmosphere.
* Bruce Cathie's Anti-Gravity Equation.
* NASA, the Moon and Anti-Gravity.
230 PAGES, 7x10 TRADEPAPER, BIBLIOGRAPHY/INDEX/APPENDIX. HIGHLY ILLUSTRATED WITH 100'S OF PATENTS ILLUSTRATIONS AND PHOTOS, $14.95. CODE: AGH

ANTI-GRAVITY & THE WORLD GRID
edited by David Hatcher Childress

Is the earth surrounded by an intricate network of electromagnetic grid network offering free energy? This compilation of material on ley lines and world power points contains chapters on the geography, mathematics, and light harmonics of the earth grid. Learn the purpose of ley lines and ancient megalithic structures located on the grid. Discover how the grid made the Philadelphia Experiment possible. Explore the Coral Castle and many other mysteries; Including acoustic levitation, Tesla Shields and scalar wave weaponry. Browse through the section on anti-gravity patents, and research resources.
274 PAGES, 150 RARE PHOTOGRAPHS, DIAGRAMS AND DRAWINGS, 7x10 PAPERBACK, $14.95. CODE: AGW

ANTI-GRAVITY & THE UNIFIED FIELD
edited by David Hatcher Childress

Is Einstein's Unified Field Theory the answer to all of our energy problems? Explored in this compilation of material is how gravity, electricity and magnetism manifest from a unified field around us. Why artificial gravity is possible; secrets of UFO propulsion; free energy; Nikola Tesla and anti-gravity airships of the 20's and 30's; flying saucers as superconducting whirls of plasma; anti-mass generators; vortex propulsion; suppressed technology; government cover-ups; gravitational pulse drive, spacecraft & more.
240 PAGES. 7x10 PAPERBACK. HEAVILY ILLUSTRATED. $14.95. CODE: AGU

ETHER TECHNOLOGY
A Rational Approach to Gravity Control
by Rho Sigma

This classic book on anti-gravity & free energy is back in print and back in stock. Written by a well-known American scientist under the pseudonym of "Rho Sigma," this book delves into international efforts at gravity control and discoid craft propulsion. Before the Quantum Field, there was "Ether." This small, but informative book has chapters on John Searle and "Searle discs;" T. Townsend Brown and his work on anti-gravity and ether-vortex-turbines. Includes a forward by former NASA astronaut Edgar Mitchell. Don't miss this classic book!
108 PAGES, 6x9 TRADEPAPER, ILLUSTRATED WITH PHOTOS & DIAGRAMS. $12.95. CODE: ETT

UNDERGROUND BASES & TUNNELS
What is the Government Trying to Hide?
by Richard Sauder, Ph.D.

Working from government documents and corporate records, Sauder has compiled an impressive book that digs below the surface of the military's super-secret underground! Go behind the scenes into little-known corners of the public record and discover how corporate America has worked hand-in-glove with the Pentagon for decades, dreaming about, planning, and actually constructing, secret underground bases. This book includes chapters on the locations of the bases, the tunneling technology, various military designs for underground bases, nuclear testing & underground bases, abductions, needles & implants; Is the Military Involvement in "alien" cattle mutilations?, more. 50 page photo & map insert.
201 PAGES. 6x9 PAPERBACK. WELL ILLUSTRATED. $15.95. CODE: UGB

24 HOUR CREDIT CARD ORDERS—CALL: 815-253-6390 FAX: 815-253-6300

email: auphq@frontiernet.net   http://www.azstarnet.com/~aup

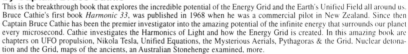

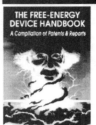

THE FREE-ENERGY DEVICE HANDBOOK
A Compilation of Patents and Reports
by David Hatcher Childress
A large-format compilation of various patents, papers, descriptions and diagrams concerning free-energy devices and systems. *The Free-Energy Device Handbook* is a visual tool for experimenters and researchers into magnetic motors and other "over-unity" devices. With chapters on the Adams Motor, the Hans Coler Generator, cold fusion, superconductors, "N" machines, space-energy generators, Nikola Tesla, T. Townsend Brown, and the latest in free-energy devices. Packed with photos, technical diagrams, patents and fascinating information, this book belongs on every science shelf. With energy and profit being a major political reason for fighting various wars, free-energy devices, if ever allowed to be mass-distributed to consumers, could change the world! Get your copy now before the Department of Energy bans this book!
292 PAGES. 8X10 TRADEPAPER. ILLUSTRATED. BIBLIOGRAPHY. $16.95. CODE: FEH

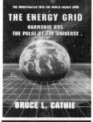

THE BRIDGE TO INFINITY
Harmonic 371244
by Captain Bruce Cathie
Cathie has popularized the concept that the earth is criss–crossed by an electromagnetic grid system that can be used for anti-gravity, free energy, levitation and more. The book includes a new analysis of the harmonic nature of reality, acoustic levitation, pyramid power, harmonic receiver towers and UFO propulsion. It concludes that today's scientists have at their command a fantastic store of knowledge with which to advance the welfare of the human race.
204 PAGES. 6X9 TRADEPAPER. ILLUSTRATED. $14.95. CODE: BTF

THE ENERGY GRID
Harmonic 695, The Pulse of the Universe
by Captain Bruce Cathie
This is the breakthrough book that explores the incredible potential of the Energy Grid and the Earth's Unified Field all around us. Bruce Cathie's first book *Harmonic 33*, was published in 1968 when he was a commercial pilot in New Zealand. Since then Captain Bruce Cathie has been the premier investigator into the amazing potential of the infinite energy that surrounds our planet every microsecond. Cathie investigates the Harmonics of Light and how the Energy Grid is created. In this amazing book are chapters on UFO propulsion, Nikola Tesla, Unified Equations, the Mysterious Aerials, Pythagoras & the Grid. Nuclear detonation and the Grid, maps of the ancients, an Australian Stonehenge examined, more.
255 PAGES. 6X9 TRADEPAPER. ILLUSTRATED. $15.95. CODE: TEG

UFOS AND ANTI-GRAVITY
Piece For A Jig-Saw
by Leonard G. Cramp
Leonard G. Cramp's 1966 classic book on flying saucer propulsion and suppressed technology is available again. *UFOS & Anti-Gravity: Piece For A Jig-Saw* is a highly technical look at the UFO phenomena by a trained scientist. Cramp first introduces the idea of 'anti-gravity' and introduces us to the various theories of gravitation. He then examines the technology necessary to build a flying saucer and examines in great detail the technical aspects of such a craft. Cramp's book is a wealth of material and diagrams on flying saucers, anti-gravity, suppressed technology, G-fields and UFOs. Chapters include Crossroads of Aerodynamics, Aerodynamic Saucers, Limitations of Rocketry, Gravitation and the Ether, Gravitational Spaceships, G. Field Lift Effects, The Bi-Field Theory, VTOL and Hovercraft, Analysis of UFO photos, more. "I feel the Air Force has not been giving out all available information on these unidentified flying objects. You cannot disregard so many unimpeachable sources." — John McCormack, Speaker of the U.S. House of Representatives.
388 PAGES. 6X9 PAPERBACK. HEAVILY ILLUSTRATED. $16.95. CODE: UAG

MAN-MADE UFOS 1944—1994
Fifty Years of Suppression
by Renato Vesco & David Hatcher Childress
A comprehensive look at the early "flying saucer technology" of Nazi Germany and the genesis of early man-made UFOs. This book takes us from the work of captured German scientists, to escaped battalions of Germans, secret communities in South America and Antarctica to todays state-of-the-art "Dreamland" flying machines. Heavily illustrated, this astonishing book blows the lid off the "government UFO conspiracy" and explains with technical diagrams the technology involved. Examined in detail are secret underground airfields and factories; German secret weapons; "suction" aircraft; the origin of NASA; gyroscopic stabilizers and engines; the secret Marconi aircraft factory in South America; and more. Not to be missed by students of technology suppression, secret societies, anti-gravity, free energy conspiracy and World War II! Introduction by W.A. Harbinson, author of the Dell novels *GENESIS* and *REVELATION.*
318 PAGES. 6X9 TRADEPAPER. ILLUSTRATED. INDEX & FOOTNOTES. $18.95. CODE: MMU

24 HOUR CREDIT CARD ORDERS—CALL: **815-253-6390** FAX: **815-253-6300**
email: auphq@frontiernet.net   http://www.azstarnet.com/~aup

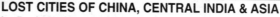

THE LOST CITIES SERIES

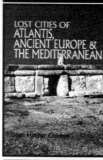

LOST CITIES OF ATLANTIS, ANCIENT EUROPE & THE MEDITERRANEAN
by David Hatcher Childress

Atlantis! The legendary lost continent comes under the close scrutiny of maverick archaeologist David Hatcher Childress in this sixth book in the internationally popular *Lost Cities* series. Childress takes the reader in search of sunken cities in the Mediterranean; across the Atlas Mountains in search of Atlantean ruins; to remote islands in search of megalithic ruins; to meet living legends and secret societies. From Ireland to Turkey, Morocco to Eastern Europe, and around the remote islands of the Mediterranean and Atlantic, Childress takes the reader on an astonishing quest for mankind's past. Ancient technology, cataclysms, megalithic construction, lost civilizations and devastating wars of the past are all explored in this book. Childress challenges the skeptics and proves that great civilizations not only existed in the past, but the modern world and its problems are reflections of the ancient world of Atlantis.

524 PAGES. 6X9 PAPERBACK. ILLUSTRATED WITH 100S OF MAPS, PHOTOS AND DIAGRAMS. BIBLIOGRAPHY & INDEX. $16.95. CODE: MED

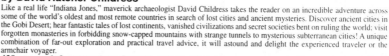

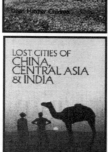

LOST CITIES OF CHINA, CENTRAL INDIA & ASIA
by David Hatcher Childress

Like a real life "Indiana Jones," maverick archaeologist David Childress takes the reader on an incredible adventure across some of the world's oldest and most remote countries in search of lost cities and ancient mysteries. Discover ancient cities in the Gobi Desert; hear fantastic tales of lost continents, vanished civilizations and secret societies bent on ruling the world; visit forgotten monasteries in forbidding snow-capped mountains with strange tunnels to mysterious subterranean cities! A unique combination of far-out exploration and practical travel advice, it will astound and delight the experienced traveler or the armchair voyager.

429 PAGES. 6X9. PAPERBACK. PHOTOS, MAPS, AND ILLUSTRATIONS WITH FOOTNOTES & BIBLIOGRAPHY $14.95. CODE CHI

LOST CITIES OF ANCIENT LEMURIA & THE PACIFIC
by David Hatcher Childress

Was there once a continent in the Pacific? Called Lemuria or Pacifica by geologists, Mu or Pan by the mystics, there is now ample mythological, geological and archaeological evidence to "prove" that an advanced and ancient civilization once lived in the central Pacific. Maverick archaeologist and explorer David Hatcher Childress combs the Indian Ocean, Australia and the Pacific in search of the surprising truth about mankind's past. Contains photos of the underwater city on Pohnpei; explanations on how the statues were levitated around Easter Island in a clock-wise vortex movement; tales of disappearing islands; Egyptians in Australia; and more.

379 PAGES. 6X9. PAPERBACK. ILLUSTRATED. FOOTNOTES & BIBLIOGRAPHY $14.95. CODE LEM

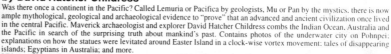

LOST CITIES OF NORTH & CENTRAL AMERICA
by David Hatcher Childress

Down the back roads from coast to coast, maverick archaeologist and adventurer David Hatcher Childress goes deep into unknown America. With this incredible book, you will search for lost Mayan cities and books of gold, discover an ancient canal system in Arizona, climb gigantic pyramids in the Midwest, explore megalithic monuments in New England, and join the astonishing quest for the lost cities throughout North America. From the war-torn jungles of Guatemala, Nicaragua and Honduras to the deserts, mountains and fields of Mexico, Canada, and the U.S.A., Childress takes the reader in search of sunken ruins, Viking forts, strange tunnel systems, living dinosaurs, early Chinese explorers, and fantastic lost treasure. Packed with both early and current maps, photos and illustrations.

590 PAGES. 6X9 PAPERBACK. PHOTOS, MAPS, AND ILLUSTRATIONS. FOOTNOTES & BIBLIOGRAPHY. $14.95. CODE: NCA

LOST CITIES & ANCIENT MYSTERIES OF AFRICA & ARABIA
by David Hatcher Childress

Across ancient deserts, dusty plains and steaming jungles, maverick archaeologist David Childress continues his world-wide quest for lost cities and ancient mysteries. Join him as he discovers forbidden cities in the Empty Quarter of Arabia; "Atlantean" ruins in Egypt and the Kalahari desert; a mysterious, ancient empire in the Sahara; and more. This is the tale of an extraordinary life on the road: across war-torn countries, Childress searches for King Solomon's Mines, living dinosaurs, the Ark of the Covenant and the solutions to some of the fantastic mysteries of the past.

423 PAGES. 6X9 PAPERBACK. PHOTOS, MAPS, AND ILLUSTRATIONS. FOOTNOTES & BIBLIOGRAPHY. $14.95. CODE: AFA

LOST CITIES & ANCIENT MYSTERIES OF SOUTH AMERICA
by David Hatcher Childress

Rogue adventurer and maverick archaeologist David Hatcher Childress takes the reader on unforgettable journeys deep into deadly jungles, high up on windswept mountains and across scorching deserts in search of lost civilizations and ancient mysteries. Travel with David and explore stone cities high in mountain forests and hear fantastic tales of Inca treasure, living dinosaurs, and a mysterious tunnel system. Whether he is hopping freight trains, searching for secret cities, or just dealing with the daily problems of food, money, and romance, the author keeps the reader spellbound. Includes both early and current maps, photos, and illustrations, and plenty of advice for the explorer planning his or her own journey of discovery.

381 PAGES. 6X9 PAPERBACK. PHOTOS, MAPS, AND ILLUSTRATIONS. FOOTNOTES & BIBLIOGRAPHY. $14.95. CODE: SAM

24 HOUR CREDIT CARD ORDERS—CALL: 815-253-6390 FAX: 815-253-6300
email: auphq@frontiernet.net   http://www.azstarnet.com/~aup

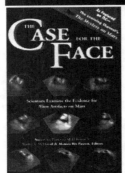

NEW BOOKS

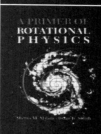

A PRIMER OF ROTATIONAL PHYSICS
by Myrna Milani and Brian Smith

Milani and Smith present a new theory of science, one based on rotational mechanics. The objective is to establish an integrated Unified Field Theory encompassing science, engineering, philosophy, medicine, and all human experience. The authors claim that rotational physics leads us to clean, safe free-energy devices and has a parallel in human thought and development. Scientific and mathematical concepts are explained in terms of everyday events and common human beliefs, enabling the reader to begin uniting various fields of endeavor into one body of thought explaining who we are, where we come from, and how our universe operates.
134 PAGES. 6X9 PAPERBACK. ILLUSTRATED. $10.00. CODE: PORP

THE PRINCIPLES OF ENERGY
And Rotational Physics
by Myrna Milani and Brian Smith

Expanding on their earlier book, Milani and Smith propose 12 principles of energy creation and collection which, if understood and applied, can lead us into an era where our basic energy forms—light, heat, sound, pressure, and potential—can be used to satisfy all our needs without depleting vital resources, producing waste, or creating hazardous conditions. Rotational physics has parallels with our feelings about ourselves and others. A great book on vortex movement, a new way of seeing time, wave function and rotational energy, free-energy concepts, how the mind influences space-time. more.
215 PAGES. 6X9 PAPERBACK. ILLUSTRATED. $12.00. CODE: POEN

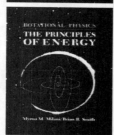

AWAKENING TO ZERO POINT
The Collective Initiation
by Gregg Braden

Ancient traditions remind us that we are living a cycle of change that began nearly 200,000 years ago: The Shift of the Ages. You are part of that change. Transcending religion, science and mystic traditions, this time cycle involves dramatic shifts in the Earth which are mirrored as changes in sleep patterns, immune systems, relationships and perceptions of time. Braden explores the following topics: mysterious glyphs appearing in cereal grain crops; the slowing of the earth's rotation; a rapid decline of Earth's magnetic fields; new diseases immune to modern vaccines; miraculous healings from "Internal Technologies," record temperature extremes; a global increase in seismic events; new patterns of healing DNA found in global population samples; more.
204 PAGES. 7X10 PAPERBACK. ILLUSTRATED. BIBLIOGRAPHY. $17.95. CODE: ATZP

JESUS CHRIST : THE NUMBER OF HIS NAME
The Amazing Number Code Found in the Bible
by Bonnie Gaunt

Mathematician and theologist Bonnie Gaunt's latest book on the amazing number code found in the Bible. In this book Gaunt says that the numerological code tells of the new Millennium and of a "Grand Octave of Time" for man. She demonstrates that the Bible's number code reveals amazing realities for today's world, and gives evidence of the year of the "second coming" of Jesus Christ. aunt says that the code was known to the ancients and has only been rediscovered in recent years. The code reveals amazing evidence that the code number for Jesus Christ has been planted in the geometry of the earth, ancient megalithic buildings in Egypt, Britain and else where and in the Bible itself. Gaunt examines the mathematics of the Great Pyramid, Stonehenge, and of city of Bethlehem, which she says bears the number of Jesus by its latitude and longitude. Discover the hidden meaning to such number codes in the Bible such as 666, 888, 864, 3168, and more.
197 PAGES. 6X9 PAPERBACK. ILLUSTRATED. BIBLIOGRAPHY. $12.95. CODE: JCNN

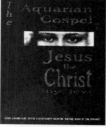

THE AQUARIAN GOSPEL OF JESUS THE CHRIST
Transcribed From the Akashic Records
by Levi

First published in 1908, this is the amazing story of Jesus, the man from Galilee, and how he attained the Christ consciousness open to all men. It includes a complete record of the "lost" 18 years of his life, a time on which the New Testament is strangely silent. During this period Jesus travelled widely in India, Tibet, Persia, Egypt and Greece, learning from the Masters, seers and wisemen of the East and the West in their temples and schools. Included in this outstanding book is information on the Council of the Seven Sages of the World, Jesus with the Chinese Master Mencius (Meng Tzu) in Tibet, the ministry, trial, execution and resurrection of Jesus.
270 PAGES. 6X9 PAPERBACK. INDEX. $14.95. CODE: AGJC

THE HISTORY OF THE KNIGHTS TEMPLAR
The Temple Church and the Temple
by Charles G. Addison. Introduction by David Hatcher Childress

Chapters on the origin of the Templars, their popularity in Europe and their rivalry with the Knights of St. John, later to be known as the Knights of Malta. Detailed information on the activities of the Templars in the Holy Land, and the 1312 A.D. suppression of the Templars in France and other countries, which culminated in the execution of Jacques de Molay. Also information on the continuation of the Knights Templars in England and Scotland and the formation of the society of Knights Templar in London and the rebuilding of the Temple in 1816. Plus a lengthy intro about the lost Templar fleet and its connections to the ancient North American sea routes.
395 PAGES. 6X9 PAPERBACK. ILLUSTRATED. $16.95. CODE: HKT

24 HOUR CREDIT CARD ORDERS—CALL: 815-253-6390 FAX: 815-253-6300
email: auphq@frontiernet.net   http://www.azstarnet.com/~aup

UFOS AND ANTI-GRAVITY:
PIECE FOR A JIG-SAW
by Leonard G. Cramp

UFOs and ANTI-GRAVITY

Piece For A Jig-Saw
by Leonard G. Cramp

Cramp's 1966 classic book on flying saucer propulsion and suppressed technology is available again. This book is a highly technical look at the UFO phenomena by a trained scientist. Cramp first introduces the idea of 'anti-gravity' and introduces us to the various theories of gravitation. He then examines the technology necessary to build a flying saucer and examines in great detail the technical aspects of such a craft. Cramp's book is a wealth of material and diagrams on flying saucers, anti-gravity, suppressed technology, G-fields and UFOs. Chapters include Crossroads of Aerodynamics, Aerodynamic Saucers, Limitations of Rocketry, Gravitation and the Ether, Gravitational Spaceships, G. Field Lift Effects, The Bi-Field Theory, VTOL and Hovercraft, Analysis of UFO photos and claims, more.
388 pages, 6x9 paperback. Heavily Illustrated. $16.95.
code: UAG

NASA, NAZIS & JFK:

The Torbitt Document & the JFK Assassination
Introduction by Kenn Thomas
This first published edition of the Torbitt Document emphasizes what the manuscript says about the link between Operation Paper Clip Nazi scientists working for NASA, the assassination of JFK, and the secret Nevada air base Area 51. The Torbitt Document talks about the roles in the assassination played by Division Five of the FBI, Defense Industrial Security Command (DISC), the Las Vegas mob, and the shadow corporate entities Permindex and Centro-Mondiale Commerciale. Also: claims that the same people planned the 1962 failed assassination of Charles de Gaul, who traced the "Assassination Cabal" to Permindex in Switzerland and to NATO headquarters in Brussels. The Torbitt document paints a dark picture of NASA, the Military Industrial Complex, and the connections to Mercury, Nevada and the Area 51 complex which headquarters the "secret space program."
242 pages, 5x8 paperback. Illustrated. $16.00.
code: NNJ

THE FREE-ENERGY DEVICE HANDBOOK
A Compilation of Patents & Reports

THE FREE-ENERGY DEVICE HANDBOOK

A Compilation of Patents & Reports by David Hatcher Childress

Large format compilation of various patents, papers, descriptions, and diagrams concerning free-energy devices and systems. A visual tool for experimenters and researchers into magnetic motors and other "over-unity" devices with chapters on the Adams Motor, the Hans Coler Generator, cold fusion, superconductors, "N" machines, space-energy generators, Nikola Tesla, T. Townsend Brown, and the latest in free-energy devices. Packed with photos, technical diagrams, patents, and fascinating information, this book belongs on every science shelf. With energy and profit a major political reason for fighting various wars, free-energy devices, if ever allowed to be mass-distributed to consumers, could change the world. Get your copy now before the Department of Energy bans this book!
306 pp. ♦ 7x10 paperback ♦ Profusely illustrated ♦ Bibliography & appendix ♦ $16.95 ♦
code: FEH

EXTRATERRESTRIAL ARCHAEOLOGY
by David Hatcher Childress

With hundreds of photos and illustrations, Extraterrestrial Archaeology takes the reader to the strange and fascinating worlds of Mars, the Moon, Mercury, Venus, Saturn, and other planets for a look at the alien structures that appear there. Whether skeptic or believer, this book allows you to view for yourself the amazing pyramids, domes, spaceports, obelisks, and other anomalies that are profiled in photograph after photograph. Using official NASA and Soviet photos, as well as other photos taken via telescope, this book seeks to prove that many of the planets (and moons) of our solar system are in some way inhabited by intelligent life.
224 pp. ♦ 8¹/2x11 paperback ♦ Highly illustrated with photos, diagrams & maps! ♦ Bibliography, index, appendix ♦ $18.95
code: ETA

MAN-MADE UFOS: 1944-1994

50 Years of Suppression
by Renato Vesco & David Hatcher Childress

A comprehensive and in-depth look at the early "flying saucer technology" of Nazi Germany and the genesis of early man-made UFOs. From captured German scientists, escaped battalions of German soldiers, secret factories in Antarctica to today's state-of-the-art "Dream-land" flying machines, this astonish-ing book blows the lid off the "Government UFO Conspiracy." Examined in detail are secret underground airfields and factories; German secret weapons; "suction" aircraft; the origin of NASA; gyroscopic stabilizers and engines; the secret Marconi aircraft factory in South America, and other secret societies, both ancient and modern, that have kept this craft a secret, and much more. Not to be missed by students of technology suppression, UFOs, anti-gravity, free-energy conspiracy, and World War II. Intro-duction by W.A. Harbinson, author of the Dell novels Genesis and Revelation.
440 pp. ♦ 6x9 paperback ♦ Heavily Illustrated. $18.95
code: MMU

THE FANTASTIC INVENTIONS OF NIKOLA TESLA

by Nikola Tesla
with additional material by David Hatcher Childress

This book is a virtual compendium of patents, diagrams, photos, and explanations of the many incredible inventions of the originator of the modern era of electrification. The book is a readable and affordable collection of his patents, inventions, and thoughts on free energy, anti-gravity, and other futuristic inventions. Covered in depth, often in Tesla's own words, are such topics as: His Plan to Transmit Free Electricity into the Atmosphere; How Anti-Gravity Airships could Draw Power from the Towers he was Building; Tesla's Death Rays, Ozone Generators, and more...
342 pp. ♦ 6x9 paperback ♦ Highly illustrated ♦ $16.95
code: FINT

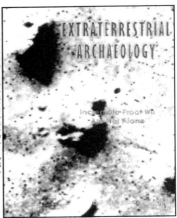

EXTRATERRESTRIAL ARCHAEOLOGY

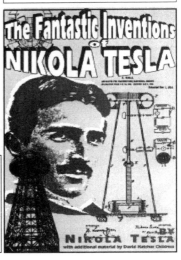

Man-Made UFOS 1944-1994
50 Years of Suppression

Renato Vesco
David Hatcher Childress

The Fantastic Inventions OF NIKOLA TESLA
BY NIKOLA TESLA
with additional material by David Hatcher Childress

One Adventure Place
P.O. Box 74
Kempton, Illinois 60946
United States of America
Tel.: 815-253-6390 • Fax: 815-253-6300
Email: auphq@frontiernet.net
http://www.azstarnet.com/~aup

ORDERING INSTRUCTIONS

➤ Remit by USD$ Check or Money Order
➤ Credit Cards: Visa, MasterCard, Discovery, &
American Express Accepted
➤ Prices May Change Without Notice

SHIPPING CHARGES

United States

➤ Postal Book Rate { $2.50 First Item
50¢ Each Additional Item

➤ Priority Mail { $3.50 First Item
$2.00 Each Additional Item

➤ UPS { $3.50 First Item
$1.00 Each Additional Item

NOTE: UPS Delivery Available to Mainland USA Only

Canada

➤ Postal Book Rate { $3.00 First Item
$1.00 Each Additional Item

➤ Postal Air Mail { $5.00 First Item
$2.00 Each Additional Item

➤ Personal Checks or Bank Drafts MUST BE
USD$ and Drawn on a US Bank
➤ Canadian Postal Money Orders OK
➤ Payment MUST BE USD$

All Other Countries

➤ Surface Delivery { $6.00 First Item
$2.00 Each Additional Item

➤ Postal Air Mail { $12.00 First Item
$8.00 Each Additional Item

➤ Payment MUST BE USD$
➤ Checks MUST BE USD$ and
Drawn on a US Bank
➤ Add $5.00 for Air Mail Subscription to
Future *Adventures Unlimited* Catalogs

SPECIAL NOTES

➤ RETAILERS: Standard Discounts Available
➤ BACKORDERS: We Backorder all Out-of-
Stock Items Unless Otherwise Requested
➤ PRO FORMA INVOICES: Available on Request
➤ VIDEOS: NTSC Mode Only
PAL & SECAM Mode Videos Are Not Available

European Office:
Adventures Unlimited, PO Box 372,
Dronten, 8250 AJ, The Netherlands
South Pacific Office
Adventures Unlimited NZ
221 Symonds Sreet Box 8199
Auckland, New Zealnd

Please check: ☑

☐ This is my first order   ☐ I have ordered before   ☐ This is a new address

Name		
Address		
City		
State/Province		Postal Code
Country		
Phone day	Evening	
Fax		

Item Code	Item Description	Price	Qty	Total

Please check: ☑

☐ Postal-Surface
☐ Postal-Air Mail (Priority in USA)
☐ UPS (Mainland USA only)

Subtotal ➤	
Less Discount-10% for 3 or more items ➤	
Balance ➤	
Illinois Residents 6.25% Sales Tax ➤	
Previous Credit ➤	
Shipping ➤	
Total (check/MO in USD$ only) ➤	

☐ Visa/MasterCard/Discover/Amex

Card Number

Expiration Date

10% Discount When You Order 3 or More Items!

Comments & Suggestions	Share Our Catalog with a Friend